W9-BKR-055

Grammar Matters

I really need to lose some weight so I will not be roast turkey, shouted Turkey Mikey.

Stenhouse Publishers
Portland, Maine

Lessons, Tips, and Conversations Using Mentor Texts, K-6

Lynne Dorfman & Diane Dougherty

DiPietro Library
Franklin Pierce University
Rindge, NH 03461

Stenhouse Publishers
www.stenhouse.com

Copyright © 2014 by Lynne Dorfman and Diane Dougherty

All rights reserved. Except for the pages in the appendix, which may be photocopied for classroom use, no part of this publication may be reproduced or transmitted in any form or by any means, electronic or mechanical, including photocopy, or any information storage and retrieval system, without permission from the publisher.

Every effort has been made to contact copyright holders and students for permission to reproduce borrowed material. We regret any oversights that may have occurred and will be pleased to rectify them in subsequent reprints of the work.

Credits
"Recipe for Writing an Autumn Poem" from *Falling Down the Page: A Book of List Poems* by Georgia Heard. Used with permission of Georgia Heard.

"Walking" by Grace Ellen Glaubitz, copyright © 1970 Highlights for Children, Columbus, Ohio. All rights reserved. Reprinted by permission.

Library of Congress Cataloging-in-Publication Data
Dorfman, Lynne R., 1952–
    Grammar matters : lessons, tips, & conversations using mentor texts, K–6 / Lynne Dorfman and Diane Dougherty.
        p. cm.
    Includes bibliographical references and index.
    ISBN 978-1-57110-991-0 (pbk. : alk. paper)—ISBN 978-1-62531-029-3 (ebook)
1. English language—Grammar—Study and teaching (Elementary) 2. Children's literature—Study and teaching (Elementary)—Activity programs. 3. English language—Composition and exercises—Study and teaching (Elementary) I. Dougherty, Diane. II. Title.
    LB1576.D656 2014
    372.61—dc23
                                                                                          2014017929

Cover design, interior design, and typesetting by Martha Drury

Manufactured in the United States of America

PRINTED ON 30% PCW
RECYCLED PAPER

20 19 18 17 16 15 14   9 8 7 6 5 4 3 2

We dedicate this book to our husbands, Ralph Abbott and Joe Dougherty, who solved our computer problems, forgave us when we became cranky, and loved us in spite of our writing habit!

Contents

Acknowledgments

Kelly Gallagher (2011) tells us: "Let's not forget that writing has become much more than a school activity; it has become a cornerstone to living a literate life" (21). Kelly's words help us explain why we wrote this book. We believe that, beginning in elementary school, knowledge of grammar and conventions is essential to our students' ability to share a literate life with peers, family members, friends, and the community at large. We didn't write this book without the help of many others, ranging in age from five to, well, let's just say, grownups. Though our learning experiences with grammar and conventions began with skill and drill, as teachers we discovered that skill and drill had little impact on our student writers. During our participation in the summer Writing Institute at the Pennsylvania Writing and Literature Project at West Chester University and our continued involvement with the project's leadership team as codirectors and course facilitators, we grew in our understanding of grammar instruction in the context of writing workshop. We thank former directors Bob Weiss and Andrea Fishman for their friendship and continued support. To Dr. Mary Buckelew, our current director, we warmly thank you for your treasured friendship, sage advice, and constant cheerleading!

Through our association with the Writing Project, we became avid readers of professional books. These works continue to inform our instruction and give us the sense that we are never alone in the classroom while teaching writing and reading. We are eternally indebted to a cadre of authors who have influenced our thinking and fueled our passion: Don Graves, Don Murray, Lucy Calkins, Nancie Atwell, Ralph Fletcher, Vicki Spandel, Constance Weaver, Kelly Gallagher, Jeff Anderson, Katie Wood Ray, Regie Routman, Laura Robb, Mark Overmeyer, Shelley Harwayne, Linda Hoyt, Stacey Shubitz, Ruth Ayres, Frank Murphy, Barry Lane, and Rose Cappelli.

We want to extend our deepest gratitude to Amy Dougherty Hicks for her wise words, which helped us define and refine our thinking in first-grade classrooms. To our friend and colleague Teresa Moslak, thank you for both of your wonderful additions to the appendices of this book. Teachers will find them so useful!

Our work in schools provided us with the classroom snapshots we needed to bring this book to life.

From Diane: Thanks to Samuel Lee, the superintendent, and Karen Snedeker, the supervisor of curriculum and instruction in the Bristol Township School District. A special thanks to fourth-grade teacher Jacqueline Hawes and her principal, Mark Wilicki, of Washington Elementary School; to fifth-grade teacher Carolyn Dutton of Buchanan Elementary School; and to the school's past principal Evy Clark.

I am also grateful to Downington Area School District superintendent Larry Mussoline; Leigh Abbott, principal of Springton Lake Elementary School; fifth-grade teacher Frank Chindemi; and third-grade teacher Amy Goulet.

Thanks to Dr. Chris Fulco, head of Woodlynde School, Maggi Koch, head of the Lower School, and teachers Barbara Barks, Carolyn Kruk, Heather Mager, Mark Miller, Denise Pritchard, Traci Sill, and Marie Van Horn.

From Lynne: Dr. Robert Milrod, the Upper Moreland Township School District superintendent; Mrs. Jenny Jehman, the assistant superintendent; Mrs. Susan Smith, the principal of the Upper Moreland Primary School; and Dr. Michael Bair, assistant principal of Upper Moreland Primary School and Upper Moreland Intermediate School, have been longtime supporters and friends. I am fortunate to be able to work with the hardworking, inquisitive children of this district. This book could not have been completed without the hard work and never-ending energy of the very special kindergarten teacher Shelly Keller, the remarkable first-grade teachers Christine Flaherty and Gail Speers, and the amazing ESL teacher Cathy McParland. A special thanks to Maribeth Batcho for her dedication, wisdom, and constant sparks of fiery imagination. Maribeth, my trustworthy colleague, collaborating with you and your two wonderful second-grade classes—the spring class of 2013 and the fall class of 2014—was such a rewarding experience for me. Thank you, Kevin Black, a third-grade teacher at Upper Moreland Intermediate School, and my dear friend and principal for over a decade, Dr. Joseph M. Waters.

I am eternally grateful to Methacton School District's extraordinary second-grade teacher Jennifer Kennedy at Woodland Elementary School and the truly amazing kindergarten teacher Alison Navarrete of Eagleville Elementary School, for their gracious welcome and collaboration. Their students were already voracious writers before I arrived on the scene. A very big thank-you to my dear friend Dr. Diane Barrie, currently the curriculum coordinator for Kutztown Area School District. Without you, I never would have met these wonderful teachers and their students!

To our families:

From Diane: Thank you for your constant belief in me—my husband, Joe; my children, Mark, Amy, and Ed; and their spouses, Jill, Brian, and Amy. Thanks to my grandchildren, Collin, Maddie, Grace, Quinn, Conrad, Callum, Neil, and Alec, who bring me joy every day.

From Lynne: How did I ever survive without you, Ralph? A big thanks and lots of love to my family, including three boisterous Welsh corgis. To my goddaughters, Alexandra Shinners and Brooke Shinners, and to my "other goddaughter," Caitlyn Shinners, and their parents, my dear friends Kevin and Jennifer Shinners, thank you for the loving words of encouragement and great joy you have brought to my life.

We want to extend a big thank-you to our friend and fellow writer Rose Cappelli for agreeing to let us continue to use the Your Turn format for key writing lessons that filled the pages of *Mentor Texts* (Dorfman and Cappelli 2007), *Nonfiction Mentor Texts* (Dorfman and Cappelli 2009), and *Poetry Mentor Texts* (Dorfman and Cappelli 2012). We believe it works with all students!

To everyone at Stenhouse Publishers, thanks for your expertise; patience; attention to detail; artistic design; and sensible, meaningful advertising in your catalogs, conference displays, and magazines. Thank you, Chandra Lowe, Chris Downey, Nate Butler, Chuck Lerch, Jay Kilburn, Rebecca Eaton, Jill Cooley, Maureen Barbieri, Elaine Cyr, Pam King, Lise Wood, and Zsofi McMullin—our extended Stenhouse family. Of course, we want to also extend our many thanks to Philippa Stratton and Dan Tobin with wishes for continued success.

Last but not least—our thanks for the quiet wisdom of our exceptional editor and friend, Bill Varner. Bill, without your insight and imperturbability, we could not have completed this work. As always, you knew what questions needed to be asked and when to grant us the precious gift of time. Thank you!

Introduction

Like everything metaphysical the harmony between thought and reality is to be found in the grammar of the language.

—Ludwig Wittgenstein

Google "grammar worksheets" and you will find 6,238 free grammar worksheets. Eighty-two worksheets are on gerunds and infinitives alone. Are you surprised? But do isolated worksheets really help our students become more successful writers? Is there a place for worksheets? If so, when are they appropriate? We believe that when we show our students how to "read like writers" (Ray 1999), we ask them to become investigators and celebrate language. We ask them to take a closer look and ask questions like, "Why did the author end his paragraph in two short sentences?" or "Why did the author choose to begin with a fragment?" or "Why did the author place her adjectives after the noun they describe?"

All these questions lead to deeper thinking about writing process and the part that editing plays. The Common Core State Standards Initiative for English Language Arts (2014) addresses the importance of writing process in "Production and Distribution of Writing" for grade five: "Develop and strengthen writing as needed by planning, revising, editing, rewriting or trying a new approach" (CCSS.ELA_LITERACY.W.5.5). When we revise our writing, we use our inner eye to see the meaning, the purpose, and the significance of our writing. Our outer eye is the editor that takes in the individual words, sentences, upper- and lowercase letters, and punctuation. The

1

outer eye, the editor, helps the writer create sentences that flow and tell our reader how we intended the sentences to be read. The outer eye ensures that our message will be communicated and understood. Constant practice with writing and engaging in the writing process will help writers gain facility and confidence. Students who can communicate their thoughts to others are empowered. They enjoy reading their pieces and can feel good about their accomplishments. Their final revisions and edits create a piece of writing that will make a lasting impression on their readers.

Our ultimate goal is to help our students also view grammar as something to appreciate, enjoy, and even admire. Joan Didion views the orchestration of composing sentences as an art form: "Grammar is a piano I play by ear since I seem to have been out of school the year the rules were mentioned. All I know about grammar is its power. To shift the structure of a sentence alters the meaning of that sentence, as definitely and inflexibly as the position of a camera alters the meaning of the object photographed. Many people know about camera angles now, but not so many know about sentences. The arrangement of the words matters, and the arrangement you want can be found in the picture in your mind . . ." (Friedman 1984, 7).

Our Grammar Backgrounds

How did the authors of this book learn about grammar and correctness in everyday speech and in their informal and formal writing? Here are our stories.

Diane's Story

I learned grammar in the halcyon days of the late 1950s and early '60s, through skill and drill. We memorized the parts of speech; we diagrammed sentences; we recited the principal parts of verbs; we distinguished the differences among simple sentences, compound sentences, complex sentences, and compound-complex sentences; we learned the difference between a participle and a gerund. In short, we became grammarians.

Did I say "we"? Now that I think about it, that pronoun is not appropriate. I learned these concepts, but I'm certain that not everyone in my classes learned them or even cared to learn them. And as I began my teaching career, I discovered that I hadn't learned them well enough to explain them to others. Knowing the subject, verb, and object of a sentence was intrinsic to me, but I couldn't begin to instruct my students about them. How could they *not* know that *run* is a verb, except, of course, when it's used as a noun in baseball?

In order to be a grammar teacher, I had to learn how to break apart a sentence in all its intricacies and how to explain these intricacies to my students. I became extremely good at it. So good, in fact, that I once boasted I could teach grammar to anyone.

Then I discovered something. I began to question the importance of the skill and drill of grammar because I, myself, wondered about the efficacy of teaching grammar in isolation. I believe in the necessity of every child's learning to write well; written communication is an essential skill. In what ways, I wondered, was I helping my students write better by teaching them the parts of speech and the parts of a sentence in isolation?

As I reflected on my own experiences in learning grammar, it occurred to me that my writing experiences were not connected to the instruction I had received in grammar and usage. None of my teachers (and I'd had some excellent English teachers in high school and college) connected the endless worksheets to our actual writing assignments. And writing "assignments" is what they were: themes about Hamlet's conflict; the effects of revenge on Chillingworth; Piggy's role in *The Lord of the Flies*, and so on. Rarely, especially in college, was there a choice about what to write or how to write it. Rarely, even in high school, were we students shown a model essay, and when we were, those models were written by consummate professionals like Virginia Woolf.

Did teachers write? We didn't see any proof of that! But teachers did grade, and their grades often seemed arbitrary. Sometimes grades were based on grammatical errors, but usually those errors were unexplained. I'd had no best practice models on which to base my teaching until I began working with the Pennsylvania Writing and Literature Project. This book reflects my philosophy of teaching writing as it has been informed by that work.

Lynne's Story

I don't remember much about writing experiences in elementary school, but I do remember that the writing we did always rewarded effort in perfect manuscript or cursive handwriting as well as correct spelling, punctuation, and capitalization. In sixth grade, Mrs. Steinberg gave us opportunities to write often and looked at other qualities of writing such as content and style—and I loved that year!

By the time I entered high school, writing mainly involved research—writing reports. The "red pen" was used to mark grammatical mistakes. The two areas my teachers often emphasized with their grading were conventions and grammar—up to 50 percent of each grade. Unfortunately, I don't remember any conferences along the way—just a final grade with few comments on how to move forward as a writer. Lessons were taught from a standard grammar book and practiced in isolation. My most vivid memory of seventh-grade writing emerged from lessons in sentence structures, especially diagramming sentences with direct and indirect objects. The exercises in the books were never connected with the writing we did in class—reports, essays, character studies, and so on.

When I reached the university, I realized there were many things I didn't know about writing and struggled with freshman year, even though every previous year I had obtained an A in English class as well as most other subject areas. How did this happen? I could diagram any sentence and knew my parts of speech. I certainly knew the difference between a fragment and a run-on sentence.

When I started teaching, we used a grammar book four days of the week and had "creative writing" every Friday. My third- and fourth-grade students entered every year insisting they didn't know what a noun or verb was, even though I knew my colleagues had taught these concepts. Every teacher complained that students lacked skills in grammar and conventions. There was no transfer of skills to their written work, even though the students had workbook pages of practice and even unit tests around each part of speech.

My work with the Pennsylvania Writing and Literature Project sent me in a new direction. I learned to address all the qualities of good writing in workshop and to teach lessons in grammar through modeling and shared and guided practice. Then came mentor sentences, paragraphs, and texts. Students tried new constructions by "walking around in the syntax" of mentor authors. I was onto something new and exciting—and it was working for my students! I realized that students could greatly improve their writing abilities by imitating the craft, organizational patterns, sentence structures, and punctuation in the model texts we used in class. These texts became mentors for my students and me and provided the gentle nudges they needed to try out new things—to take risks in their writing.

I became fascinated, too, with writers who "broke the rules." Sometimes when I found a fragment or run-on sentence, I paused to rewrite it in my head for correctness and found that the fragment or run-on was very purposeful. I questioned why authors would begin a sentence with the word *and* or string a list of items together repeatedly using *and* instead of just a comma. Katie Wood Ray's *Wondrous Words* (1999) and Edgar Schuster's *Breaking the Rules: Liberating Writers Through Innovative Grammar Instruction* (2003) became mentor texts for me. I began to delight in reading almost anything like a writer as well as a reader. Suddenly, my writing started to improve and my writing workshops took on a new meaning.

Grammar Instruction: Traditional or Innovative?

Grammar doesn't have to be the rule-bound, bland, boring subject of past decades. Of course, there certainly are rules of English syntax that should be honored. A common student error is to use the pronoun *me* as the subject of the sentence and to further compound the error by placing it first within a compound subject: *Me and Diane rode horses at the farm.* Our ears hurt when we hear these words spoken aloud, and yet our students see this construction in some of the children's books they read because the authors are trying to imitate how children speak in conversations with friends. Pronoun usage may be tricky, but *me* should not be used as the subject of the sentence in writing because it will dominate the student's usage in everyday talk as well.

Our book offers classroom snapshots of grammar and conventions lessons embedded within the context of teaching units of study as well as Your Turn Lessons to show how these rules can be taught in ways that empower students and enable them to write with confidence and gain self-esteem. Students' work needs the look and sound of literacy in order to be taken seriously in the real world. Schuster (2003) cautions us that the regular use of nonstandard English in the contemporary adult world will most likely limit the user both economically and socially (55). However, there are other rules, taught for hundreds of years, that have become entrenched in the traditional grammar but infrequently followed outside of the classroom. Schuster has a list of what he calls "mythrules" and explains that some usage rules are not followed by society at large in speech and/or in writing but are rules that grammarians and others believe should be followed by educated people. For example, imagine the following scene: You are knocking on the door of a friend's house and he calls out, "Who's there?" How do you respond? "It's me." *OR* "It is I." Consider the case of the split infinitive. Is it okay or even better to say, "I'd love to actually play in the final championship game instead of watching the game from the sidelines!" In this case, the word that is emphasized is the adverb *actually* that splits the infinitive *to play*. Splitting infinitives is a common mistake and only desirable when the sentence construction would be awkward or the meaning would be fuzzy without doing so. By showing examples of the best contemporary writing that sometimes breaks the rules in meaningful ways, we hope to put "traditional" grammar myths to rest. We aim to give all our writers the opportunity to write with authority and precision.

News About Grammar

The Common Core State Standards are explicit about the "Conventions of Standard English" at each grade level. Through the "Knowledge of Language" strand teachers are guided toward helping students apply those conventions in their writing throughout the day and in all content areas. Looking at the standards alone, however, will not provide a curriculum for writing or grammar and conventions. In *Pathways to the Common Core*, the authors nudge us to "regard these standards as an invitation to explore, invent, and pilot some new ideas" (Calkins, Ehrenworth, and Lehman 2012, 168). They do not view the Common Core standards as mandates; rather they impel us to view them as a "call to action." Teachers need to be creative in how they apply the standards in their everyday writing workshops. The way we deliver grammar instruction will have a significant impact on how students retain the information and apply it in various contexts. A good writer is a lover of words. Studying grammar in isolation does not make someone a lover of words or a better speaker and writer. Neither will isolated grammar lessons and workbook pages create confidence and proficiency in grammar and mechanics. There is ample evidence to support this:

- "The teaching of formal grammar has a negligible or, because it usually displaces some instruction and practice in actual composition, even a harmful effect on the improvement of writing." (Braddock, Lloyd-Jones, and Shoer 1963, 37–38)
- "If students write well, it is mostly due to wide reading, the rich use of language in the home and classroom, and the continued efforts of teachers to guide their students through the writing process. Good writing is not, however, produced by mere grammar study, as research has shown again and again." (Weaver and Bush 2008, 28)
- "The study of traditional school grammar . . . has no effect on raising the quality of student writing." (Hillocks and Smith 1991, 248)
- "The meta-analysis [of grammar instruction involving the explicit and systematic teaching of the parts of speech and structure of sentences] found an effect for this type of instruction for students across the full range of ability, but surprisingly, this effect was negative. This negative effect was small, but it was statistically significant, indicating that tra-

ditional grammar instruction is unlikely to help improve the quality of students' writing." (Graham and Perin 2006, 21)

It is astounding that, after thirty years of noncontradictory research showing us that isolated grammar instruction does not work, educators and politicians are still having this conversation. The purpose of this book is to provide a close look at teaching grammar and conventions through the context of student writing, giving teachers the knowledge and tools to help their students become proficient and compelling communicators.

New Mentors

What pedagogy is on the front burner of education today? Certainly, Jeff Anderson is a mentor for teachers everywhere. His *Mechanically Inclined* (2005) and *Everyday Editing* (2007) provide a wealth of information regarding effective practices in teaching grammar and mechanics. Jeff's books serve as references for teachers and provide practical strategies for embedding grammar into daily instruction. His teaching methods are student centered, and reading his books will put you at ease with the teaching of grammar. The organization of both of these books makes them easy for teachers to use regularly as teaching tools.

Donna Topping and Sandra Hoffman, in *Getting Grammar: 150 Ways to Teach an Old Subject* (2006), breathe life and even fun into practices that help students use grammar and gain writing fluency. Their work is useful for novices as well as for experienced teachers.

In *Funner Grammar: Fresh Ways to Teach Usage, Language, and Writing Conventions* (2012), Sandra Wilde addresses the idea of learning about language for its own sake while also addressing conventions, usage, and what Wilde calls "nitty-gritty" grammar. Chapter 5, "Language Diversity and Social Justice," is certainly food for thought and worth reading.

Harry Noden's *Image Grammar: Teaching Grammar as Part of the Writing Process* (2011), uses visual imagery to motivate students to write and rewrite, trying out new sentence patterns and structures. Each teaching point is clearly aligned with a specific strategy to improve writing, a good way to help teachers learn to embed grammar in the context of writing process and a workshop approach.

Teachers may need several books like these to serve as references and jumping-off points for embedded grammar and mechanics instruction in their daily transactions with student writers across the day. Students will even be able to use books by Ruth Heller such as *A Cache of Jewels and Other Collective Nouns* (1987), *If You Were a Conjunction* by Nancy Loewen (2007), or *The Girl's Like Spaghetti: Why, You Can't Manage Without Apostrophes!* by Lynne Truss (2006).

Grammar Matters: The New Kid on the Block

Our book will demonstrate how to embed grammar instruction into units of study in the writing workshop classroom. It is divided into three parts that correspond to the text types and purposes featured in the Common Core State Standards, and a fourth part that explores grammar and conventions conversations. The first part includes the study of the narrative, including fiction. Within that part we explore the use of wordless books as a scaffold for writing fiction; the use of personal or fictional narrative; and the use of a touchstone text for writing fiction. Part 2 is devoted to informational writing. In it we have chapters on description, compare/contrast, and procedural writing. Part 3 includes opinion writing—book reviews and shared opinions about subjects important to students. Within the classroom snapshots we include teaching points (strategies for classroom management and/or aspects of teaching writing) and grammar references (explaining grammatical terms in plain language). Part 4 is a plan for the entire year and includes attention to whole-class conversations about grammar using mentor texts, one-on-one conferring about grammar and mechanics issues, and ways to assess student growth. Each of the first three parts is followed by five Your Turn Lessons, which focus on aspects of grammar instruction. The reader of this book will find appendices for use as a quick reference to grammar and punctuation rules with particular attention to parts of speech and their jobs in the well-written sentence. In addition, we provide a "Treasure Chest of Books" specifically dedicated to the teaching of grammar and conventions useful for students and teachers.

How to Use This Book

Goals

Our main purpose for this book is to help elementary teachers, K–6, embed the teaching of grammar and conventions within units of study in the writing workshop. We provide specific examples of embedded instruction in the three text types and purposes as stated in Common Core State Standards: argument (opinion writing in grades K–5), informative/explanatory, and narrative (CCSS.ELA-LITERACY.CCRAW.1,2,3). Using this book will support teachers' efforts to move away from isolated grammar instruction and toward more effective teaching methods. Daily grammar instruction within the context of a unit of study helps students retain knowledge of grammar and conventions and carries over to their everyday writing. This is the crux of the matter—that students transfer their newly acquired skills to the work they do in the classrooms and beyond. We hope this book will assist teachers in two important ways as they teach grammar related to improving writing across the curriculum and school day. First, it will help teachers move through different units of study, offering tips about teaching narrative, informational, and opinion writing and embedding grammar and mechanics instruction. Second, it is an important grammar resource—a quick and easy guide to rules and examples that will help teachers instruct their budding writers.

Organization

Within each of the three text types, teachers will find units of study. We chose to begin this book with narrative units because telling stories is a natural way for teachers to get to know their students and to begin building a writing community. Everyone has a story to tell. Each day we wake up with a new page to write on. In the real world, genres are blended (Romano 2000), and story is a powerful vehicle to deliver information or to argue a point. Informational and opinion writing often use anecdote and other story characteristics like dialogue to emphasize big ideas. Since we typically begin the year with the narrative writing genre, we believe that this book should begin that way, too. The narrative chapters include wordless books, personal or narrative fiction, and use of a touchstone text. For the informational chapters, we include descriptions, compare and contrast, and procedural pieces. For opinion writing or argument, we focus on composing book reviews and point-of-view opinions based on a particular topic or text.

To create an authentic scenario and bring our readers right into the classrooms as we work with children, we have included classroom snapshots in every grade level. Additionally, each of the first three parts concludes with Your Turn Lessons—larger writing lessons that follow the gradual release of responsibility model and end with reflection (see Dorfman and Cappelli 2007, 2009, 2012). These lessons require more explicit teaching and are an effort to support educators as they help students become effective communicators.

Within the chapters readers will find Grammar Reference and Teaching Point sections. Grammar references explain grammatical terms that coincide with the embedded grammar lessons in that particular unit of study. We want teachers to be able to proceed with the lesson without necessarily referring to another grammar textbook. Teaching points provide organizational and management tools for the smooth-running writing workshop classroom.

Be sure to visit the appendices, including information about homophones (Appendix C) and other useful lessons for the English language learner (ELL). It might make the most sense to begin to use these lessons in the last stage of the writing process. As we start the school year, we often ask students to engage in an eye conference (sitting side by side to edit) or a self-conference (to look at conventions such as spelling, grammar, capitalization, and punctuation) as the last thing they do before publishing. Editing, however, can occur in any or all parts of the writing process. Students should do what they are comfortable with, but it is always a good idea to do a final edit right before publishing. Even the tiniest mistake could make your audience misunderstand what you are trying to say! Above all else, we should remember that grammar and punctuation help writers build sentences that make sense to our readers.

A Writing Community

Successful writing workshop classrooms rely on a number of factors. These include, of course, sufficient time, choice of topic, and constructive feedback. Equally important, however, is the establishment of a writing community—a safe environment in which students and teacher share their struggles with writing, experiment with possibilities, and take risks knowing that their efforts are valued. This environment does not occur by magic, nor is it established in one day or one week; community building is continuous. The wise writing teacher makes community building a priority throughout the year. Each school year should be a new beginning for everyone, teachers included. How we begin that year and how we nurture our students throughout the year are the scaffolds upon which we build success for all.

What exactly is meant by "building community"? Community building is not team building; it's not fun and games; it's not boosting self-esteem. Although there are elements of all of these in a good community-building activity, the primary purpose of community building is education: students in a nurturing writing community have a better chance of becoming committed readers and writers than those who do not have that advantage. Any activity that brings students as equals to the writing table can be a community-building activity. Whenever possible, community-building activities should be tied to an academic purpose. However, any activity that leads to students' getting to know one another, their teachers, and themselves as learners has justification since writing workshop requires a certain level of trust and cooperation among its members in order to be successful.

Anyone with access to a computer and the Internet can find multiple beginning-of-the-year exercises for students and teachers, and Lynne and Diane voice no opposition to teachers using them. Their objections lie in the use of team building only during the first week or two of school and the attitude that this one week is all it takes to build a learning community. Nothing could be further from the truth.

Community building needs to be ongoing; it needs to be embedded in every action—from greeting students at the door each day to making an effort to know each child individually. Donald Graves, in *The Energy to Teach* (2001), suggests putting a checkmark in your grade book next to a student's name when you know something about him or her that is not classroom related and putting a second checkmark next to the name when the student knows that you know this fact. Admittedly, this is a difficult task, but difficult is not impossible. We teachers need to know more than our students' names; we need to know their goals and their dreams as well as their learning styles. How lucky we are to be writing teachers! When we read and respond to student writing we learn a great deal about our students—information that can easily get lost in the everyday march to cover the curriculum. How we encourage students to write and share begins on the very first class meeting and continues each day thereafter.

Following are a few community-building activities that have proven successful for the writers in Lynne's and Diane's workshops.

Quick Facts

A writing classroom supposes that students will write—that they will explore multiple topics and genres, confer about their writing, and revise and edit their pieces. Ask each student to jot six to ten facts about themselves, including one plausible lie. Share your own facts/lie with the class.

- I am a good cook.
- I once won a contest for baking the best apple pie.
- I have three grown children and eight grandchildren.

- I have been married for forty-eight years.
- I have never lived outside of the state of Pennsylvania.
- One of my favorite pastimes is reading the Sunday *New York Times* and doing the Sunday crossword puzzle.

As students read their lists, ask the class to try to determine which of the "facts" is the lie. Students enjoy trying to guess correctly, but the real purpose of the activity is to help students to grow their lists of topics for writing. You can expand this activity by asking students to write a paragraph developing content about one of the truths and another developing content about the lie. These can be shared or used as examples for conferring later.

Another surefire community-building activity uses a poetry scaffold (with embedded grammar!) encouraging student participation. Ask students to form pairs. If there is an odd number of students, the teacher partners with a student to make an even number. Students interview each other, asking questions about hobbies, likes and dislikes, favorite places, and so on. For some classes it may be beneficial, or even necessary, to brainstorm a list of questions for this activity. Encourage students to take notes about what their partner tells them. After the interviews are completed, ask students to write poems about their partners using the following scaffold:

Line 1. Two adjectives connected by "and"
Line 2. A verb (activity or sport is optional) followed by an adverb
Line 3. A simile starting with "As _____ as . . ."
Line 4. If-only statement

Here are some student examples:

Intuitive and observant,
Plays soccer skillfully
As bright as a cardinal on a wintry day
If only I could be as enthusiastic as Sean.
              —Geoffrey, grade five

Comical and thoughtful,
Paints pictures beautifully,
As funny as a carload of clowns
If only I could be as witty as Jessica.
              —Jamal, grade four

Giving and friendly,
Ice skates smoothly,
As fast as a penguin on ice,
If only I could be as athletic as Timmy.
—Garcia, grade two

Depending on your grade level, you can adjust the instructions to focus on verbs and adjectives only or omit a step such as the simile or if-only statement. This activity could follow a mini-lesson on adjectives within your reading workshop when you might create an anchor chart of character traits. The work here will support the creation of this poem in writing workshop. It is easy to embed some grammar lessons on adverbs here. Consider reading *The Maestro Plays* by Bill Martin, Jr., or *Suddenly!* by Colin McNaughton as a read-aloud to introduce the use of -ly adverbs in narratives. Then ask students to return to an anchor chart of verbs that relate to the person they chose to describe in their poem and add an adverb to each verb to tell how the person paints, skates, sings, writes, reads, or bakes—to name a few. Additionally, students can continue to partner with their classmates to write more poetry using this scaffold. Post their poems around the room in the beginning of the year so students can read about their peers and get to know one another.

The Learning Community

Our writing workshops have changed from year to year, depending on a number of factors. While the basic framework stays the same, with focus lessons, guided practice, writing time, and sharing, how we organize the classroom and how we deliver instruction may vary according to our students' needs. Some years we may be able to rely on students' peer conferring more than other years. Some days writing time may take most of the writing block; other days we may allot fewer minutes because students need to spend more time on the focus lesson and guided practice. This may be particularly true when the focus lesson is an aspect of grammar for which students are woefully without a frame of reference. Don't expect that your writing workshop will look the same every day or even from year to year. What should not change, however, is time for sharing because sharing writing and taking risks with writing are both ways that our student writers gain confidence and become better writers. Unless we have fostered a community of learners, students will be hesitant to read their pieces to the class, and their classmates will be unwilling to offer praise or suggestions.

Furthermore, sharing helps writers recognize problem-solving strategies they and their fellow writers are using. When Braden shares how he revised his piece of writing for sentence variety, for example, and explains why he did it, his classmates see a strategy that they can appropriate as their own. It's one thing to have a conference with the teacher; it's another to know that, as a writer, you have the entire class with whom to confer and to problem-solve. It is important to note here that errors can actually be viewed as positives—even as gems—since mistakes often mean that writers are showing growth and developing in sophistication because they tried something new. Smith and Wilhelm tell us that "all significant learning requires risk taking and mistake making" (2007, 58). As students are challenged by new genres, formats, organizational patterns, and sentence structures, they are probably going to make errors. During conferences, teachers must decide which errors should be addressed. In order to do this, teachers need to know what their students (sometimes on an individual basis) are ready to learn, understand, and apply. Often, the focus is on an error that is repeated frequently and by a significant number of the students in the class. When an error diminishes the readers' understanding of the text, the error should be addressed. Other errors take away from the author's voice of authority. If, for example, the student is writing about a famous person such as Abraham Lincoln and misspells that person's name, the writer will not be seen as an expert in the minds of the readers, regardless of the quality of the content. In whole-group or small-group conferences, the teacher and the students are given the opportunity to offer praise first and suggest refinement or polish second. Here are a variety of ways to make good use of share time in writing workshop:

- Talk about what you as a teacher have noticed during conference time.
- Ask your students to share some things they've noticed during peer conferences.
- Take a quick survey. Popcorn around the room: students read a line of their piece when they're ready to, in no particular order. Like speakers in a Quaker meeting, they read "when the spirit moves them." Choose a student to be first, and then have students continue to share aloud the one line they really loved from the piece they are currently working on (almost all students will participate, as well as the teacher).
- Ask students to perform collaborative pieces in reader's theater format or another interesting way (possibly use background music or create backdrops or props).
- Use share time to conduct a group conference using praise-ponder-polish.

- Share snippets from your writer's notebook and ask the students to share from their notebooks.
- Lengthen the writing time and ask the students to write down a line that was a stretch for them—where they tried out something new—or that they were surprised came from their "pen." Collect as a quick survey.
- Build in time for students to turn and talk with a partner about something they struggled with today—something that was difficult for them to do.
- Ask students to share something that a peer or peers had tried out that they would like to try, too.
- Suggest to your students that they find one word from their draft that they consider to be a "gem" and share it aloud (works well when everyone does this and you can collect on a poster that you pass around to be displayed).
- Have students share one thing they have learned from an author they are reading—and you can do that, too, as their teacher.
- Give students multiple opportunities to complete this thought: "As a writer I have learned . . ."
- Have students share what their plans are for the next workshop. Ask them, "Where are you headed?"
- Ask students to share one thing they are going to work on as they revise their piece.
- Encourage students to share a connection they've made between the text they are working on and a book they've read.
- Students share fingerprints—what they naturally do as writers.
- Students share a tip for a successful peer conference.
- Students share something about their writing that surprised them!
- Ask students to share the most important sentence in their piece. Ask, "Why did you choose it?"
- Students share the emotion that drives this piece. Ask, "What were you feeling when you decided to write?"

The structure of writing workshop is predictable and, therefore, comfortable for students. They know what to expect. When we really get into the groove, students think about writing throughout the day. We often hear someone in the class say, "Maybe you should write about that," or "You should put that in your writer's notebook." Students don't have only one writing teacher; they come to recognize how their own classmates may be experts. When Matthew wants to know something about hockey rules, he knows he can ask Bryce. When Jada wants to know if her description of the waterfall in the hotel's pool works, she can ask Gia to listen to it, and Jada knows she will get specific feedback. How does all this happen? Only by building community! Don't neglect this important factor.

Final Thoughts

As we begin to move through units of study, or cycles, throughout the school year, we should start to push a certain amount of editing skills further and further back. That is to say, once a skill has been taught and revisited, students should be responsible for attending to this skill in their earlier drafts in writing workshop, then across the day in science or social studies, and, finally, in their writer's notebook and anything they compose—even a note to a friend. Students should eventually be responsible for using the skills they have learned all the time, giving the "look of literacy" to all written work, formal and informal. Since we believe in a culture of correctness, it is important to push back skills so they become a matter of habit.

Often, you need to examine the writing to know what a particular student or class really needs to be able to do. If your fourth graders are trying to use conversation in their narratives but don't use quotation marks or have no idea where to place end punctuation within quotations—or they don't begin on a new line each time the speaker changes—then it's a good opportunity for a small-group or whole-group conference. Many times, only a few students need to be able to do this skill at that moment. In such cases, creating a flexible small group to do some mini-lessons on writing conversations will move these writers forward.

Tuck in editing skills throughout the year in several places. Word study work can include a look at a sentence from a novel or picture book. Encourage the students to "walk around in someone else's syntax." For example, take the first sentence from *Owl Moon* by Jane Yolen: "It was late one winter night, long past my bedtime, when Pa and I went owling." Notice that Yolen tells when in the first part of her sentence, elaborates on the when (in an appositive phrase), and then tells who and what in the second part of the sentence (an adverbial clause). Have the students copy her lead sentence in their writer's notebook and try it out—walk around in Yolen's syntax. Here is Lynne's example: *It was a sticky, uncomfortable July afternoon that should have kept everyone holed up inside air-conditioned malls or homes, but I was wilting at the Warrington Horse Show with my students, waiting for the next division of competition to begin.*

At the beginning of the year, start to make a list of grammar and editing skills you think your students need. Talk with your grade-level partners, who may have some of the same needs and some different ones. Consult Common Core State Standards as well. Decide what is necessary to move the writer, not the individual piece of writing, forward. Dorfman and Cappelli state, "The best way to encourage students to take risks with grammar and mechanics, as well as develop an understanding of sentence, is to embed this teaching into daily practice" (2007, 256).

We can make the instruction of grammar and conventions skills and concepts part of our teaching across the day—not just in writing workshop. And in order to keep it real and doable, we must remember, writing cannot be taught in a year! Use your best judgment to decide when a student absolutely needs more instruction in grammar or conventions in order to communicate with the target audience clearly and precisely. Differentiate instruction by providing lessons in small, focused groups or in a one-on-one conference. These differentiated lessons often come from your conference notes. As you review them, areas of need and readiness will jump out at you. Remember that mentor texts (see Appendix A) such as picture books, novels, newspapers, magazines, and song lyrics can help all students—including our ELLs (see Appendix F)—improve sentence fluency and gain insights into language (sentence structure, idiomatic expressions, use of punctuation) while amassing a larger vocabulary base. Mentor texts will help bring language to life, promoting active engagement of all students to learn the subtleties of the English language effectively and to experience the joy of learning to love words!

Part 1
Narrative Units of Study

Chapter 1

Writing the Narrative

Introduction to Narrative Writing

How can we use narratives to teach grammar and conventions? What can students learn about grammar by writing fiction, personal narratives, memoir, and folktales? What kinds of stories can beginners write and tell? How can more advanced students learn to tell sophisticated and complex stories for many academic purposes? Narrative writing is an important tool for students of all ages. Stories are told for many purposes. "Indeed, it is imaginative literature that offers readers a chance to think about the human issues that concern us all: love, hate, hope, fear, and all the other emotions, problems, situations, and experiences of living" (Beers and Probst 2013, 17).

What is true for readers is also true for writers. They explore the human condition through compelling plots and larger-than-life characters, using story to illustrate how people make decisions, solve problems, and affect their world. Story helps readers to fashion their moral compass (Gallagher 2003). Sometimes, as in novels, stories are told simply to be stories—to entertain readers. Other literary forms in the tradition of oral storytelling, such as the folktale or myth, are composed to illustrate principles and, in fables, to provide examples. Good stories, however subtle, always teach the reader something, their endings resonating in their readers' minds long after they've read the last word.

Stories are a powerful and engaging vehicle for delivering opinions and information, sometimes acting as bookends to frame expository writing and bring the text to life, as is the case in *Skyboys: The Building of the Empire State Building* by Deborah Hopkinson. Narratives show up in all types of academic writing. Even the process through which research is done appears as a narrative in social studies textbooks.

Teachers who see the big picture, looking at the "forest" rather than the "trees," begin their grammar and conventions instruction by clustering certain lessons in particular modes (text types) of communication.

One of the easiest ways to embed grammar and conventions instruction in narrative is through observing the patterns used in writing stories. Narratives tend to feature the use of:

- past tense verbs (mostly simple past but also past perfect)
- adverbs
- chronological order (signaled by those adverbs and adverbial clauses)
- proper nouns (for the names of people and places)
- personal pronouns (to refer to those people and places)
- use of apostrophes to indicate possessive forms
- use of apostrophes with contractions—often used in informal speech that is more common in story than in any other text type
- sense of sentence—how a sentence looks, with a subject and predicate and various sentence structures
- dialogue—a true characteristic of narratives—with quotation marks and commas to separate explanatory words from what is spoken

Additionally, the narrative structure follows a basic story map that teachers, students, and readers of all ages are familiar with, including the identification of the main character(s), setting, problem or goal, episodes (events), and solution/resolution. This is the basic structure that students often use with teachers, parents, and peers when retelling a story they've just read. Generally, a narrative story uses simple past tense verbs and is in chronological order with occasional flashbacks or flash-forwards; but sometimes an entire story is told in the present tense as in the case of *Shiloh* by Phyllis Reynolds Naylor or *Roller Coaster* by Marla Frazee.

A narrative story also has background information that the author weaves into the text. Most of the time, this information includes what the writer thinks his readers will need to understand the story and may include opinions, generalizations, descriptions, and even previous events that influence the story map. The background information is often more complex than the story map and tends to be more difficult for students to write than the basic story. It may contain, for instance, myriad verb tenses, such as present tense for generalizations that are still true in the present and past perfect tense for events that happened prior to the time of the story. In addition, determining what your reader doesn't know is a very difficult task for any writer and certainly daunting for a student writer.

No matter what the level of the reader (beginner or advanced), all stories include these same two major parts: the basic story map structure or plan and the background information that the author feels the reader will need to understand, enjoy, and remember long after he is finished reading it.

Stories have the same grammar no matter what level of reader they are written for. Differences in complexity lie in the vocabulary used (the number of multisyllabic words), the length of the sentences, the length of the complete text (the number of words used), and the themes and conflicts presented. Furthermore, there can be a substantial difference in the amount of background knowledge given, depending on the target audience, since stories about places, events, and themes that are familiar to the reader are easier to understand and require less explanation than stories about strange new people and events. Text complexity is also reflected in the task the reader is assigned to complete during and after reading the text, but it's not about the grammar. All narratives have similar clusters of grammatical and mechanical features.

Chapter 2

Wordless Books Create Story and Opportunities for Grammar Lessons

Everybody has a story to tell. It's part of the human experience. Since the time of cave dwellers, human beings have needed to tell their stories, leaving behind pictures on cave walls. In the Middle Ages, minstrels traveled from town to town, telling their stories with the help of musical instruments. Considering this remarkable history, we believe that narrative writing is a good way to begin the school year. Children enter school filled with stories to tell (many that their parents wish they wouldn't!). The story is a vehicle to building a writing community. As students listen to one another, respond, and continue to imagine, the community becomes tighter and the possibilities emerge. There is no better time to begin to embed the teaching of grammar into your writing classroom. How does a teacher make this magic happen?

We believe that modeled and shared writing provide opportunities to teach focused lessons and create anchor charts so that the writing can be revisited often and new lessons presented. Anchor charts (displayed as figures throughout this book) usually contain information posted on large pieces of chart paper so that students can use the new learning independently and teachers can return to them, adding new thinking or revising and editing. Modeled and shared writing provide a place in the writing classroom for students to play with language, experiment with words, and take risks in a supportive environment with teacher guidance.

The modeled and shared experiences are perfect occasions to highlight grammar issues. Begin with the basics: recognizing the sentence unit; applying structures of sentences; understanding the importance of nouns and verbs, including their placement in effective sentences; and using appropriate end punctuation. The Common Core State Standards (CCSS) for Language Arts K–5 (Common Core State Standards 2014) addresses these skills as early as kindergarten with increasing development across the grade levels. For example, in kindergarten, CCSSA.ELA-LITERACY.L.K.2.A states, "Capitalize the first word in a sentence and the pronoun I." CCSS.ELA-LITERACY.K.2.B. states, "Recognize and name end punctuation." By first grade, CCSS.ELA-LITERACY.1.1.J requires students to "Produce and expand complete simple and compound declarative, interrogative, imperative, and exclamatory sentences in response to prompts." CCSS.ELA-LITERACY.1.2.B states, "Use end punctuation for sentences." Clearly, to meet these standards, children as early as in kindergarten need to begin to develop a sense of sentence—it begins with a capital letter and ends with an appropriate mark of punctuation. First graders are asked to be able to write the four types of sentences. In order to do that, students will need a sense that sentences, for the most part, require a noun and a verb to be complete.

Teaching Point: Keep alert for those areas where a particular class consistently misuses the English language. For example, your students (like ours) may struggle with pronoun usage. The shared writing will highlight these errors. You can choose to conduct a mini-lesson immediately using the writing on the anchor chart, or you can decide to return to it the next day in the form of a larger, more formal lesson.

Students will often write the way they speak. During class discussions and writing or reading conferences, it may be advantageous to keep a clipboard handy. As you hear common usage errors such as "Me and my friend played ball yesterday" or "I brung the note in from home," make a note of it. Those errors can help you decide which grammar lessons to embed in your current unit of study. Review your notes weekly to get a handle on mistakes that are repeated often by multiple students. Of course, a glaring error belonging to only one or two students can be addressed individually through conferences or small flexible-group instruction. Set a grammar or conventions goal when it is crucial for readability; that is, when the writing cannot be clearly understood or the message is muddled. Formative assessment such as clipboard cruising (walking around the classroom to observe writing behaviors and noting areas of concern, as well as skills and strategies the students are already using that you can praise) is another excellent way to monitor students' needs and progress. As your students are drafting and revising, circulate and stop to read small parts or to ask questions to guide their writing of the narrative. Note errors that you are seeing for *later* grammar and conventions lessons. It is important to let your writers get their ideas down on paper first before addressing conventions and syntax.

Teaching Point: Remember to embed the teaching of grammar into your daily writing lessons through mini-lessons, larger-focused lessons, feedback during conferences, and in whole-group, final reflections (but this teaching may not occur every day in all of these places).

Getting Started: Using Wordless Books

Wordless books are motivating choices for younger and older students. The pictures will help your struggling writers and nonwriters (students who can write but choose not to write) to invent narratives that help them feel successful as writers. We suggest beginning with a read-aloud. In this case, the students will read the pictures with you. Displaying the book on a document imager may be an easy way to provide the whole-class experience. If you have several copies gathered from various libraries, some students can take a "lead" or "teacher" role and share the book. "Reread" the book by asking questions as you turn or display the pages. You might want to pay attention to the story grammar—in other words, who are the characters, where and when does the story take place, what is the problem or conflict, and how is it resolved? Your questions will help your students form a story in their heads. You can model the first time you use a wordless book, orally writing the story as you turn the pages. You can record your storytelling as a video and play it back to students or let them view it later. You can choose to write the story down as you go, or you can write it the second time you go through the pages. Your students may notice that your story has changed slightly or includes new details. Here is a good place to talk about how oral rehearsals are part of the prewriting experience, but the written draft(s) can change slightly or, in many cases, significantly. Students should feel comfortable to explore many possibilities and need to know it is okay to do so.

As you write in front of your students, you can make note of some of the grammar choices, particularly in punctuation and capitalization. If you've used dialogue, you could even talk about the quotation marks you needed. Or you could decide to revise by combining two simple sentences to create a compound sentence. Hopefully, your students will begin to see the necessity for grammar rules and conventions in the context of creating a piece of writing that will be clearly understood by the reader.

Good Dog, Carl by Alexandra Day is a nearly wordless book but does frame the story with the mother speaking to the dog on the first and last page. Here is Diane's model from her work with fifth graders at Springton Manor Elementary School and at Clara Barton Elementary School:

On the first page I am noticing a big black dog named Carl, a mother, and a baby who is in his crib but not asleep. I know someone is talking to the dog because the author uses a comma. This comma is called a comma of address because it helps the reader understand that a character is speaking to someone else directly (CCSS.ELA-LITERACY.5.2.C, "Use a comma to set off the words yes and no, to set off a tag question from the rest of the sentence, and to indicate direct address."). Let's read the sentences together and pause when you come to the comma: "Look after the baby, Carl. I'll be back shortly." The quotation marks tell us that the mother is speaking these words to the dog (CCSS.ELA-LITERACY.3.2.C.). What other marks of punctuation do you notice on this page? (If the students do not notice the apostrophe, point it out to them. First, ask your students to explain the job of the apostrophe. If they don't know, you may have several follow-up grammar lessons to do that week. The apostrophe is a language standard for grade two.)

We know the main characters and have an idea of the setting, so I am going to tell the story as the pictures help me to imagine it. As I go along, I will record it on chart paper. (Diane tells the story, shows the pictures, and records):

"Carl watches out the window as Mother leaves the house. Immediately, Baby stands at the side of the crib, climbs over the bars, and hops onto Carl's back. Carl, a big, strong Rottweiler, can easily carry the weight of the diapered baby. Baby rides

Carl into the adjoining bedroom, and they have fun bouncing on the bed. Carl jumps over the baby, and Baby giggles.

"Afterward, Baby climbs onto the dresser, and he uses the powder puff to powder Carl's nose. Then he makes himself a hat out of the powder puff and the dresser doily. He also adorns Carl's head with beads and the lid to the powder container. They admire themselves in the mirror. How pretty! Suddenly, Baby has an idea . . . he sits on the edge of the laundry chute.

"Alarmed, Carl races down the steps taking giant leaps to cover the ground as quickly as possible. He finds Baby safely nestled in the pile of dirty laundry and carries him back up the steps. In the living room Carl comes to a screeching halt, sliding across the room on a throw rug, scattering papers all over the floor. What fun!

"Next, Baby rides Carl to the fish tank where he takes a swim with the fishes. Carl holds him up above the water with his teeth and pulls him out. Carl realizes that Baby needs exercise. He turns on the music, and they sway to the beat. Carl dances beautifully. In the kitchen they snack on grapes, chocolate milk, and cookies. What a mess they make!

"Afterward, Carl carries Baby up the steps and into the bathroom. Once he fills the tub with water, he bathes the baby—clothes and all! Using a hair dryer, he dries Baby and plops him into his crib. Carl spends the rest of the time cleaning up: throwing away bread wrappers, lapping up the milk, making the bed, and putting away the powder puff and doily.

"When he looks out the window, he sees Mother approaching and runs back to lie beside the crib. He is very tired. Mother is pleased with her babysitter. She says, '"Good dog, Carl!"'"

Your writing lesson for this narrative unit of study is to show that to tell a story, you need a lot of content. Things happen. Using the wordless book, we are not just describing the pictures, we are telling a story. For younger students, you may teach organization and a sequence of events. For older students, you may focus on elaboration, adding specific details in key places, or you may choose to explore possibilities for building effective beginnings and endings. Regardless of your purpose, remember to embed some instruction in grammar. Let's look at Diane's story and notice some grammar lessons in sentence structures as well as sentence patterns. We will discuss exclamatory sentences, interjections, complex sentences, and compound sentences for this model since it contains so many examples.

 Grammar Reference: More than any other punctuation mark, the exclamation point tells the reader how to read the sentence. Students like to use the exclamation point, many times to excess. It can be used following one-word or sometimes two-word interjections such as: Hurray! Ouch! Fire! Help! Stop! Wow! Hallelujah! Wonderful! Oh! Hey! Yuck! Gross! Oh no! What fun! How pretty! Just wonderful! Look out! (CCSS.ELA-LITERACY.5.1.A: "Explain the function of conjunctions, prepositions, and interjections in general and their function in particular sentences.") The exclamation point can also be used at the end of an exclamatory sentence, as in the sentences from Diane's model: What a mess they make! Once he fills the tub with water, he bathes the baby—clothes and all! How pretty! (Note: The interjection "How pretty!" does need an exclamation mark, as do most interjections. However, sometimes an interjection does not use an exclamation mark, as in the sentence, "Oh, well, that's the way it goes.")

Teaching Point: Encourage students to save the exclamation mark for those times when they want to show real surprise or strong emotion. Students can use sticky note strips or colored dots to return to their narrative to find one or two places where the exclamation point would make a difference. When they are making this writing decision, it probably would be helpful to read the piece aloud just the way they would want their readers to imagine it.

In the anchor chart in Figure 2.1, students worked in small groups with piles of books to discover sentences containing exclamation points. This activity reinforces the notion that exclamation points are rare beasts, not commonplace.

Figure 2.1
Discovering Sentences with Exclamation Points

- "April, listen to this. April!" From *Hey World, Here I Am!* by Jean Little
- "Suddenly a voice called out above the others, '"I caught one!"' From *Fireflies* by Julie Brinckloe
- "'Boss!'" he cried in horror when he saw Gasper." From *The Monsters of Morley Manor* by Bruce Coville
- "My grandmother's arms flew into the air. '"Shoo! Skedaddle! Scat!"' she said." From *Mick Harte Was Here* by Barbara Park
- "'The poor things!'" Sophie cried." From *The BFG* by Roald Dahl
- "'Oh, look!'" cried Winnie. '"Water!"' From *Tuck Everlasting* by Natalie Babbitt
- "Grandma is some actress!" From *The Wednesday Surprise* by Eve Bunting
- "''Course. Wood's a superb Keeper!'" Lee Jordan told the crowd as Flint waited for Madam Hooch's whistle. '"Superb!"' Very difficult to pass—very difficult indeed—YES! I DON'T BELIEVE IT! HE'S SAVED IT!'" From *Harry Potter and the Prisoner of Azkaban* by J. K. Rowling. (Notice that, in this case, there are several exclamatory sentences and two one-word interjections. In addition, the author uses variation of print in the form of all capital letters to heighten the emotion.)

Grammar Reference: A complex sentence uses at least one independent and one dependent clause. For example, the first sentence in Diane's model is a complex sentence: *Carl watches out the window as Mother leaves the house.* In this sentence, "*Carl watches out the window*" is the independent clause since it can stand alone as a complete sentence representing one complete thought; "*as Mother leaves the house*" is the dependent clause, in this case, an adverb clause because it tells when something is happening. It is not a complete thought and cannot stand alone.

Ask students to find examples of complex sentences in Diane's model. Record the independent clauses on sentence strips in one color of marker or crayon and the dependent clauses on strips using a different color. Students can stand with a partner, one student reading the independent clause and the second student reading the dependent clause. Extend the lesson by asking students to reverse the order in which the clauses are read. For example, in the aforementioned sentence one may read, "As Mother leaves the house, Carl watches out the window." Ask students to notice the punctuation to see how it changes when the sentence is reversed. Finally, ask partners to return to their notebook to create several sentences using an independent and dependent clause. Write one of them on two sentence strips following the aforementioned procedure and present them at the end of workshop time or display them on the bulletin board (CCSS.ELA-LITERACY.3.1.I: "Produce simple, compound, and complex sentences.").

Grammar Reference: When the dependent clause comes first in the sentence, the comma separates it from the independent clause. However, if the dependent clause follows the independent clause, no comma is typically needed.

The next day ask your students to return to a writer's notebook entry or the narrative piece they are currently working on. Instruct them to look for complex sentences or places where sentences can be combined to create one or several complex sentences for sentence variety, reader interest, and rhythm (CCSS.ELA-LITERACY.5.3.A: "Expand, combine, and reduce sentences for meaning, reader/listener interest, and style). Also, ask them to check to be sure they used the comma correctly. Students can bring their examples to whole-class share. Sometimes, it can be a good idea to place their models on an anchor chart or bulletin board for easy reference. Figure 2.2 is one fifth-grade classroom's anchor chart for complex sentences.

- "When I opened my eyes again, it was Sarah standing there." From *Sarah, Plain and Tall* by Patricia MacLachlan (adverb)
- "When the tinkling little melody began, Winnie's sobbing slowed." From *Tuck Everlasting* by Natalie Babbitt (adverb)
- "He had to work fast or the snowflake would evaporate before he could slide it into place and take its picture." From *Snowflake Bentley* by Jacqueline Briggs Martin (adverb)
- "He picked up the chopper and was about to start chopping away again when he heard a shout behind him." From *James and the Giant Peach* by Roald Dahl (adverb)
- "When Sam goes, she and I do the dishes." From *The Wednesday Surprise* by Eve Bunting (adverb)
- "The screen door banged behind me as I ran from the house." From *Fireflies* by Julie Brinckloe (adverb)
- "When she raised the squeaky lid of the aquarium to shake some shrimp flakes onto the water, Joshua jumped up and came to the top, just as cats and dogs will come running when their food dishes are being filled." From *Every Living Thing* by Cynthia Rylant (adverb)
- "Tonight I'm sleeping on the bottom bunk with Roger, who is afraid of monsters and the dark." From *Someday* by Eileen Spinnelli (adjective)
- "Sometimes he howls at herring gulls until the painter tells him to stop." From *Painting the Wind* by Patricia MacLachlan (adverb)
- "When I tiptoed to the top of the stairs, my heart was racing in my chest." Daijahn, grade five (adverb)
- "When my brother climbed onto the roof of the shed, I knew there would be trouble." Justine, grade five (adverb)
- The snow, which fell for hours, covered the town in a white blanket. Maddie, grade five (adjective)

Figure 2.2
Discovering Complex
Sentences

Notice that students have added their own examples from narratives they had been working on for this unit of study. See the Your Turn Lesson "Expanding a Sentence Using Complex Elements" in Part 3.

Grammar Reference: Help students recognize the different kinds of dependent clauses in order to increase their understanding of how language works. Two choices for dependent clauses are adjective and adverb. Adjective clauses modify or describe nouns or pronouns. They tell which ones, what kind, or how many. They often interrupt the flow of the sentence and are separated by commas because they must be placed next to the noun they modify. Adverb clauses tell when, where, or how and describe verbs. They are more commonly used by young writers.

Another sentence structure Diane uses in her story is the compound sentence. The last sentence of the first paragraph is an example: *Baby rides Carl into the adjoining bedroom, and they have fun bouncing on the bed.*

Grammar Reference: A compound sentence consists of at least two independent clauses, joined by a comma and a coordinating conjunction—*for, and, nor, but, or, yet, so.* A commonly used mnemonic device used to remember these conjunctions is FANBOYS. Both clauses must have a subject and a predicate. Furthermore, the clauses must be able to stand alone.

Ask students to find a few more examples of compound sentences in Diane's story or one you have created for your students such as, "Afterward, Baby climbs onto the dresser, and he uses a powder puff to powder Carl's nose." You might want to point out the difference between a compound sentence and a compound predicate like "He finds Baby safely nestled in the pile of dirty laundry and carries him back up the steps." While this sentence contains two separate actions, the part of the sentence after the conjunction (and) cannot stand alone. Instruct students to return to notebooks, portfolio pieces, or the narrative they are working on for this unit of study and find compound sentences or sentences that can be combined to form a compound sentence. Ask them to read the sentences that come before and after their revised sentences to hear how all the sentences flow. Remind them that a piece contains many kinds of sentences and different lengths of sentences. Too many long sentences may leave the reader breathless or confused. Take some sentences from your model and make them shorter or longer and read the passage aloud to hear the flow of the language. As Vicki Spandel says when discussing sentence fluency, "You must hear the writing—put it in motion" (2013, 191). Sentence fluency is not an issue of grammar; however, in order for students to achieve sentence fluency, they must have a sense of sentence structure or syntax. Students need to learn to trust their ears because language is an oral imprint first and foremost. While they are revising and reading aloud, ask them to explain what kinds of sentences they are creating and how they know. Let's return to the first paragraph of the Carl story:

Carl watches out the window as Mother leaves the house. Immediately, Baby stands at the side of the crib, climbs over the bars, and hops onto Carl's back. Since Carl is a big, strong Rottweiler, he can easily carry the weight of the diapered baby. Baby rides Carl into the adjoining bedroom, and they have fun bouncing on the bed. Carl jumps over the baby, and Baby giggles.

Now we'll create a new paragraph of simple sentences and read the paragraph aloud to and with your students. Ask them to "think-ink-pair-share" in their writer's notebook. Did the revision improve the paragraph? Why or why not?

Carl watches out the window. Mother leaves the house. Baby stands at the side of the crib. He climbs over the bars. He hops onto Carl's back. Carl is a big, strong Rottweiler. He can carry the weight of the baby. Baby rides Carl into the bedroom. They have fun. Carl jumps over the baby. Baby giggles.

A discussion followed, eliciting these comments:

"The second paragraph sounds like a first grader wrote it. It makes you stop too many times. You can't get going."
"It all sounds the same."
"You almost felt like you were reading a fill-in-the-blank workbook page."
"It made you feel like you were taking a bumpy boat ride."

The anchor chart in Figure 2.3 has text examples, teacher examples, and a fifth-grade student example. Anchor charts can be posted in a spot in the classroom where all students can see them and use them. Anchor charts will reduce the number of questions a teacher needs to answer during writing workshop. Many times, the answer can be found by studying the information collected on the chart. Remember, you can always ask students to continue to add to an anchor chart and to revisit it for future mini-lessons throughout the school year. If you have created a real gem, consider laminating the chart so that you can use it in future years as well!

Encourage your students to notice compound and complex sentences in their independent reading books and reading anthologies or guided readers. Add examples to a bulletin board or anchor chart displayed for easy access.

Teaching Point: Ask your students to continue to find examples and add them to the anchor chart as well as the list they are creating in their writer's notebook. These sentences can be used as a quick mini-lesson review over the next several weeks or months. If it is easier for you and your students to access, you may want to keep a small loose-leaf binder or composition book for grammar and conventions notes and make it available to your students. This binder is very useful to students who are absent or are pulled out to attend another class (math or reading support, for example); see Appendix J for more tips.

- "He collapsed next to Sarah, and the lambs pushed their wet noses into us." From *Sarah, Plain and Tall* by Patricia MacLachlan
- "No one else saw, but I found him behind the barn, tossing the pieces of hair into the wind for the birds." From *Sarah, Plain and Tall* by Patricia MacLachlan
- "Sasha is shy about being painted, so the painter puts Charlie on her lap, Emmet at her feet." From *Painting the Wind* by Patricia MacLachlan
- "It was squatting on a low stump and she might not have noticed it, for it looked more like a mushroom than a living creature sitting there." From *Tuck Everlasting* by Natalie Babbitt. (This sentence contains three independent clauses. The comma is used only before the conjunction *for* because the reader needs take a breath here. The first two clauses are closely connected and can be read in one breath. The conjunction signals that an explanation is going to follow. This sentence is probably a good one to challenge the thinking of sixth-grade writers. It is not the best choice for upper elementary school writers who are just learning about how to sprinkle their writing with complex sentences.)
- "I knew I would not have to hide from him, so I walked up and sat down beside him." From *My Side of the Mountain* by Jean Craighead George
- "I was alone in the store but I wasn't afraid." From *Hey World, Here I Am!* by Jean Little. (When students are reading, they may find examples where the comma isn't used before the conjunction such as in the example above. Authors may do this when either clause or just the second clause is short. We should tell students that even though they may find these kinds of sentences in their reading, they should make use of the comma before the conjunction in their own writing for correctness. It is never wrong to use the comma, but by choosing to eliminate it, they could have erred.)
- "We waited a long time to see Santa, yet it was all worth it!" Diane's example
- "I could have gone riding, or I could have earned money babysitting." Susan's example, grade five
- It was not the best time for a picnic, nor was it the best time for a family feud." Lynne's example. (The conjunction *nor* is most commonly used when paired with *neither*. "I like neither sweet things nor salty things." This sentence, however, is not a compound sentence. Students will have difficulty finding examples of compound sentences using nor as the conjunction. It appears that *nor is an endangered species!*)

Figure 2.3
Discovering
Compound Sentences

Other possible lessons from Diane's narrative based on *Good Dog, Carl* include the following:

- Why "baby" is capitalized sometimes (when it is used as the character's name) and not other times (when it is simply a descriptor)
- The use of commas in a series
- The use of exclamation points and interjections
- The use of quotation marks
- The subject-verb sentence
- Subject-verb-indirect object–direct object sentence
- Verb tense
- Possessive nouns
- Proper nouns

- Coordinating and subordinating conjunctions
- Compound predicates
- Shifting word order
- Using active voice
- Appositives

As you can see, myriad opportunities for grammar and punctuation lessons can be found in Diane's model.

Teaching Point: Save your modeled and shared writing experiences to use again and again throughout the school year.

In Christine Flaherty's first-grade class at Upper Moreland Primary School, Lynne used the nearly wordless book *Tuesday* by David Wiesner. First, she "read" *Night at the Fair* by Donald Crews to introduce students to a nearly wordless book. She showed how it could be used to create a narrative, orally telling the *story* behind the pictures. Then she introduced Wiesner's book. Lynne chose this book as one way the students could learn about developing a narrative. The first several pages lend themselves to a great beginning that makes use of description of setting, an important element of story that many students pay little attention to as they compose. The class began by looking at the cover and identifying what they noticed in order to develop a sense of setting. The most important things they noticed are that it was dark and it looked like the story took place in the suburbs. The town clock shows the time as nine o'clock, and the porch light helped students infer that the story took place at night, also a part of setting. The first page identifies the day and time: Tuesday evening, around eight. The next page offers three illustrations of the same scene minutes apart. The students noticed how the light changed: the sunset, the moon beginning to rise, and the moon higher in the sky. Some students said they were at a pond, and others thought it was a swamp. They all noticed the turtle in each drawing. Tyler pointed out that the turtle seemed to be looking at something in the sky in the final picture. At this point, the class helped Lynne write a good beginning for this story as a snapshot of setting. Lynne told them they would return to their opening paragraph to revise for other possible leads after the entire book was shared:

The purple and pink sky was beautiful. A full moon was beginning to show as night came. Lily pods floated near a log in the middle of the water. One turtle sat on the log. He stared at something in the sky.

The rest of the book was shared on a document imager so that students could clearly see the pictures and imagine what was happening in their heads. No one spoke while the pictures were viewed.

Lynne returned to the book the next day to revise the lead paragraph to embed instruction on regular and irregular verbs and to link the choice of verb tense to style (CCSS.ELA-LITERACY.2.1.D: "Form and use the past tense of frequently occurring irregular verbs" and CCSS.ELA-LITERACY.3.1.D.: "Form and use regular and irregular verbs."). They began by rereading the snapshot of setting that they had composed the day before. Lynne decided that she would have the students take a second look at their snapshot of setting before they wrote the remainder of the story. The goal, to "prime the pump" for more vivid writing around the verb of choice, also would demonstrate that revision can occur throughout the writing process. Lynne asked them to look at the first sentence: "The purple and pink sky was beautiful." Lynne noted that it was a telling sentence and asked students to talk about what made the sky so beautiful—what was happening to cause the sky to change colors. Many students immediately noted that it was the sunset. Lynne asked them to start with that and finish a sentence. Hannah came up with, "The sunset made the sky yellow, pink, and purple." After writing the sentence on the board, Lynne asked them to read the original sentence and the revised sentence aloud, then turn and talk about which one they liked better and why. The students liked the second sentence. Lynne asked them to think of a word to replace the verb "*made*." She wrote on chart paper: *The sunset _____ the sky yellow, pink, and purple.* The students volunteered these verbs: *turned, changed, colored, painted*, and *streaked*. The students almost unanimously agreed that the verb *streaked* should replace the verb *made*. Lynne asked them if she could add the word "*with*" after the verb "*streaked*." The students read the sentence. Lucy said it sounded right. The students talked about how the verbs showed that something had already happened. Owen noticed the *-ed* endings on verbs such as *streaked, floated*, and *stared*. They talked about the verb they had discarded—"*made*"—and Lynne said, "Yesterday I made a cake. Today I _____ a cake." The students recognized that the past tense for make cannot be formed by adding an *-ed*.

Teaching Point: If students have difficulty recognizing verbs, ask them to change the time of the sentence from present to past or past to present. The word that changes when you change the time is the verb (CCSS.ELA-LITERACY.3.1.E: "Form and use the simple verb tenses.").

The students talked about the verbs that changed and ones that did not change. Lynne charted them on the board. A discussion with partners followed about verbs, and Lynne asked students if they could think of any other verbs that did not use *-ed* to show past tense. She asked them to frame their thinking with two sentences: Today I _____. Yesterday I _____. The students talked in small groups and came up with a list that included bring-brought, keep-kept, see-saw, sit-sat, swim-swam, sing-sang, buy-bought, make-made, sell-sold. Lynne thought their combined list was quite impressive for first grade.

The first graders continued with their oral writing; however, Lynne asked them to take one more look at their opening paragraph to add a different kind of sentence as a closing sentence for their snapshot of setting. On the board, she quickly reviewed the four kinds of sentences. She suggested trying out an interrogative or exclamatory sentence. In their writer's notebooks, students experimented writing a closing sentence with a partner that was not a declarative sentence (statement). The class liked Nigel's question: What was it?

Grammar Reference: There are four kinds of sentences according to purpose. The most common sentence is the statement or declarative sentence. Its purpose is to give the reader information as either showing or telling. The next most commonly used sentence is the question or interrogative sentence. Its primary purpose is to get information, not give it, or to get people to think more deeply about something (as is the case with rhetorical questions). Exclamatory sentences show strong feeling about a subject and use the exclamation point. An imperative sentence is a request or a command. If strongly stated, an exclamation point would be used (Get here right now!).

The following day Lynne returned to the wordless book to write a whole-class shared experience based on the next six pages of illustrations. Chris and Lynne decided that the students would do better by describing the pictures aloud in whole group or with a partner and then using their writing journal to record their thoughts. After a discussion and time for writing for each individual picture, students shared aloud in whole group. Lynne chose one student's response to record in their shared story, often asking students if they wanted to add or change anything. Here are a few sentences from the whole-class shared experience:

From Shannon: when he looked out his kichen window he sal fling frogs. The fling frogs crashed into the clothsline. Most of the frogs crashed into white shets. They did not look like frogs any mour . . . they looked like gosts!

Lynne and Chris praised Shannon's description and her ability to write in sentences. She used the exclamation mark sparingly. Lynne walked over to Shannon's journal and asked her to circle "sal" and then write "saw" above it. While this spelling error is probably created by a pronunciation error, Lynne felt this word needed to be spelled correctly by a first grader. The word "flying" could be explored at a later date in whole group.

From Nigel: Outside one frog was roketing down the lane when he saw a big dog coming his way. The frog stopped his lileypad and truned around and the frog rased back down the path with the big dog ganing on him. The frog was feeling scard . . .Tarafiyed! The all of asoten hontreds of frogs apeard out of nowere. Then the dog felt TARAFIYED!

After Nigel shared aloud, Chris showed how Nigel had used the ellipsis and how he used all capitals to emphasize how the dog felt. The entire class read Nigel's last sentence aloud. Lynne loved his action words: *appeared, raced, gaining,* and *rocketing.* Lynne asked Nigel to consider rewriting his longer sentence with commas like this: *The frog stopped his lily pad, turned around, and raced back down the path with the big dog gaining on him.* Nigel read the sentence aloud with Lynne several times and agreed to make the changes. Lynne told Nigel that commas are useful when the writer is trying to list more than two things—in this case—three consecutive actions.

From Owen: The sun was coming up in the morning sciy. the frogs wer tubuling onto trees and sum frogs wer on chimnes and ruft ops. The lily pads wer all arond the naberhud.

Lynne loved the way Owen chose to use *morning* as an adjective to describe sky. She pointed out his use of the verb *tumbling,* which evoked a strong picture for her as a reader. Lynne asked Owen to read to find a place where he needed a capital letter, and after reading aloud and pointing to every word, he discovered that the *t* in the word *the* in his second sentence needed an uppercase letter. Lynne asked Owen to circle the word *sciy* and write *sky* above the misspelled word. She felt that was a word Owen could learn how to spell and would most likely need again.

Maribeth Batcho's second-grade class began their study of wordless books with *Night at the Fair* by Don Crews. After sharing the picture book, Ms. Batcho "reread" the book with the help of her second graders. She reviewed the graphic organizer for narrative writing on the board and students shared the elements of story. Maribeth asked them to think about the importance of setting for this story. She also asked them for names for two main characters. The students felt it would be fair to make one character a girl and one a boy, and they wanted them to be brother and sister. Milo and Olivia were chosen as character names. As they developed their lead sentence, they returned to *When I Was Young in the Mountains* by Cynthia Rylant to study how she created a sense of setting. The second graders volunteered their descriptions of the night (the when) and the location (the where). After several sentences were shared, the group decided on Mikey's unique description and combined it with Chris's opening phrase: *One starless night, when the sky was as black as the spots on a cow, Milo and Olivia bought tickets for Funland Fair.* As Lynne recorded the sentence, she asked for help with capitalization. Julianna knew that names of people need uppercase letters and Jayla helped with the name of the fair. (The next day Lynne returned to this lead paragraph and students brainstormed a list of proper nouns for a reference page in their writer's notebook.) Maribeth talked about the simile and told the students that a simile is a comparison between two very different things that are alike in one way. Mikey told the class that he used cows because cows are sometimes at fairs like the fair described in *Charlotte's Web.* Lynne and Maribeth pointed out the use of alliteration in the name "Funland Fair." They used tongue twisters to illustrate what alliteration does. The second graders would return to study similes in spring.

Students continued to orally compose by turning to talk with a partner or two about each picture displayed under the document imager. They had many discussions. Dashawn had described the crowded fair by sharing that Milo felt "like a cushion about to be squooshed." Lynne and Maribeth talked about how sometimes authors make up words. Right away Mikey thought of the Dr. Seuss books. When Maribeth asked what other real words might mean the same thing, Kadden came up with *squashed* and Jayla was pretty sure that *squished* was also a word. In this way, the students engaged in a rich discussion about language. Developing a love of words is key to good writing and to a study of grammar and the musical rhythm created by combining words and sentences.

Since dialogue is a key element of narrative, Lynne and Maribeth found some places where they encouraged the students to speak the words they imagined the characters would say to each other or just out loud to themselves. When the students volunteered these sentences, they referred back to their early November "Turkey Talk" conversations (where students wrote dialogue in the persona of turkeys) and checked the reference pages in their writer's notebook for rules to help them write conversation correctly (see Chapter 16, "Using Mentor Texts for Whole- or Small-Group Discussion" and the Your Turn Lesson "Adding Conversation to a Narrative" in Part 1).

In addition, they decided that certain words needed all capital letters for emphasis, such as in the dialogue, "I WON!"

Maribeth and Lynne also talked about the importance of well-chosen and well-placed adjectives like *sour-sweet* to describe the taste of the lemonade and *salty* to describe the taste of the peanuts. They also talked about the use of effective repetition when JuneSeo suggested: *They looked up, up, up and saw the COLOSSAL Ferris wheel.* Again, Kadden thought the word *colossal* should be written in uppercase letters to make the size of the Ferris wheel even bigger in the readers' minds.

When they finished the shared experience, Lynne made copies for everyone with plenty of empty space so they could draw their own illustrations with colored pencils. They took their books home as holiday presents to share with family members. The class also teamed up to create large illustrations for the panels of text that Maribeth had created with their words in order to display the entire story along the wall in the hallway where teachers, students, and visitors could stop to read their narrative. Like Don Crews, the class was the writer and the illustrator for the shared story included here:

"The Night of the Ferris Wheel"
by Ms. Batcho's Second Graders

One starless night, when the sky was as black as the spots on a cow, Milo and Olivia bought tickets for Funland Fair. They walked through the main entrance. Their hearts were pounding with joy!

It was so crowded that Milo felt like a cushion about to be squooshed. Even though their stomachs growled when they passed the pizza stand, they kept pushing through the steady stream of people.

They forced themselves to keep marching forward past Frozen Delight, funnel cakes, and corndogs. They didn't stop for sour-sweet lemonade or salty peanuts. Milo and Olivia had one thought in mind: the giant Ferris wheel!

"Go ahead. I'll meet you later," Milo told his sister. "I'm going to try to win that monkey with the big red lips." When the man blew the whistle, Milo's duck raced ahead. His duck was the first one to cross the finish line. "I WON!" Milo shouted. He pointed to the one-tooth monkey with big red lips. "That one!" he grinned.

While Olivia was on the way to the Ferris wheel, she saw all the great prizes at "2 IN WINS." She thought, "I'll play to win the parrot with huge yellow wings for my brother." She threw overhand, and her red ball bounced off the back of the booth. Next, she tossed the second ball up in the air and watched it bounce off the pole and ricochet off the bucket. She took a deep breath, closed her eyes, and made a wish. Finally, she threw the next ball high in the air. Olivia held her breath as the third ball went up, up, up! To her amazement, it came down, down, down into the bucket! "I WON!" she shouted. "2 in wins a prize!"

The siblings met at The Twirling Twister. At the same time, Olivia and Milo shouted, "SURPRISE*!*" They exchanged their prizes. Then they sprinted past the carousel, the Whirler, and the bumper cars.

Finally, they stopped. They looked up, up, up and saw the COLOSSAL Ferris wheel. It was so enormous it seemed to touch the sky. It was round and shiny. The ride seemed to be spinning fast. The bright lights were flashing on and off like a thousand lightning bugs. Olivia started to shake and sweat. She thought to herself, "I can't do this!"

"Come with me, Olivia! It's our turn!" Milo squealed excitedly as he took a seat inside the teacup.

Olivia walked slowly with her head down, her heart pounding like a drum. The attendant shut the door. No turning back now. . . .

On the way up, Olivia squeezed her eyes shut tightly. She hugged her brother like a boa constrictor. "Let go!" I can't breathe!" Milo gasped.

At the top of the ride, it paused for one moment, and Olivia opened her eyes. She could see the entire fair! Suddenly, she wasn't afraid anymore! Their teacup began its descent. Milo screamed, "MOM*!*"

A moment later, Olivia pointed and screamed, "DAD*!*"

They wildly waved at their parents and yelled their lungs out all the way down. When the ride came to a stop, Olivia said, "Let's go on again!" Milo grabbed her hand and they raced to the end of the enormous line at the base of the Ferris wheel.

Lynne moved on to a new wordless book, *Tuesday,* by David Wiesner. After sharing the book as a read-aloud, Lynne and Maribeth shared it one more time, allowing the students to make comments about the story through the striking illustrations. The students were so enthralled with this text that many of them asked the librarian for copies of *Tuesday* and other books by David Wiesner.

As they fashioned the lead paragraph, they used Wiesner's three panels to create this paragraph:

The sun was setting over the pond. The sky was painted in purples, pinks, and oranges. The moon was coming up. It looked like an eggshell white ball. A turtle was walking along a fallen log. It was floating among the lily pads. On Tuesday night something mysterious was about to happen. The turtle saw something strange out of the corner of his eye . . .

Maribeth returned to this lead paragraph the next day to see it again with new eyes. She asked the students to read it aloud with a partner several times and make suggestions for revision. The revision focused on two questions:

1. Can you change the order of the sentences to make it more powerful?
2. Are there any sentences that can be combined to improve this lead paragraph?

The students decided to flip-flop the first two sentences and combine them with the word *as* and change the order of the last two sentences, also moving the ellipsis so that it would remain as the final mark of punctuation for the paragraph. Kadden wanted to describe the moon as full and round. Lynne wrote this sentence on the board: *It looked like a full, round, eggshell-white ball.* Then she asked the students if they could move any of the describing words to a different spot. Maggie suggested that "full" and "round" could go at the end. Lynne agreed that sometimes adjectives can come after the noun they describe and rewrote the sentence: *It looked like an eggshell-white ball, full and round.* Aliece thought that another sentence pair could be made into one sentence: *A turtle was walking along a fallen log that was floating among the lily pads.* Lynne returned to the original paragraph on the chart paper and used a different-color marker to edit, using arrows and other editing marks such as the caret. The class orally reread their lead paragraph. Everyone was pleased! Deshawn commented, "Writing sure is hard work!" Maribeth and Lynne readily agreed.

Maribeth asked the student writers to again give the lead paragraph a close read, noticing what changes they had made. Together, they created an anchor chart noting their revisions (Figure 2.4).

As the students continued to examine the pictures, they wrote orally with a partner and sometimes individually in their writer's notebooks. As they began to describe the major events in the plot, Maribeth and Lynne turned the writers' attention to a close look at the verbs and the verb tense.

Figure 2.4
Student Editors of Ms. Batcho's Class Do a "Close Read" of the Lead Paragraph for the Shared Writing for *Tuesday*

1. We changed the order of our last two sentences because it made more sense.
2. We moved the ellipsis to our new final sentence to build suspense and get our readers to read on!
3. We joined (or combined) the first and second sentence using the word *as* and flipped the order.
4. We had to eliminate the pronoun *It* to combine the fourth and fifth sentence by adding the connecting word *that.* The combination helped the paragraph to flow better.
5. We thought about another possibility to combine the first three sentences and change the phrase *coming up* to *rising* (the antonym for *setting*): *The sky was painted in purple, pink, and orange while the moon was rising and the sun was setting over the pond.*
6. We talked about another possibility for the sentence described in number 5. We decided to move the prepositional phrase *over the pond* to follow the word *while* because it sounded better.
7. Looking at the lead, we decided we could move *over the pond* to the very beginning of the sentence and change the basic sentence structure to *the sun painted the sky in.*

The rest of the text was divided into four sections of about four pages of pictures. Maribeth managed one group and Lynne took a group assigned to a different section. Their task was to orally write collaboratively, maintaining their chosen verb tense (past or present) and then rewrite it in the other tense. On the board, Maribeth wrote a reminder and asked a question:

1. During share time, be prepared to share your paragraph.
2. How do you think your choice of verb tense worked for you in this story?

Lynne and Maribeth wanted to find out how students were handling verbs and verb tenses. Students were encouraged to take turns and equally contribute ideas as much as possible. Parts of four different collaborations are shown here. Maribeth and Lynne recorded their groups' responses on chart paper, and then Lynne made copies and circulated the stories so that students could reflect on which verb tense created a more interesting story.

(Past tense) At 11:21 p.m. a man sitting at his kitchen table saw them. "What's that outside the window? Is that frogs on lily pads? I must be dreaming," he thought. The frogs didn't stop. They floated by through the back yards. Some got tangled in the sheets hanging on the clothesline. Others just kept going on. On and on they went.

(Present tense) The frogs pass through open windows and down chimneys. They stop to watch TV with a sleeping grandmother. At 4:38 a.m. one frog is chased by a German shepard. The dog ends up being chased by the frogs! The frogs jump on top of roofs and through the air until daylight. Then, they all begin to fall. Back to the pond they go and sit on their lily pads.

(Past tense) Frogs flew like Superman with bed sheets flowing behind them. They approached the dark houses. Some floated through windows left open on this hot summer night. Others managed to float down the chimney. One frog found a TV remote control and changed the channel with his long, sticky tongue. The old lady sleeping in the chair never woke up. The frogs' eyes were glued to the TV screen watching a movie about Kermit and Miss Piggy. Outside, a frog ran from a German shepard. When a flock of frogs approached, the terrified dog ran for his life.

(Present tense) Ambulances and police cars scream down the wide streets. A puzzled detective scoops up a flattened lily pad. His dog sniffs one lying in the street. They dot the road like flowers in a field. The TV camera crew with a reporter interviews a man still dressed in pajamas. He says he saw frogs floating by his window. What could've happened here? The next Tuesday at exactly 7:58 p.m. strange shadows glide over the red barn. Pigs are floating through the town . . .

A rich discussion followed during reflection time at the end of writing workshop. Students decided that the present tense gave immediacy to the writing, putting the writer and the reader "right there" in the story. They also noted that it was easier to write in the past tense and stay in the past tense. Some teams had trouble maintaining present tense and had to revise some verbs when they reread their pieces. One second grader, Kadden, said he liked the present tense because at the end of the story the whole thing was starting all over again but this time with pigs. Emily agreed and added that the past tense makes you feel that the story is over and this one isn't. So, she felt present tense was the better choice. This is the kind of conversation teachers want to have with their students. Writers need to understand the reasons for the decisions they make in writing.

Teaching Point: With your students create an anchor chart that students can continue to add to throughout the narrative unit of study. You may choose to use a three-column chart like Lynne did, displaying present, past, and past participle. See chart in Figure 2.5.

Figure 2.5
Principal Parts of Irregular Verbs (created by Ms. Batcho's second-grade class)

Present	Past	Past with Helper "Have"
rise	rose	risen
bring	brought	brought
sing	sang	sung
write	wrote	written
think	thought	thought
see	saw	seen
teach	taught	taught
ring	rang	rung
run	ran	run
break	broke	broken
come	came	come
do	did	done
go	went	gone
say	said	said
give	gave	given
fly	flew	flown
swing	swung	swung
speak	spoke	spoken
eat	ate	eaten
fall	fell	fallen
grow	grew	grown
know	knew	known
shake	shook	shaken

Grammar Reference: Irregular verbs form their past and past participle in different ways from regular verbs. Sometimes the spelling is completely changed, as in *go, went,* and *gone.* Other times the spelling remains the same, as in *set, set,* and *have set.* A past participle uses a helper word such as *have, has, had,* or any other helper. Although the chart will not note present participle, students may be using present participles in their writing. For example, the present participle of the verb *go* would be *(is) going* or *(are) going.*

Teaching Point: Before you send your writers off to do guided or independent writing, make sure they know what they should be thinking about and what they will be asked to share so they are prepared to reflect and take part in the discussion at the close of workshop.

Here is the entire story the second graders developed, revising and editing as a shared writing experience. Wiesner's wordless book was a perfect choice for them—highly engaging!

The Magical Moon

(A fantasy based on David Wiesner's Tuesday)

by Ms. Batcho's Class

The sky was painted in purples, pinks, and oranges while the sun was setting over the pond. The moon was coming up. It looked like an eggshell–white ball, full and round. A turtle was walking along a fallen log that was floating among the lily pads. The turtle saw something strange out of the corner of his eye. On Tuesday night something mysterious was about to happen.

The turtle tucked his head into his shell and looked up. Everywhere there were frogs flying up into the air on their lily pads like airplanes. The fish, balancing on their tails, looked up out of the water in amazement. "Oh my goodness! FLYING FROGS!" thought the fish.

The full moon was shining brightly on the clock tower. It was a few minutes past nine. Ravens perched on telephone wires like a church choir when suddenly, the flying frogs came into view. The ravens screeched as they flapped their wings and flew away as fast as lightning bolts. The frogs felt excited when they discovered they could fly their lily pads with the birds.

The flying frogs headed toward the houses where families were sleeping. In one house a man got up to have a midnight snack. While he was eating his peanut butter sandwich, he heard the soft croaking of frogs. He felt like there were eyes watching him! He got up slowly and tiptoed toward the window. Frogs were tangled in the sheets hanging from the lines and looked like ghosts flying through the air. One frog tunneled through a leg of jeans hung on the line while another grabbed on as his lily pad floated away.

In a nearby house a small amount of light glowed from the window. Frogs wearing capes were flying on their lily pads toward an open window. Others floated down the chimney and out of the fireplace like jolly old St. Nick. Frogs hovered like helicopters around the sleeping grandma to watch television. One frog had the TV controller and used his long, sticky tongue to change the channels.

Another frog was flying along outside when he suddenly saw a four-legged creature with a big, spiky collar. The frog leaned back and pushed out his feet to try to stop the lily pad. The furry creature was only two steps away. The frog turned around and started to fly away with the dog close behind.

The game of dog-chase-frog backfired. Suddenly, all the frogs that were watching TV heard soft croaks and fierce growls coming from the yard. They knew their friend was in trouble. They poured out of the old lady's house and chased the panicking dog down the street until he disappeared into his doghouse where he stayed until the sun came up.

As soon as the sun started to come up, the frogs began to fall from their lily pads. One lily pad hung from a chimney. Others fell onto the branches and rooftops. Surprised and disappointed frogs began to fall from the sky like green rain. They hopped from town through the cornfield, down the country lane, and back to their pond. SPLISH-SPLASH!

Early that morning the police came to see lily pads scattered over the quiet neighborhood after receiving a call from a man who reported seeing flying frogs. He pointed to the sky. "Frogs were flying through the sky on lily pads!" he told reporters. A detective was trying to figure out why wilted lily pads greened the road while his canine that had been chased by frogs earlier sniffed one lily pad nearby. If only dogs could talk!

The following Tuesday night a mysterious shadow appeared above the barn door. As the full moon continued to rise, so did the pigs . . .

Students were given the option of returning to Wiesner's *Tuesday* to write an entire story on their own or choose another wordless book from the school or classroom library. Lynne and Maribeth conferred to brainstorm possibilities for other grammar lessons (new or revisited) that could come from the collaborative and independent pieces. Here is that list:

- Sentence combining
- Sprinkling dialogue in a narrative (quotation and punctuation)
- Kinds of sentences by purpose
- Playing with word order in sentences
- A complete sentence has a subject and predicate
- Helping (auxiliary) verbs
- Using verbs in contractions
- "To be" verbs
- Adding adjectives after the noun they describe
- Using prepositional phrases to begin a sentence (for variety and to add details)

In Cathy McParland's kindergarten ESL classroom in late spring, Lynne shared *Night at the Fair* by Donald Crews. The book has some text (often in the form of signs such as "Main Gate") but relies heavily on illustrations for meaning. Almost every child has had some experiences with fairs, boardwalks, and amusement parks—but even if they haven't, Crews's drawings evoke a sense of what a fair is like. Lynne shared the book with the students gathered close to her on a rug. She asked them what they saw in the pictures, and Lynne charted their thoughts. On the first page they noticed families waiting in line for tickets. They said that everyone was happy because fairs are fun. Son said that the sky was as black as chocolate candy. Alfredo added that it looked very crowded. On subsequent pages, they described many things:

> different kinds of food and games
> bright lights
> nighttime
> people eating ice cream and candy
> stuffed animals from games
> merry-go-round ride (carousel)
> tilt-a-whirl
> swings
> giant Ferris wheel
> leaving the fair

Lynne read the text that appeared on some of the pages, often in the form of fragments such as, "So many things to eat and drink." She read the signs, too. The next day she returned to the book and took a picture walk. Lynne modeled with her sentence for the first page of text: *Many families stand in line for tickets to the fair.* Then she asked her class to think about what was happening on the next page. Here are some responses:

> A family is ordering pizza. They are very hungry.
> The kids aren't going to eat because everyone knows you should do the rides first.
> People are smiling, talking, looking, and walking.
> Kids are happy because it is summer and they are out of school.
> There is a game with whales. There are prizes!

Lynne asked the ESL students to begin to think about a lead paragraph and name two characters. They decided on "Linda" and "Jake." She asked the students to give her some sentences that would tell the "where" and the "when" of the story. Lynne also asked the kindergartners to tell her how they would feel if they were about to enter the main gate of the fair on a summer night. She recorded their thinking and moved on to continue to describe the setting in the first several pages of pictures on subsequent days. Lynne used chart paper to record their sentences, one sentence for each page (illustration). Her purpose for the lesson was to have students write sentences beginning with a capital and ending with a period or question mark (CCSS.ELA-LITERACY.K.2.A.: "Capitalize the first word in a sentence" and CCSS.ELA-LITERACY.K.2.B: "Recognize and name end punctuation."). While students were contributing their sentences, Lynne and Mrs. McParland helped them, doing a little editing if the sentence was a fragment or a run-on, although they didn't label their attempts as such. Mrs. McParland called her young writers to the chart paper to underline the first letter in the first word of every sentence and to notice that it began with a capital letter. She asked other students to come to underline the end punctuation mark in a different color. Lynne mentioned that every sentence has a "who" or a "what" and the rest of the sentence tells more about the "who" or the "what" (CCSS.ELA-LITERACY.1.1.J: "Produce and expand complete simple and compound declarative, interrogative, imperative, and exclamatory sentences."). She told students that a sentence has a "who" or "what" called the subject. The rest of the sentence is called the predicate and is about what the "who" or "what" is doing. In kindergarten, it *is* important to give students a basic idea that a sentence has a "who" or "what" that does something, but it is not important that the students name the parts of the sentence as subject and predicate (see Appendix B).

The following day, Mrs. McParland gave each student a partner. She gave partners one copy of *Night at the Fair* and a small frame made out of Popsicle sticks. The same page was marked with a sticky note so that all students opened their book to the same illustration. She asked them to decide which part of the picture was most interesting to them and place their picture frame over that part. Then students were asked to turn and talk about what was in their frame. Next, they were asked to help each other write down their sentence(s) in their writer's notebooks. Lynne reminded them to begin with a capital letter and to end with a mark of punctuation such as a period, question mark, or exclamation mark. Mrs. McParland and Lynne circulated to help students with spelling. Here are some student sentences:

I can win the monkey! (Joon Woo and Katherine)
Linda is throwing balls into a basket. (Alfredo and Lizbett)
Jake gives the man money to play the game. (Nathaniel and Son)

Students read their sentences in share time. Mrs. McParland asked the student pair to show where they had used a capital to begin their sentence and the end punctuation mark. She asked Katherine and Joon Woo to explain why they had used an exclamation mark to end their sentence. Joon Woo said winning a prize is very fun. Lynne agreed that this sentence shows how exciting it is to win a prize.

Teaching Point: In order to move quickly around the room to help with difficult spelling, carry index cards with you. Use a ruler to divide the card in half on both sides. When students need a big word, copy it onto the index card, leave it with the student, and move on rather than stay in one spot and spell letter by letter while the student writes it down. Then you can use the same index card for the same child four times. If you choose, you could have a spelling section or ABC spelling notebook so that students can eventually take the words from the cards and copy them into a permanent notebook to use again.

Lynne and Mrs. McParland continued to show different pages to the students who were gathered on the rug in front of the chart, and during the next week students orally wrote individual sentences for many of the illustrations. The students particularly noticed the flags. They discussed the use of capital letters to name the flags from individual countries. When they came to the page that showed the Ferris wheel, Lynne asked them to use describing words to help her see the Ferris wheel in Crews's illustration. Son said it was big. Lynne asked them to think of synonyms, and the students thought of *large, huge, giant, gigantic, humungous,* and *enormous.* Nathaniel liked the lights that "looked like tiny stars." Lynne wrote that down. "Wow! Nathaniel, that works so well here because it is night and stars come out at night. Perfect!" Lizbett liked the blue, yellow, and orange spokes, but she didn't have the word for the arms that extend from the center to the outer wheel so she pointed to them. Mrs. McParland told her that they looked like the spokes on a bicycle wheel, so she could call them that.

When Lynne asked how the main characters probably felt as they reached the top of the ride, Alfredo raised his hand right away. "You can see the whole universe!" he exclaimed. Lynne used all their descriptions and recorded their sentences. Sometimes, Lynne and Mrs. McParland had to ask a few more questions to pull details from the students. They tried to give attention to capital letters and end punctuation. When Lynne asked specifically for the exact words that Linda or her brother might say about riding the bumper cars, she showed the students the quotation marks and explained to them why she needed them.

Lynne copied their final version along with their chosen title and left room for illustrations on each page. The students sat in a big circle and read their story. They practiced reading aloud several times so they could share the story with parents and siblings. All the sentences created a story about a night at the fair. Here is their entire story:

The Giant Ferris Wheel
by Mrs. McParland's Kindergarten ESL Class

Jake and Linda stood in a long line to buy tickets for the fair. They felt happy and excited. They wanted to ride the Ferris wheel.

They passed the pizza stand and The Whale Game. They saw the American flag, the Korean flag, and the Mexican flag. One red flag had a big yellow star on it. Jake knew it was the flag for Vietnam. They walked by candy, ice cream, and the lemonade stand but didn't stop.

They stopped to watch the carousel. Jake pointed to a horse, small and white. On the next ride, children sat on swings that went up into space. They were flying around in circles like bats.

When they came to the bumper cars, Linda said, "I don't like this ride. It hurts!" Her brother laughed. He liked to crash into other bumper cars.

The Ferris wheel was humongous! The bright lights were blinking. There were hundreds of lights like teeny tiny stars. The seats looked like teacups.

Jake and Linda sat down in a teacup. Their hearts beat hard and fast. They grabbed the bar tightly. The Ferris wheel started to spin. Jake and Linda went up, up, up! They were so high they could see the whole universe! They started coming down. They started to scream. "YEAH!"

Jake and Linda were sad the ride was over. Jake said, "Let's ride it again!" Linda was dizzy, so she watched while her brother rode the Ferris wheel two more times before they went home. The fair was so much fun!

Mrs. McParland and Lynne talked about possible lessons that could immediately follow using *Night at the Fair*. See the Your Turn Lesson: "The Job of a Verb Is to Show Action" at the end of Part 1. They came up with lots of possibilities for grammar and mechanics lessons within the narrative study to be addressed in spring when the students would have had more practice with writing:

- The pronoun *I* is always capitalized.
- A noun is a naming word.
- A verb is an action word.
- Adjectives tell about nouns.
- A period is used at the end of a telling sentence.
- A question mark is used at the end of an asking sentence.
- An exclamation mark is used at the end of a strong feeling sentence.

- Variation of print—all capitals—to show excitement and/or to say the words in a louder voice ("And now, on to the RIDES!")

Bibliography of Wordless Books

Because wordless books provide young writers with a natural scaffold upon which to build a story, we recommend having multiple copies of wordless books on hand. Here are some that Lynne and Diane have found useful in grades K–6.

Baker, Jeannie. 2004. *Home*. New York: Greenwillow Books.

_____. 2010. *Mirror*. Somerville, MA: Candlewick.

Becker, Aaron. 2013. *Journey*. Somerville, MA: Candlewick.

Boyd, Lizzy. 2013. *Inside Outside*. San Francisco: Chronicle Books.

Briggs, Raymond. 1986. *The Snowman*. New York: Random House.

Catalanatto, Peter. 1993. *Dylan's Day Out*. New York: Scholastic.

Cole, Henry. 2012. *Unspoken: A Story for the Underground Railroad*. New York: Scholastic.

Crews, Donald. 1998. *Night at the Fair*. New York: Greenwillow Books

Day, Alexandra. 1989. *Carl Goes Shopping*. New York: Farrar, Straus and Giroux.

Day, Alexandra. 1991. *Good Dog, Carl*. New York: Simon and Schuster.

de Paola, Tomie. 1978. *Pancakes for Breakfast*. New York: Voyager Books.

_____. 1981. *The Hunter and the Animals*. New York: Holiday House.

Frazier, Craig. 2011. *Bee and Bird*. New York: Roaring Book Press.

Idle, Molly. 2013. *Flora Flamingo*. San Francisco: Chronicle Books.

Keats, Ezra Jack. 1999. *Clementina's Cactus*. New York: Viking.

Lee, Suzy. 2008. *Wave*. San Francisco: Chronicle Books.

Lehman, Barbara. 2004. *The Red Book*. Boston: Houghton Mifflin.

_____. 2008. *Trainstop*. Boston: Houghton Mifflin.

McCully, Emily Arnold. 2007. *Four Hungry Kittens*. New York: Penguin.

Newgarden, Mark, and Megan M. Cash. 2007. *Bow-Wow Bugs a Bug*. New York: Harcourt.

Pett, Mark. 2013. *The Boy and the Airplane*. New York: Simon and Schuster.

Pinkney, Jerry. 2009. *The Lion and the Mouse*. New York: Little, Brown Books for Young Readers.

Raschka, Chris. 1993. *Yo! Yes!* New York: Scholastic.

———. 2011. *A Ball for Daisy*. New York: Schwartz and Wade.

Rathmann, Peggy. 2002. *Good Night, Gorilla*. New York: Putnam.

Rogers, Gregory. 2004. *The Boy, the Bear, the Baron, the Bard*. New York:
    Roaring Brook.

Rohmann, Eric. 1997. *Time Flies*. New York: Dragonfly Books.

Staake, Bob. 2013. *Bluebird*. New York: Schwartz and Wade Books.

Tan, Shaun. 2007. *The Arrival*. Melbourne, Australia: Lothian Books.

Wiesner, David. *Tuesday*. 1991 New York: Clarion Books.

———. 1992. *June 9, 1999*. New York: Houghton Mifflin.

———. 1999. *Sector 7*. New York: Houghton Mifflin.

———. 2006. *Flotsam*. New York: Houghton Mifflin.

———. 2013. *Mr. Wuffles*. New York: Houghton Mifflin.

Chapter 3

Writing the Personal or Fictionalized Narrative

In the past, primary-grade students often read lots of stories and had many stories read aloud to them. Over the past decade, however, the picture has slowly changed. Teachers are giving up some read-aloud time each day to fulfill other content demands. Lynne surveyed a dozen primary school teachers from several school districts. They were very honest about the lack of time to read aloud to their students. The majority of teachers confessed that read-aloud time was the first activity they had to cut for special assemblies, guest speakers, field trips, and time to administer myriad assessments including DIBELS, DRAs, and running records for progress monitoring. Reading programs highlight guided readers that are controlled for vocabulary and word count. The stories are not highly motivating or filled with the rich details that readers love to gobble up! Anthologies are at least 40 to 50 percent nonfiction text, and Common Core State Standards have turned the spotlight on nonfiction reading and writing in a big way. Parents' work schedules are on overload, too. They often lament the short time they have to get their kids to after-school activities, prepare and eat dinner, and help with homework. There is little time or energy to read aloud to their children. As a result, many students are unfamiliar with fairy tales, folktales, and other stories. Read-alouds help young children develop a sense of how stories go, how they are developed, and what ingredients a writer needs to use to be successful. Hearing the written word aloud is important because language is an oral imprint first. The young writer begins to internalize the syntactical progressions of various sentence patterns, learning to expect a noun here and a verb there, even if he cannot identify those parts of speech. For all these reasons, teaching the narrative should be a slow and deliberate process with plenty of modeling and shared experiences. Within each shared experience, group conference, and one-on-one conference is an opportunity to embed instruction concerning grammar and conventions.

Lynne partnered with second-grade teachers in the Upper Moreland Primary School and Woodland Elementary School in Methacton School District to develop and teach a narrative unit of study. The teachers recognized the need to break down narrative instruction around the narrative's basic components using the traditional story map as a guide. Although it seemed like their students should be natural storytellers at this age and stage, students often engaged in recounting the infamous "And then I" story that was boring to all but the author who wrote it. Students lacked conflicts, problems, goals, and big events. Many stories retold trips or weekend events and read more like a time schedule.

Lynne asked second-grade teachers Maribeth Batcho and Jen Kennedy what grammar and conventions lessons were needed based on their observations. They came up with similar lists. They were concerned with students' having a sense of sentence and with the use of a capital letter to begin the sentence and some mark of end punctuation at the close of the sentence. Their list of mini-lessons included pronoun use (particularly naming oneself last and not using "me" as the subject pronoun), using end punctuation, punctuating dialogue, capitalizing names of pets, holidays, cities, states, and specific places such as Empire State Building, Missouri River, Grand Canyon, and Great Adventure Amusement Park. Apostrophe use in contractions and possessive forms was problematic. The students knew almost nothing about when to begin a new paragraph and did not use time/order words (transition words and phrases) to help the reader move through a piece of writing. Lynne added use of variation of print, so effective in the narrative form. She also added a strategy that would highlight a strong verb and enhance the writer's voice. Teachers also contributed correct usage of the homophones your/you're, their/there/they're, to/two/too, and hear/here. Common Core standards for Grade 2 include capitalization rules (CCSS.ELA-LITERACY.2.2.A), use of the apostrophe in contractions (CCSS.ELA-LITERACY.2.2.C), and expect students to write sentences beginning with a capital letter in kindergarten (CCSS.ELA-LITERACY.K.2.A), and ending with an appropriate end mark in first grade (CCSS.ELA-LITER-ACY.1.2.B). Lynne had plenty of food for thought so she started by reading aloud to them. The students heard two favorite narratives, *Widget* by Lyn Rossiter McFarland and *Crab Moon* by Ruth Horowitz. When she read *Widget*, Lynne stopped on the page that contained these words: *Mrs. Diggs was saved*. Lynne asked the second graders to think about endings for stories. This sounded like an ending, but was it a good one for this story? Students talked with one another and came up with the thinking that since the book was really about the dog, they thought it should end by telling us what happened to Widget. Lynne readily agreed and showed them only the illustration on the last page. She had the students give their thoughts and feelings about what was happening in the picture. Together, they wrote a satisfying ending for the story. Ms. Batcho's class contributed this shared writing experience:

The cats gathered around Widget. They purred loudly and waved their tails proudly in the air. They looked at Widget with love. They rubbed their fur against his back. They wanted him to stay forever. Widget had saved the day and he would always have a home!

Although Ms. Batcho's class would not return to work on endings for their own stories for another week, Lynne felt that starting with endings might help students think about them differently. Too often, students lose energy by the closing of a story and don't spend time writing the perfect ending for their story. Lynne talked about the strategies the students had used, including final actions, what the characters were thinking and feeling, and a final promise or decision. She returned to other books they had read such as *Crab Moon, Shortcut* by Donald Crews, and *Fireflies!* by Julie Brinckloe to talk about strategies for writing endings. Lynne started with endings because she wanted to stress the importance of writing a satisfying ending and how writers often used more than one strategy to accomplish this feat.

When they returned to the shared experience, Lynne taught them a strategy for highlighting the verb. The technique can be found in *Love That Dog* by Sharon Creech. It's a great method for writers of all ages to use because it helps them focus on action verbs in their writing. Verbs are the muscles of a piece of writing. Author Frank Murphy shared this technique of replacing weak verbs with powerful ones with Lynne. He explained that this strategy adds song and poetry to any piece while at the same time adding emphasis to a particular thought, feeling, or action. For example, if a sentence about a snow day reads, "My brother and I went down the hill on our sleds," the first thing to do is revise. The verb *went* is weak. The writer would brainstorm substitutions such as *slid, raced, zoomed, rocketed*. If the writer chose *raced*, then the sentence would be rewritten to repeat the base form of the verb two times before the *-ed* or *-ing* form. "My brother and I race, race, raced down the hill on our sleds." If the student chose *rocketed*, the sentence would look a little different. Since *rocket* is a two-syllable word, the writer would use the first syllable and change the sentence to: "My brother and I rock-rock-rocketed down the hill on our sleds."

Lynne directed students to locate the action words or verbs in their shared writing experience (CCSSELA-LITERACY.L.1.1.E specifies the recognition of verbs). The students chose *looked*, *rubbed*, and *purred* to try out this strategy. After rereading the paragraph with revisions, the second graders concluded that one time was probably enough. The sentence they selected to keep read, "They purr, purr, purred loudly and waved their tails proudly in the air." Lynne encouraged them to try out this strategy as they wrote their narrative or returned to revise it. For additional practice, she asked them to return to their notebooks to find an entry where they could add this strategy. The young writers located several strong verbs or replaced weak ones with better choices. Then they tried out the strategy once or twice and shared in whole group. Later, she would ask the second graders to try out this strategy within the text of their narrative, either while drafting or revising. Although this strategy definitely contributes to the style of a piece of writing, it also helps young writers think about their verbs, revising their writing to replace weak ones as they try out this skill. Nothing is as critical as the use of action verbs in a narrative piece of writing. Students must learn to paint pictures with verbs, substituting stronger ones for overused, weak ones.

Teaching Point: When writers learn a new strategy or craft, they will most likely overuse it until they reach a comfort level with the new technique. It's okay to let them do that in the beginning. Then wean them off using a strategy that really should only appear once or twice in a story that is one or several pages. Let them know that in the books they read, they may find a strategy used many times, but the book may have thirty pages or more!

The shared writing experience was rich in other opportunities to teach grammar and mechanics. Lynne noted that the students might be ready to talk about adverbs since they used two adverbs in their shared ending. (See the Your Turn Lesson "The Movable Adverb" at the end of Part 3 of this book.) Other possibilities include a mini-lesson on the homophones *their/there/they're* and an introduction to prepositional phrases and what they add to the sentence (see Appendix C). Finally, Lynne wanted to eventually return to this piece of writing to talk about pronouns and the job they do as well as the overuse of a pronoun leading to some confusion for the reader.

The next day Lynne returned to mentor texts to help students get their stories started. One way to write a good beginning for a narrative is by describing the weather. The weather is something that everybody talks about daily. Students of all ages are able to describe it. Since setting is such an important element of story, details about the weather can also help readers determine time of day and the season. Lynne shared the beginning from *Best Little Wingman* by Janet Allen:

> Janny pressed her fingers against the icy kitchen window, watching for the headlights on the road. She knew that when her fingers melted the ice, her father would come to take her for a ride in the big snowplow. "Come away from that window and eat your supper," her mother called as she pulled hot biscuits from the oven. Janny was tempted by the smell but she couldn't leave her window.

Lynne asked the students to find nouns that helped describe the weather or setting. (See more discussion in *Mentor Texts: Teaching Writing Through Children's Literature, K–6* [Dorfman and Cappelli 2007].) The students listed *ice, headlights,* and *snowplow.* When she asked for verbs, they came up with *melt.* She asked if any adjectives helped to describe the season or setting, and immediately they found *icy.* Originally, they had placed *kitchen* in the group of nouns. Lynne showed them why *kitchen* acted like an adjective in the sentence from the story. A quick mini-lesson on testing for adjectives followed: the (a or an) _____ noun. If the word fits in the space between the noun marker and the noun, it is an adjective. Lynne showed the young writers that just a sprinkling of the right words help readers to understand the setting.

Introducing primary students to basic parts of speech helps teachers and students talk about how to improve sentences or revise for specificity. She wrote in front of the students:

As I walked through the doors, the air became quite muggy. A strong smell of chlorine filled my nostrils, but all I could really think about was the high dive. I wiped my clammy hands on my towel and sat down on the bench next to my friends. My knees were knock, knock, knocking together and my heart raced inside my chest. I wondered if I would be able to do a dive that would qualify me for the swim team. "Calm down," I thought to myself.

Lynne asked the second-grade writers to look for nouns that helped them discover the setting for the story. They found *chlorine, high dive, bench,* and *swim team.* Max was excited because he found the "highlighting a verb technique." Lynne asked him if he thought she made a good selection. "Yes!" Max answered. "It helps me know that you were really nervous about the dive." Stephanie added that Lynne could have picked *wiped* as the verb to highlight because it would also show how nervous she was about making a good enough dive. Lynne pointed out that she used a "thoughtshot" (what someone is thinking; see Barry Lane's *After "The End": Teaching and Learning Creative Revision* [1993]) to show what she was thinking inside of her head instead of speaking the words aloud. Showing what the characters are thinking is also a characteristic of narrative. Lynne felt the second graders were ready to have a go at a shared writing experience for a good beginning. Their teacher, Maribeth Batcho, asked them to think about why lead paragraphs are so important. Brandon shared that if the beginning is good, then you want to keep reading. Ms. Batcho asked them to think about a setting for a story that they could all help to write. It is very important in the shared experience to try to find that common ground so everyone or almost everyone can participate. They chose their field trip to the Mercer Museum. Ms. Batcho asked them to listen while she reread the beginning of *Best Little Wingman.* Then she asked them to think about the weather for that particular day of their recent field trip and give her a lead sentence. Slowly, they built a beginning while Lynne recorded it on a chart:

When we took our trip to the art museum, it was a sunny, windy day. The clouds looked like fluffy cottonballs. I was really excited to see the artwork. I chattered away the entire bus ride. When the bus arrived, my classmates were chanting, "We're here! We're here!" Nothing could go wrong on this wonderful day!

The students evaluated their beginning. Sarah pointed out that they had described the weather and even used a simile, something Ms. Batcho had taught them earlier that year and revisited several times. Jake noticed some strong verbs like *chattered* and *chanting*. At this point in time, Lynne and Maribeth did not talk about auxiliary or helping verbs. Aidan liked the dialogue. He had actually suggested it. Lynne said it would help readers recognize this piece as a story. Maribeth applauded Aidan's use of contractions and knowing how to spell *we're* correctly. The second graders had learned many contractions, but they had not yet mastered them. Still, they enjoyed trying them out in their writing (see the Your Turn Lesson "Contractions Using Pronouns" at the end of Part 2 of this book). The students used the rest of writing workshop time to brainstorm choices for their own narrative or to look back in their writer's notebooks for possible ideas from their heart maps or authority lists (see *Mentor Texts* [Dorfman and Cappelli 2007] and *Nonfiction Texts* [Dorfman and Cappelli 2009]).

The next day the class shared ideas for narrative. Lynne and Maribeth talked about the personal narrative and how writers often write about what they know best—their own lives. Lynne tried to explain the difference between an autobiography and a personal narrative. She talked about a "slice of life" and gave some examples from her own life. Maribeth and Lynne encouraged the second graders to fictionalize their stories in order to create a problem or goal or to be able to build to an exciting event that would compel their classmates to read on. Lynne returned to *Best Little Wingman.* "The 'About the Author' information on the back inside flap of the cover tells the reader that Janet Allen grew up in the state of Maine [she pointed to Maine on a map] where the winters can be cold and snowy. It also says she traveled around the countryside with her dad. I'm thinking that 'Janny' in the story is Janet Allen and that this story is based on things she really did with her father." Then Maribeth and Lynne both orally wrote a quick sketch for a story. Lynne's fishing story with her Uncle Earl and her grandfather took place on Lake Wallenpaupak in the Poconos, but nothing exciting happened. They didn't even catch any fish. Lynne changed the story and fictionalized it to add an incident where she fell over the side of the boat in an attempt to catch a fish and was rescued by her grandpa but still had her fishing line with a fish on it! Maribeth and Lynne gave the students permission to embellish—they actually encouraged it. It may seem odd, but elementary school students sometimes have to be told that they can write a story that is based on truth but is mostly fiction.

They began to write a sledding story that would become their mentor text they could refer to as they wrote their own narrative. The beginning of their shared experience would create a sense of setting, use a weather lead, and let the readers in on what the main character was thinking or feeling. Lynne reminded the young writers that they could use a splash of dialogue or a thoughtshot to accomplish this. Additionally, the beginning would point the reader in the right direction—the path the story was taking. If students do this, it helps them stay focused and not begin at a point so far away from their big event that they have to write ten pages to get there, losing their readers along the way! Here is the beginning of the shared experience:

It was a cold, white day. The snowy rooftops in the neighborhood looked like vanilla ice cream. I dreamed of racing down the Cold Spring hill on my sled. "Dad, let's go sledding!" I shouted into the kitchen. Before I knew it, we were on our way.

After commending the second graders for a strong beginning, Lynne and Maribeth talked about the use of dialogue and how to punctuate it correctly. Lynne called attention to the comma placed after "Dad" to show the reader that the main character is actually talking to him (comma of address). (Even though the CCSS does not specify mastery of comma of address until grade five, this was an opportune time to introduce this class to the concept.) They took a few minutes to write some additional sentences that looked like the mentor sentence in the lead paragraph, paying attention to the quotation marks and the comma of address. There was some confusion when they wrote a sentence where the direct quotation was a statement or a question. The students were confused about where to place the mark of punctuation or whether a statement ended in a comma when it came before the explanatory words. For now, they were held accountable for quotation marks and a comma after the name of the character they were directly addressing. The lead paragraph was rich in opportunities for other grammar lessons. Maribeth did a mini-lesson on proper nouns—what they are and how to capitalize them—during reading workshop time that day when they were reading about Memorial Day and its meaning. She referred to their lead paragraph in writing workshop where they had capitalized "Cold Spring" to refer to the sledding hill behind what had once been Cold Spring Elementary School. Lynne used the apostrophe in "Let's" to do a Your Turn Lesson on apostrophes and contractions. (See the Your Turn Lesson "Contractions Using Pronouns" at the end of Part 2.)

 Grammar Reference: Quotation marks are used around the exact words a speaker says. A comma follows the part that introduces the exact words of a speaker if those explanatory words come first. If the words the speaker says come first, a comma follows those words inside the final quotation mark. A capital letter begins the direct quotation wherever it is located in a sentence. When the spoken words are at the end of a sentence, the period, question mark, or exclamation mark goes inside the quotation marks.

Teaching Point: When teaching students about quotation marks, it may be easier to write sentences that end with explanatory words; however, teach sentences that begin with the explanatory words rather than end with them at another point in time. Don't teach both structures simultaneously—it's too confusing for young writers.

The students had time to plan and write a beginning for their narrative. They were asked to orally rehearse with a partner before actually writing. Lynne reminded them that the beginnings for narratives usually talked about the setting, introduced the main character in some way, and pointed the reader in the right direction. Here are some examples:

One hot summer morning I was at Upper Moreland Swim Club so I could take my band test. "Dad, can I take my test?" I asked, and he said yes. So I walked over but then I was shaking with fear because the pool water was so deep and so far. I thought I was going to be sick. (Kaylee, grade two)

It was dark and hot—hot—hot. I was on the boardwalk. After I went on the kid's race track and bumped into everything, I took some pictures and ate a snack. My sister yana and I were ready to go into the scary house . . . or at least we thought so. Our parents told us to wait until we're older. We should have listened. But we said at the same time, "Mom, we're ready!" We should have listened. (Stephanie, grade two)

The entire class saw many examples on a document imager. They looked at the use of direct quotations and the punctuation that was necessary. At this point, we also talked about the various proper nouns the students had used. Katie's story took place on Christmas morning, Will went to Disney World and wrote about his ride on Space Mountain, Julia's story had a pet kitten named Fluffy, and Kaylee's setting was the Upper Moreland Swim Club. Brianna's story had names for specific amusement rides like Tower of Terror and Ring of Fire. Marcus named the two soccer teams, UM United and FC Barcelona. Aidan's hiking story took place in the Adirondacks. The students recorded a few mentor sentences in their writer's notebooks under a page called "All About Capitalization" and wrote down their thinking—what they felt they needed to remember.

Teaching Point: When the students are using their writer's notebooks to study craft, conventions, and grammar, they can start at the back of their notebook and work their way toward the middle. They can also use the back pages for things such as authority lists, heart maps, memory chains, and brainstormed lists (like the smells and sounds of Christmas or things that are blue in June). When the notebook pages are created to serve as a reference for them, instruct the students to print a large capital "R" in the upper right- or left-hand corner of their notebook page, depending on which page they are currently working on. Ask students to draw a large square around the "R" and then fill in the square with yellow highlighter. This system allows the students to quickly flip through their notebook pages and find the ones that serve as references or helpful tips as they engage in drafting or revision.

The second graders and teachers spent the next several days talking about the middle of the story and what kinds of things could be found there. In both Jen Kennedy's second-grade classroom and Maribeth's classroom students struggled with where to go next. In oral rehearsals, the students often jumped right to the main event or most important thing they wanted to tell their reader, so their stories were over before they really got started. Lynne returned to *Crab Moon* by Ruth Horowitz. She read the paragraph that carried the reader from the beginning of the story into the next segment. Lynne suggested they call this paragraph a "bridge" paragraph because it forms a connection from the beginning of the story into the middle where all the action is. This paragraph from *Crab Moon* is a rich description and appeals to the senses:

> That night, the fat, round face of the full moon wavered on the surface of the water. The path felt cool under Daniel's feet. As the beam of their flashlight swept the beach, he drew a sharp breath. Everywhere they looked horseshoe crabs crowded and pushed, like restless cobblestones. Under the sandy shuffle of the surf, he could hear the clack of the crabs' shielded backs bumping and scraping together.

Lynne shared other examples from *Roller Coaster* by Marla Frazee and *Widget* by Lyn Rossiter-McFarland. Then she returned to their sledding story and asked the students to help each other write another paragraph for their shared story. She asked them to try out highlighting a verb strategy and possibly add another splash of dialogue:

When we arrived, the gigantic hill was empty. We had the entire hill to ourselves. I climb, climb, climbed up the snowy mountain with my sled dragging behind me. "Let's race, Dad. It will be fun!" I shouted.

Lynne applauded their use of *climb, climb, climbed* to highlight the verb and the use of dialogue, a characteristic of the narrative. She made sure they understood that even though there are two sentences here, quotation marks do not have to be placed around each individual sentence if the speaker does not change and just keeps talking. She also pointed out that she placed a comma before the word *Dad* as she scribed for them since the main character was addressing him (talking to Dad directly). She changed the sentence on the board and rewrote it to read: *"Dad, let's race. It will be fun!"* I shouted. She asked the writers to notice where the comma was written when the sentence started with the name of the person the character is addressing. Since so many students write dialogue and include the name(s) of the person they are speaking to, Lynne felt it was appropriate to teach the comma since it helps the reader understand the sentence clearly. Students looked at their lead paragraph and their beginning of the middle of their story, the bridge paragraph, and checked to see if they used the comma of address or if they needed to add it. They shared some of their findings with the whole group. In Will's "Space Mountain" story he wrote: *"Will, we have the front seat!" my brother shouted.*

Jen Kennedy's class was writing a snow day / sledding story, too. You can see that they both used effective repetition. Jen's class chose not to highlight a verb yet but repeated "up" to emphasize the height of the sledding hill. They may have borrowed it from Frazee's text where the author slows it down even more by placing a period after every word: *Up. Up. Up. And then . . .* Jen's class also hinted of the problem in their bridge paragraph when they included a sentence about a big rock. Lynne talked with them about where writers of narratives place the problem in their story. Sometimes it is in the lead paragraph. You know the problem in *Widget* right from the start. In *Crab Moon,* the problem does not occur until the middle of the story— after the bridge paragraph and the first real event.

When I finally got there, I saw the giant hill covered with snow. The big rock would be fun to go off on my sled. No one else was sledding yet. A crowd of people started up the hill. I spied Evan and plodded through the snow to get to him. My best friend and I stood at the bottom and stared up, up, up. We trudged up the hill, pulling our sleds behind us. "Let's race!" I shouted to Evan.

Lynne asked them to revise the dialogue so they wouldn't need the explanatory words, *I shouted to Evan*. After writing just the direct dialogue on the board, the students were able to revise it two ways: *Let's race, Evan!* and *Evan, let's race!* Students looked back at their own stories for possible revisions. Lynne pointed out that the use of the exclamation mark showed excitement and indicated that probably the words were being spoken in a loud voice, too, so the use of the explanatory words might be unnecessary.

During the next writing workshop session, Lynne worked with both second-grade classes on completing the middle of their stories. She returned to *Crab Moon, Shortcut,* and *Roller Coaster* to show students how the authors "exploded a moment in time" (see Barry Lane's *Reviser's Toolbox* [1999] and *Mentor Texts* [Dorfman and Cappelli 2007]). The students noticed the use of description, dialogue, appeal to the senses, and thought-shots. Lynne took time to talk about how authors sometimes wrote certain words or phrases in all capital letters to let readers know that they should read these words with a louder voice or to recognize an intense feeling in the speaker such as fear, excitement, or anxiety. In Don Crews's *Shortcut* (1996), the kids are all on the train tracks to take a shortcut home when one of them shouts: "I HEAR A TRAIN!" Lynne had the writers turn and talk about why he decided to use all capitals. They looked at Marla Frazee's use of variation in print to describe the actual roller-coaster ride. It begins with a single-word sentence, *WHOOSH!* and ends with a single-word sentence, *WHEEEEEEEEEEEEEEEEEE!* She asked the students to explain why the author repeated the final letter *e* so many times. Marcus explained that if you were on the ride, you probably would say that word all the way down the steepest slope. Students agreed that you would definitely draw out the word to show how exciting the ride is and how much fun you are having. Lynne asked them to try it out somewhere in the middle section of their narrative if it seemed to naturally fit. She added that strategy, variation in print, to the anchor chart that also contained "highlighting the verb" and "using a splash of dialogue." Then she returned to their shared writing experience about a sledding day to finish the middle part of their story. Maribeth's students wrote the rest of their middle and the bridge paragraph is also included here:

When we arrived, the gigantic hill was empty. We had the entire hill to ourselves. I climb, climb, climbed up the snowy mountain with my sled dragging behind me. "Let's race, Dad. It will be fun!" I shouted.

I dove onto my stomach and my sled started to pull me down the hill like a giant magnet. Dad was behind me. "I'M GOING TO BEAT YOU!" he shouted. I know I was zoooooooooooming down the hill, but I didn't feel like I was going that fast. Suddenly, I soared through the air. I felt like my stomach went up to my head. Was I falling out of the sky?

When I landed, I tumbled off my sled right into an enormous snowbank—head first! Someone was yanking me out of the snow, pulling hard on my legs. When I stood up, I looked like an evil Frosty the Snowman!

The writers easily were able to agree on a spot to use all capital letters and even stretch a word by adding more letter "*o*" vowels to the word zooming, but could they do this when they wrote independently? Here are several examples from a part of the middle sections of the second graders' writing:

In Max's story, "The Big Soccer Game," he wrote:

It was the second half and the score was one to one. It was our turn. I passed it back, then my teammate passed it to me. Then I shot and scored. "YES! I scored TWO times!" I shouted.

Michael wrote about a baseball game. Here is the entire middle of his narrative:

The baseball game was starting. I was really nervous about my first baseball game. I was playing outfield. My parents were here in the stands watching me play outfield. I hoped they would see me. "Batterrrrr up!" the tall umpire shouted. In the outfield I hoped I could catch the ball. I did! "OUT!" the umpire yelled. Strike one, strike two . . . HOME RUN! It was one to zero. The other team was ahead. Finally, I was batting. Bases were loaded. The score was 4 to 5. CLACK! I slam, slam, slammed the ball over the fence! It was a triple. We won!

In Ryan's piece about a summer afternoon at the beach, he also made use of both strategies in the middle section of his story:

"I bet it will be a lot more fun than last year," I told my family. We got into the car. My heart was beating with excitement. I was jummmmmmmping up and down in my seat! When we got there Mia and I went straight to making sand castles on the most bright and sandy spot on the beach. We were pretty close to the water. "Oh, nooooooooo!" A gigantic wave tackled our umbrella and took Mia out to sea. I raced out of the sand and tried to get Mia out of the water, but the current pulled me out, too. I told her to climb on my back and kick as hard as she could. "KICK–KICK–KICK!" I chanted to keep her calm. I swam as hard as I could to shore. We collapsed on the sand. I saved my sister and my own life. I was scared, too. I couldn't stop shivering!

As you can see, the writers were able to use these techniques to make their writing even better. Some of the students were able to hit their stride and incorporate these variations in print as they drafted, but most of them were more comfortable adding it in when they returned to do some revision. One problem that arose throughout the unit was the question of when to use the exclamation mark. Most of the second graders were fond of using an exclamation point to end a sentence. When is its use overdone? Lynne and Maribeth embedded a mini-lesson on the use of exclamation marks within a narrative. They explained that the exclamation mark is used to show a wide range of emotions—love, anger, happiness, confusion, fear. Maribeth told her second graders that exclamation marks are reserved for powerful feelings, so you won't find them used to express a matter-of-fact emotion, and you won't find them often. They're common in everyday speech, but exclamation marks need to be used sparingly in writing. Lynne told them to be careful not to overdo. She told the writers to read their sentence or sentences aloud several times, voicing the end punctuation in the way they read their sentence(s). She asked them to imagine what it would be like for their readers to read line after line of sentences that ended in exclamation marks.

Teaching Point: When it comes to academic writing, such as essays and reports, instruct your students not to use exclamatory sentences at all, unless they are using them in quotations.

Grammar Reference: For older students, tell them that formal English requires exclamations to begin with either the word *what* or *how*. In everyday informal English you'll find exclamations can begin with any word. When the exclamatory sentence contains a plural noun, always choose to begin with "What" instead of "How." Here are two examples: How beautiful you are! What creative students you have!

Students of all ages can sprinkle their writing with appropriate exclamatory sentences, especially in narrative genres where excitement, fear, and joy are expressed in character's thoughts, dialogue, and actions. They just need to keep in mind that a little goes a long way. If your writers are emphasizing everything, they end up emphasizing nothing. Writing of any kind should always be honest and sincere, so encourage your students to use exclamatory sentences to show sincere, honest feelings to pull their readers into their words.

Finally, it was time to look at endings. Maribeth and Lynne asked the students to turn to the reference page (marked with a capital R enclosed in a square in the top right- or left-hand corner of the page) in their writer's notebook where they had listed strategies for satisfying endings. The students had created this page after they shared their endings for *Widget,* using only the final picture in the story to compose an ending. The strategies the students discovered they had used included: a final action, a promise or final decision, a self-discovery or lesson learned, a hope or wish for the future, and what the main character(s) is thinking or feeling. Lynne reread the endings from several mentor texts and placed the pages under a document imager so that all the students could read the words, too. *Crab Moon,* for example, uses several final actions and a wish for the future. The author of *Widget* uses what the characters were thinking/feeling as well as an inferred final decision or promise (see *Mentor Texts* [Dorfman and Cappelli 2007] for more information and lessons about endings for narratives). Lynne returned to their shared experience story about sledding. After the students reread the story with Lynne and Maribeth, the students were asked to turn and talk about what strategies they thought they could use for this story. Lynne reminded them that not every strategy worked well with every story. It's up to the writer to find the perfect match. The final paragraph is the ending they decided worked the best. Lynne wrote some reminders on the board and asked the students to use the anchor charts they had previously created as they worked through the narrative unit. The reminders included using a splash of dialogue or a thoughtshot using quotation marks, the possible use of highlighting a verb strategy, and variation in print—using all capital letters to emphasize an action or an emotion. Here is their finished narrative:

It was a cold, white day. The snowy rooftops in the neighborhood looked like vanilla ice cream. I dreamed of racing down the Cold Spring hill on my sled. "Dad, let's go sledding!" I shouted into the kitchen. Before I knew it, we were on our way.

When we arrived, the gigantic hill was empty. We had the entire hill to ourselves. I climb, climb, climbed up the snowy mountain with my sled dragging behind me. "Let's race, Dad. It will be fun!" I shouted.

I dove onto my stomach and my sled started to pull me down the hill like a giant magnet. Dad was behind me. "I'm going to beat you!" he shouted. I know I was zooming down the hill, but I didn't feel like I was going that fast.

Suddenly, I soared through the air. I felt like my stomach went up to my head. Was I falling out of the sky? When I landed, I tumbled off my sled right into an enormous snow bank—head first! Someone was yanking me out of the snow, pulling hard on my legs. When I stood up, I looked like an evil Frosty the Snowman!

Dad and I cracked up. I was laughing so hard I fell over into the snow. "Come on, Dad. Let's go again!" We dragged our sleds up, up, up the hill and ZOOMED down.

Maribeth asked the students to turn and talk about the strategies they used to create this ending. Emily said they used dialogue to show feeling. Lynne asked why she thought so, and Emily explained that the use of the exclamation mark showed how excited the narrator was to do it all over again. Stephanie said that the main characters were both laughing really hard, so the readers would know that they were happy and having lots of fun. Jake said there were two final actions. Marcus explained that they zoomed down the hill, and Ryan added that they had to drag their sled back up the hill first. Lynne was thrilled that Katie had instructed her to capitalize all the letters in the word zoom to emphasize the action and that Ryan had suggested the addition of the word *up* two more times to remind the readers that it was a really big sledding hill. Maribeth and Lynne thought the students were ready to write their endings. Here are some examples:

> We enjoyed the rest of our day at home with each other. Our parents kept giving us hugs and kisses. They were scared, too. They called me a hero. (Ryan, grade two)
>
> I was so excited. Everyone piled on top of me and knocked me to the ground. I was a hero! I'll never forget the time I scored the winning goal. (Max, grade two)
>
> We are so lucky for such a cute cat. Don Gato is the cutest, fattest cat in the world. He is part of my family. I'm so glad Mom surprised us with a cat! (Lilia, grade two)
>
> We ran into our parents' arms. They said they were worried sick. But in my mind I was saying, "Mmm–Hmm! I saw you laughing." My sister told me she would rather die than go in there again. But I said, "There's always next year." I LOVE TO BE SCARED! (Stephanie, grade two)
>
> We got off the ride. My hair was sticking straight up and I felt so sick I fell on the ground. My dad said it was a kiddy ride for him. "Are you kidding me?" I thought to myself. I'm NEVER going on that ride AGAIN! (Will, grade two)

Lynne and Maribeth asked the students to share their writing with each other in peer conferences and revise to make sure their endings matched their stories and helped their readers have a sense that the story was over. In the final five minutes of workshop, Lynne and Maribeth asked the students to think about the strategies they used to create a satisfying ending and what they had learned. When they met in whole group, the students read their endings and shared their strategies. Most of the students had used a combination of final actions, what the character(s) was thinking and feeling, and a wish for the future. A few students used a lesson learned or a self-discovery. Lynne and Maribeth were excited that the students could actually talk about the strategies they had used.

The next day they asked the students to read over their entire narrative to note other strategies involving conventions and grammar as well—listed on several anchor charts in the room and on reference pages in their writer's notebook. The students found and talked about the following strategies: using contractions in dialogue to imitate oral speech, highlighting a verb, variations in print (such as using all capital letters to show emotion or importance), the use of dialogue or a thoughtshot with quotation marks, and the use of exclamation marks to show extreme emotion. Lynne and Maribeth asked the students to do a final edit for correct homophone use, including two/to/too, there/they're/their, and your/you're. The students had a homophone page as a reference page in their writer's notebook with mentor sentences as models (see Appendix C). After a final edit, the students began the hard work of publishing their pieces. If they needed another conference at this point before they began their final draft, they simply had to request one. They were also free to confer with peers.

Teaching Point: Some grammar and conventions needs can be best met through individual or small-group conferences. When a student continues to make the same mistake over and over again, or he does something that really takes away "the look of literacy," the teacher can spend some time addressing that issue. Often the errors are spelling matters such as forgetting to double a final consonant when adding a suffix as is the case in *fat* to *fattest* or *swim* to *swimming*. Other times, the error is directly connected to how the student hears or pronounces a word, as is often the case in writing *are* instead of *our*. Make a few brief notes in a log/notebook you are keeping with the student's name and the date of the conference so that you can refer to it the next time you confer with that student. Look for evidence that the student has demonstrated the advice and instruction you gave to him. Sometimes, the same advice or instruction must be repeated.

The students celebrated their hard work with small-group shares, thunderous applause, and Popsicles. Here are two examples of completed stories. Spelling errors the students did not fix have not been corrected.

The Unexpected Visitor
by Sarah, grade two

Once I was going camping with some of my friends and one mom was bringing us to the campground. "Okay, Mom! I'm ready to go!" I said. "Isn't it a great day? It's very sunny. You should putt on some sunscrean," Mom said. I got my bags and we got in the car. On the way we ran into the mom that was taking me to the campground. I steped out of the car, got my bags out of the trunk, then hopped in my friend's car, and before I knew it, we were on our way!

I had butterflies in my stomach because it was a long time since I've been camping. Next thing I knew, we were there! The campground was far away from home and I was nervous. We saw a playground across the street and play, play, played there for two hours strate! "Okay, girls. We're going to dinner," she said.

But before we could even open the door, THERE WAS A SKUNK! Everyone was shriek, shriek, shrieking at the top of their lungs. My friends ran away and left me there — all alone. I picked up a tall box, putt lettuce in it, then putt a stick under the box to make a trap. I climbed the oke tree. The skunk stepped into the trap! The skunk stayed still inside. I climbed off the tree.

I didn't know what to do. The skunk sat there confused, eating the fresh greens in the box. My friends came back and saw I cawt the skunk. Mrs. Smith called the park ranger to deal with the skunk.

Everyone was proud of me. I was proud of myself too. We moved to a different place. Thankfully, no one got sprayed! Everyone enjoyed the rest of their weekend! No more skunks appeared—thank goodness!

Space Mountain
by Will, grade two

When our family took a trip to Disney World I rode in my first rollercoaster. It was called Space Mountain. I was waiting in a long line and hearing people scream at the top of their lungs! "Will, we have the front seat!" my brother shouted.

We finally got on the ride. It was too late to change my mind. The guy who controlled the ride released the brakes and the ride started. I was going so fast my skin was flapping. I screamed so loud my brother called me a sissy, but he was screaming louder than me. My mom said we were going 100 miles per hour!

We got off the ride. My hair was sticking straight up and I felt so sick I fell on the ground. My dad said it was a kiddy ride for him. "Are you kidding me?" I thought to myself. I'm NEVER going on that ride AGAIN!

Chapter 4

Using a Touchstone Text to Write Fiction

In order to embed craft and grammar lessons throughout a unit of study, Diane used a story scaffold with fourth, fifth, and sixth graders at the Woodlynde School, a private school in suburban Philadelphia for K–12 children with learning differences. The purpose was to direct the students in writing a piece of fiction that contained everyday characters, a setting, a problem, and a possible solution. The students had a chance to imagine a story that used the following list:

Maggie's kitten
the park
a big dog
a tall tree
too frightened to meow
a ladder
the fire department
a bowl of milk

Diane reminded the students that all stories have a beginning, a middle, and an end. Using that scaffold, the students identified the story elements and where these elements would likely first appear in a narrative. Students talked about possible ideas for their stories with a partner before they started writing. Some students drew pictures to help them visualize their story. One student even decided to use an outline as a prewriting activity to organize his thinking.

Diane reviewed good beginnings, suggesting that setting a scene might be a particularly good way to start this story. She reminded them to "show-not-tell" the setting and modeled by doing a shared writing of the setting of their own classroom. Then she directed them to think about the seasons and time of day to establish their setting.

While they drafted their beginnings, Diane and their teachers circulated to check in and confer. The sixth graders drafted on laptops and didn't seem to need help with spelling. Fourth and fifth graders were encouraged to write and use phonetic spelling. Diane modeled by showing them how she uses a squiggly line under words she is not sure how to spell. That way she can keep drafting and getting her ideas down on paper. Later on, she can check with a dictionary or peer to edit her paper for spelling errors. As Diane moved about the room, she wrote words on sticky notes if the students asked for help. She could see the relief on the students' faces when they could immediately get the spelling help they needed.

 Teaching Point: Some students become paralyzed with indecision and cannot move beyond the word they need to spell. By writing those words on notes or cards, teachers can provide help and quickly move on. Standing there and spelling the word one letter at a time is time-consuming, noisy, and counterproductive.

When the students finished drafting, they shared their lead paragraphs with a partner. The listeners were told to find something in their partner's narrative to praise. Diane reminded students to think about elements of a story—character, setting, problem, solution—and to ask themselves some questions such as, "Can you see the characters?" or "Do you know where and when this story is taking place?"

The next day Diane returned to model the development of the plot—the events of the story. She returned to the scaffold (beginning, middle, end) to identify what could happen in the middle. They talked about specifics, such as what kind of dog might be in the story, what things could happen in the park, and how Maggie was feeling as she looked for her kitten. They reviewed time/order words and how events in a story follow a meaningful sequence. Together, Diane and the students looked for places where students could slow down time and make the reader feel like he was there. Students suggested various places in the story where time could be slowed down: when Maggie searches for her kitten, the dog-and-cat chase, or when the kitten climbs the tree. Students began to plan and draft the middle paragraphs for their story. They shared with a partner, but this time the partner was listening for chronological order to see if the story made sense.

Then, Diane talked about satisfying endings, specifically how the author creates an ending through final actions, final decision, and what the character(s) is/are thinking and feeling. She shared *Widget* by Lyn Rossiter McFarland, *Shortcut* by Don Crews, and *Crab Moon* by Ruth Horowitz.

Teaching Point: Throughout a unit of study, students may be at different points in their writing at the same time. The question teachers often ask is, "What do I do when students tell me they are finished while most of the class is still drafting?" Of course, a writer is really never "finished" a piece of writing. Revisions and edits can truly be endless. Provide students with a writing checklist (Figure 4.1) in order to have a self-conference. Encourage them to be critical readers of their own writing. Occasionally, ask students to highlight or underline changes they have made during a self-conference and be prepared to talk about them during a teacher-student conference or final reflection time at the end of a writing workshop session. Some of the items in the checklist, such as *whispering parentheses* and *taffy* sentences, are mentioned in *Wondrous Words* by Katie Wood Ray (1999). When writers include information in parentheses, they often want you to think they are whispering a secret to you (their reader). This technique establishes a sense of intimacy and makes a reader feel like he's the author's close friend—for example, "The big bully (who would rather have lots of friends but didn't know how to make them) terrorized the playground." A *taffy sentence* is a sentence that is constructed through repetition of some part of the sentence (often the subject noun) and stretching it by adding an adjective or two: "On the day, on the cold, stormy day, on the cold, stormy, gloomy day an unexpected visitor knocked on our door." You can inform your students that they may not be familiar with all of the skills on the writing checklist at the start of the year, but it is hoped they will acquire these skills as the year progresses. As a teacher, you can change the number of optional choices.

Figure 4.1
Writing Checklist for
Narrative, Grades 4–6

Narrative Name _____

Writing Checklist

My narrative is at least four to six paragraphs and includes some of the following skills.

A combination of appropriate leads:

_____ Weather lead   _____ Snapshot of setting   _____ Snapshot of character

_____ Action/suspense   _____ Dialogue or thoughtshot   _____ Appeal to the senses

A combination of effective techniques:

_____ Appeal to senses   _____ Exploding moment   _____ Dialogue

_____ Vivid adjectives   _____ Strong verbs   _____ Precise nouns

_____ Show-not-tell   _____ Personification*   _____ Simile*

_____ Metaphor*   _____ Hyphenated-adjectives*   _____ Taffy sentence*

_____ Whispering parentheses* _____ Thoughshots   _____ Adjective interrupters
                                                                (adjectives after
                                                                the noun)

_____ Rich description of   _____ Highlighting the verb* _____ Alliteration*
       people, places, objects

                                                         *Optional techniques

A satisfying ending that includes a combination of at least two of the following:

_____ Final action

_____ Final decision/promise

_____ Lesson learned

_____ Hope, wish, or dream for the future

_____ Memory that lasts (always remember . . . , never forget . . .)

_____ Main character—thinking and feeling (thoughtshot, show-not-tell, dialogue)

_____ Reflection—now I realize how others will view me; I know or learned about myself

Diane embedded some grammar lessons within the process of revision. For a lesson on verbs, she reproduced the following version of the student-generated story "Maggie's Kitten" that contained both exact verbs and weak verbs as well as intentional inappropriate shifts in verb tense. She wanted to know if the students could recognize the difference in order to make good revision choices:

Maggie walked down the street for the third time that morning. Even the green grass and pretty flowers did not cheer her up. She was looking for her lost kitten, Harry. He had slipped out the door that morning and Maggie was afraid she'd never see him again.

Just then, she saw a small ball of fur in the park across the street. That was Harry! She is sure of it. She ran to the park to get him.

Maggie was happy to see Harry, but she knew she had to be careful not to scare him away. She carefully walks toward Harry who does not seem to notice her. As Maggie approached the kitten, she saw a man with a big dog on a leash. When the dog saw Harry, it began to bark. Harry starts to run.

The dog ripped the leash from his owner's hand and began to chase the cat. Down the path they run, with the dog following close behind. Maggie watched as Harry leaped over a big rock in the path. The dog barked and barked. What could Harry do to escape? Harry ran to a big tree in the middle of the park. When it looked like the dog would catch Harry, Harry jumped onto the tree. His claws stick to the bark like Velcro. Up Harry climbed inch by inch to a tall branch. There he sat, stuck and too frightened to meow.

Maggie said to the man, "Can you help me get my cat down from the tree?" The man used his cell phone and called the fire department. They were there in minutes. One firefighter went up the fire-engine ladder to the branch and rescued Harry. Maggie was happy. She took Harry home and gave him a bowl of milk.

Diane asked her students for help in revising the piece by using strong, vivid verbs to replace the ordinary verbs in the piece. First, they read the piece through, underlining the verbs that might be revised such as "walked," and "was looking" in the first paragraph; "saw" and "ran" in the second paragraph; "was," "[carefully] walked," and "saw" in the third paragraph; "ran" and "jumped" in the fourth paragraph; and "said," "were [there]," "went [up]," "took," and "gave" in the final paragraph.

Diane encouraged students to use strong verbs that show specific actions. She asked, "How did Maggie walk down the street? She's unhappy and worried. Would she skip? Would she run? Why not? What are some verbs that might describe how she would walk?" Sixth graders suggested *dragged, moped, trudged, hiked, plodded, marched, slogged,* and *trotted* as some examples. They continued brainstorming for each nonspecific word. For "jumped," they came up with *leaped, dove, catapulted, hurled* (himself), threw (himself), and *hurtled* (through the air and onto the tree bark). Their word choices for "ran" ("Harry ran to a big tree in the park") included *sprinted, galloped, rocketed, raced, zoomed, sped, whizzed, zigzagged, dashed, flew, tore, bounded, hurtled.* All suggestions were placed on an anchor chart. Students were encouraged to create a space in their writer's notebook to list precise verbs and group them by synonyms. (As early as grade two, Common Core standards suggest that students be able to distinguish shades of meaning among closely related verbs [CCSS.ELA-LITERACY.L.2.5.B]. Student writers in upper grades can improve their writing styles by concentrating on strong verbs that mean exactly what they want to say.) Later, students and their teacher could return to these lists to review spelling patterns such as doubling the final consonant before adding a suffix such as *-ed* or *-ing* in words like *whiz, trot, trod, plod,* and *drag.*

Teaching Point: Brainstorming means exactly what it says! Students should always try to push themselves to imagine all the possibilities before giving up. That way, they have choice and can make the best choice (in this case, word choice) for their piece of writing. Too often, students stop the brainstorming process after one or two ideas or words are listed. Although those choices may be excellent ones, and ultimately the ones they use, they may have stopped short of finding the best choice of all.

After the students completed the shared writing experience with Diane, they returned to their own "Maggie's Kitten" stories to revise for exact verbs.

Here are some of Aidan's revisions:

(Original)
While I was running I could hear the leaves crunching under my feet. I carried Joseph in his pet holder as I ran. It was a great run. I was getting thirsty so I went over to a bench to have a Gatorade. After a couple of sips, I put it down to play with Joseph. I looked in his pet holder but he was gone. I was worried.

(Revision)
Leaves crunched under my feet as I sprinted on the path carrying Joseph in his pet holder. It was a great run. I paused at a park bench to chug a Gatorade and put Joseph in his carrier beside me. For a minute I was distracted by a noisy nest of birds in the tree above my bench. I peeked in at Joseph, but his pet holder was empty. He had disappeared.

Grammar Reference: Some students may have difficulty recognizing verbs. If this is the case, ask them to change the time of the sentence (such as past to present). For example, the lead sentence "Maggie walked down the street for the third time that morning" is written in the past tense. Ask students to change it to the present tense, as if it were happening now. "Maggie walks down the street . . . " The word that changes (in this sentence, "walked" to "walks") is the verb. Students should note that a verb is the part of speech that changes tense or tells time—present, past, future.

The following day, Diane stayed with verbs to address inappropriate tense shift, a common error with upper elementary students in grades three through six (see the Your Turn Lesson "Verb Tense Consistency" at the end of Part 3). She began by asking the fourth graders to read through the story again and tell her if the story was taking place in the past, present, or future. The students knew the story was written in past tense by identifying verbs using the *-ed* suffix and irregular past tense verb forms. Then she asked them to examine the second paragraph to find a verb that is not in the past but the present. One student found the sentence *She is sure of it* and identified the verb *is* that needed to be changed to past tense (*was*). Diane realized some students were still having difficulty identifying verbs unless they were action verbs. She quickly reviewed state of being verbs—listing them on a chart paper.

Grammar Reference: The most common linking verb is the verb *to be*, which has the following forms: *am, is, was, were, be, being, been*, and all verbs ending in *be, being*, or *been*, such as *can be, is being, could have been*, and so on. Ask students to try as much as possible to substitute more powerful alternatives for these bland verbs.

Diane divided the class in two. Half the class partnered up and looked at paragraph 3, and the other half of the class partnered to examine paragraph 4 to hunt for tense shifts. In paragraph 3, they found three examples of inappropriate tense shifts. *She carefully walks toward Harry who does not seem to notice her* and *Harry starts to run* use present tense verbs: *walks, does*, and *starts*. Students changed these verbs to *walked, did*, and *started*. In the fourth paragraph, students changed *run* to *ran* and *stick* to *stuck*.

Working with a partner, they looked at their own pieces to determine if they used the same tense throughout their narrative.

On subsequent days throughout the narrative unit, the reproducible "Maggie's Kitten" was used to show how to incorporate dialogue for a lesson on proper punctuation of quotations with the fourth-, fifth-, and even sixth-grade classes (CCSS.ELA-LITERACY.3.2.C, "Use commas and quotation marks in dialogue," and CCSS.ELA-LITERACY.4.2.B, "Use commas and quotation marks to mark direct speech and quotations from a text."). Diane asked her fourth- and fifth-grade students to think about why dialogue is used in narratives and to share their thinking with a partner or small group. She made a list of their responses:

Why Authors Use Dialogue in Works of Fiction

1. It's more fun to read.
2. It gets you into the story quickly.
3. It makes you feel like you are right there in the story.
4. It makes it seem like it is really happening (lends authenticity to the piece of writing).
5. It tells you about the characters and how they feel about things.
6. It tells you what kind of people the characters are.
7. All the fiction and fantasy books we like have lots of dialogue in them, such as the Harry Potter books and Roald Dahl's books, such as *Matilda* and *The BFG*.
8. It gives the reader a break from reading descriptions and telling events.
9. It gives the reader a break because it is quicker to read with more "little" paragraphs because you need to start on a new line every time the speaker changes.
10. We get to know the main characters by what other characters say about them and by what they say themselves.

In the "Maggie's Kitten" story sample, Diane used one splash of dialogue: *Maggie said to the man, "Can you help me get my cat down from the tree?"* Diane asked the students what they noticed about how this sentence is punctuated and how the punctuation helps the reader to understand. Students noticed that quotation marks surround the words that Maggie actually speaks, "can" is capitalized even though it appears in the middle of the entire sentence, the question mark comes before the end quotation mark, and a comma was used to separate the words that Maggie does not say aloud from the direct quotation. She asked the students to work with a partner to mark one or two places within the sample where dialogue could possibly be used. Their examples were written on the board. If the students needed some help with punctuation rules, they chose other students to assist them. Here are some of their examples:

(Within the second paragraph) Maggie yelled, "Harry! Is that you?"

In the final paragraph, many students included a small conversation between Maggie and the firefighter. Here is one example from Lily and Victor.

The firefighter gave the kitten to Maggie and said, "Here he is. He's not hurt, just frightened."
   "Thank you," Maggie said shyly as she hugged her kitten tightly. "I'll make sure Harry doesn't get away again."

The students returned to their drafts to find at least one place where they could use dialogue and tried it out. After they were finished, they gathered in whole group to talk about whether the dialogue improved their story. It's important for students to realize that inserting dialogue into their story does not necessarily make it better.

Grammar Reference:

1. The rule of thumb for punctuating quotation marks is that the punctuation comes before the quotation mark. Therefore, the comma that sets off the explanatory words from the direct quote comes before the direct quote. The end punctuation for the words spoken as dialogue comes before the end quotation mark. (Exceptions to this rule of thumb are colons and semicolons, which are always placed outside the closing quotation marks. For example, "Mary," my mother scolded, "you need to finish your homework"; then she told me to make my bed.) Such constructions are rare among primary- and intermediate-level writers.

2. If the dialogue comes before the explanatory words and it is a statement, the direct quotation ends with a comma, not a period. ("That's my cat," Maggie said to her friend.)

3. If the quotation is a complete sentence, the first word is always capitalized, even if it comes after the explanatory words. (The firefighter handed Maggie the kitten and said, "Here he is . . . safe and sound!")

4. Quotations introduced by the word "that" are not put in quotation marks. For example: Maggie said that her cat was lost.

5. Begin a new paragraph every time the speaker changes.

6. If the direct quote is interrupted by explanatory words, the punctuation still comes before the quotation marks. For example, "Here is your kitten," said the firefighter, "safe and sound!" Notice that the word "safe" is not capitalized because "safe and sound" is not a sentence but a continuation of the quote that was interrupted by the explanatory words. Teach fifth and sixth graders how to do this to add some variety of sentence structure to their pieces.

The touchstone text may also be used as a lesson in precise nouns, by asking students to look at the story and change generic terms like *flowers* to specific kinds of flowers. If this is spring, what flowers would Maggie likely see as she trudges down the street? What kind of "big dog" might be at the end of the street? What kind of tree did Harry, the kitten, climb? Ask students to make lists of specific nouns in their writer's notebooks to use as a reference for future work.

Diane reviewed adjectives with the fifth graders and asked them to describe what adjectives do in a sentence and where they are usually found. They hunted through their independent reading books to find examples of sentences with adjectives. The students agreed that adjectives describe nouns and are usually located just before the noun they describe. Diane used an example from *Harry Potter and the Chamber of Secrets*: "Not only were there a dozen frost-covered Christmas trees and thick streamers of holly and mistletoe crisscrossing the Great Hall, but enchanted snow was falling, warm and dry, from the ceiling." The students could see that the adjectives *warm* and *dry* follow the noun *snow*. The students also talked about how position of the adjectives slowed down the rhythm of the sentence and helped them think about the importance of the adjectives. Real snow is cold and wet, but enchanted snow is something else. (See the Your Turn Lesson "Adjective Interrupters" at the end of Part 1.) Diane returned to "Maggie's Kitten" and found a spot where the sentence could use adjectives to add specificity to the description. *One firefighter climbed the ladder to the branch, leafy and long, to rescue Harry.* Diane's revision also changed the verb. You might point out to students that good revision often leads to several changes. Diane asked her students to look with a partner to find another spot where adjective interrupters might fit. One pair came up with: "His claws, tiny and sharp, stuck to the bark like Velcro." Another pair volunteered: "The Saint Bernard, immense and powerful, ripped the leash from his owner's hand." Finally, another pair came up with this sentence: "Harry ran to an oak tree, tall and leafy, in the middle of the park."

Students were asked to find one or two places in their narratives to slow down the flow of the sentence by interrupting it with an adjective pair. Diane reminded them that commas are used to set off the adjective interrupter pairs from the rest of the sentence.

Here are some student revisions:

Jake, tiny and frightened, sprinted just ahead of an angry English bulldog. (Ellie)
Maggie watched, frightened and desperate, as Ava climbed the tall oak tree in the park. (Samantha)

Back home they snuggled, warm and safe, by the fireplace. (Alex)
He snatched the kitten, small and weak, and carried her safely down to Maggie. (Ben)
Maggie's kitten, slender and supple, slipped through the fence and disappeared. (Sophia)

Using adjective pairs is a stylistic device, but it is an opportunity for a grammar lesson as well. Parts of speech cease to be mysteries for students when we can give them multiple opportunities to understand their uses in everyday writing, speaking, and listening.

When students began writing their own narrative pieces, Diane returned to the touchstone text to teach both strategies for adding detail (dialogue, description of setting, and description of character) as well as strategies for grammatical correctness.

Following are two sixth-grade samples of "Maggie's Kitten." The first is Aidan's.

Leaves crunched under my feet as I sprinted on the path carrying Joseph in his pet holder. It was a great run. I paused at a park bench to chug a Gatorade and put Joseph in his carrier beside me. For a minute I was distracted by a noisy nest of birds in the tree above my bench. I peeked in at Joseph, but his pet holder was empty. He had disappeared.

I asked the first person I saw if he saw an orange and white kitten. He said, "I did see one being chased by a Labra doodle over by the water fountain." I ran to find Joseph and saw him zooming down the path with the dog close behind. The dog dashed at Joseph and they bolted to the tall, green Cyprus tree in the middle of the park. Joseph climbed the tree, crouching on a skinny branch way up high. He was cornered!

I grabbed my phone and called the fire department. In less than ten minutes they arrived with a ladder. Unfortunately, when Joseph heard the commotion, he climbed up even higher. I thought they'd never get him down from there.

One of the bystanders said, "Don't worry. They'll get your kitten for you." I wasn't so sure. I watched and worried. One of the firemen climbed the ladder and carefully coaxed Joseph into a carrier. When the fireman and Joseph were safe on the ground, I walked over to say thanks. I took Joseph home in his carrier and gave him a bowl of milk. I decided to go jogging alone from now on.

Aidan has a good beginning and a satisfying ending. He sprinkled just enough dialogue for interest. He did a great job with action verbs as well. Look at all the synonyms for *run* that he uses: *chased, zoomed, dashed,* and *bolted,* for example. His story has a clear beginning, middle, and end. He definitely has a good sense of what it takes to create a narrative.

The next sample is from Lauren:

Izzy found herself in the park on a beautiful sunny day. She saw people feeding the ducks, walking on the paths lined with colorful flowers, and having picnics. Birds chirped overhead in the trees. Izzy had bolted out the back door this morning when her owner Maggie wasn't looking. She was beginning to get worried that she was lost.

Izzy suddenly froze in fear. In her path was a big black German Shepard dog. Compared to Izzy, the dog was a giant. When Izzy finally got the courage to move, the dog looked her way. Suddenly he began to growl. Izzy ran followed closely by the dog. Izzy began to grow tired but she spied a tall tree in the center of the park. She jumped and began to climb. Up she went with the Shepard snapping and barking at her.

Eventually all that barking was noticed. The helpless kitty in the tree was rescued by the fire department. At first Izzy was still afraid that another dog might come along but then she saw Maggie and she felt safe again.

After that Izzy and Maggie returned home glad to still have each other in their lives. Maggie stroked Izzy's fur. Izzy was happy to be home. She decided that instead of trying to chase down a ball of string in a dangerous world of big dogs and people, she would just stay home and drink her bowl of milk.

Lauren's beginning and ending are appealing. She sets the scene in the beginning and develops a satisfying ending. She could work some more with her verb choices, and in the final sentence of the first paragraph, the pronoun *"she"* is indeterminate. Lauren could also use help with punctuation, but all in all, this sample shows that the writer understands the concept of narrative.

The final sample is from Danny, grade four.

One cold Saturday morning Maggie went for a walk in the park. She was deprest. It seemed like she was the only one in her class without a pet. She wanted a kitten. She would name the kitten Abby.

During the walk Maggie heard a faint "meow." Her eye caught sight of a little kitten. She took the kitten home and asked if she could keep it. Maggie's mom said she could. Maggie was very happy.

The next morning Maggie took Abby outside and a bird caught her eye. She chased it out of the yard and accros the street into the park. As soon as she got there, she was chased by Mr. Brill's dog, Rufus. The dog was a huge German Shepard. Abby raced to a tall tree. The tree was bigger than three of Maggie's dads! Maggie didn't know what to do, so she climbed up after Abby. Maggie captured the kitten and put her in her lap.

"At least we are together," thought Maggie. She yelled and yelled. Finally, Maggie's mom heard her cries and saw what happened. She called the fire department. They came and rescued

Maggie and the kitten. Maggie's mom took them home. She gave Abby a bowl of milk. Maggie promised never to climb a tree again.

Danny has a beginning, a middle, and an end. He uses dialogue and has used quotation marks correctly. He has several spelling errors that need correction. He can be encouraged to work on varying sentence length and type. Some of his sentences can be easily combined, for example.

These examples demonstrate how the students took the writing lessons and the grammar lessons and applied them to their own writing. Students constructed the touchstone narrative with a "set the scene" beginning, a chronological-order middle, and a satisfying ending. Almost all the writers used dialogue; most of them remembered to use quotation marks. The writers worked hard to provide their pieces with specific nouns and strong verbs. They also experimented with using adjective interrupters for style. These lessons transferred to their own narratives once they began writing them.

Here, for example, is the beginning of Brenna's narrative about her experience skydiving with her mother.

"Are you ready?" the pilot shouted. My mother held tight to the safety bar. I was ready but my stomach wasn't. I was about to jump until I saw how high up we were. The grass below looked so green and the hot air blasted my face as I stood there at the edge. My mom and I were harnessed together, but she would not budge. I closed my eyes and jumped. I fell and my mother had no choice but to come with me.

Notice how Brenna uses dialogue as the attention-getting opener to her narrative. She remembered to place the question mark inside the quotation because it is the pilot asking the question. She can revise later for verbs, though she does use some strong ones: "shouted," "blasted," and "budge," for example.

As the narrative unit continued, Diane returned to the lessons on specific parts of speech (verbs, nouns, and adjectives) and correct punctuation of quotations. Remember that teaching any grammar skill requires repeated practice. Don't be discouraged if your students make mistakes even after you've taught the concept. Once they have a frame of reference for the grammatical terms, and you all speak the same language, you will find it easier to point out their errors in conference, and they will find it less onerous to make the corrections.

Adding Conversation to a Narrative

There are many ways authors build content for their stories. For students, the most satisfying stories are often rich in conversation. Students can relate to the story through these conversations. Understanding that dialogue often reveals what the main character is thinking or feeling about his own actions or the actions of another character or reflections on a lesson learned or a wish for the future is important for our young writers. Dialogue can help reveal a character's personality.

Hook: Choose some of the mentor texts you have been using in the classroom and examine the conversations closely with your students. Important: Look for books that have the kinds of conversations you think your students can imitate in their own stories. If you write these out on chart paper, they can be posted in the classroom. You might try underlining only the exact words that the character(s) is saying. Read *Elinor and Violet: The Story of Two Naughty Chickens* by Patti Beling Murphy as a read-aloud. Return to it as a hook to teach writing conversation correctly. Use the conversation that follows. Read it aloud to the class. Then ask for student volunteers to play the parts of Violet and Elinor, only read the exact words their character speaks.

> "How about we pretend we're evil pirates and bury lots of treasure?" Violet said. "And we'll pinkie-swear not to tell where it is!"
> "Yes, yes!" Elinor replied.
> They gathered up pieces of treasure and hid them in nooks and crannies all over the house.
> "Now we need just one more special treasure," said Violet, eyeing Aunt Lucy's purse.

Purpose: *As we have been discussing, conversations are a very important part to any narrative. Since conversations are often sprinkled throughout a story, they should be purposeful and satisfying and not used just to fill up lines on a page. However, conversation can be confusing if the writer does not use the proper punctuation to communicate clearly with his readers. Today I will show you how you can write that kind of dialogue in your own stories.*

Brainstorm: In this case, brainstorming is closely tied to the use of literature in the hook. As students examine books and discover conversations they are actually engaging in a type of brainstorming. Copy part of a conversation into the writer's notebook or mark the page(s) with a sticky note.

Model: Either read a previous notebook entry of your own or compose a new entry in front of the students. You must be able to display your notebook entry or the writing you do so that everyone can see your use of punctuation marks and paragraphing. When you are finished, reread the conversation and talk about why it would be important to include in this notebook entry. If it is a personal narrative, be sure to include your thoughts and feelings as the main character and perhaps combine it with a final action, a future wish, a lesson learned, or perhaps a memory. Ask for students to volunteer to role-play the parts of your two (or three) characters and only read the words the characters speak. Make sure the students notice that every time a new speaker talks, the writer must indent and begin on a new line.

Guided Practice: Ask students to return to a previous notebook entry that contains conversation or a splash of dialogue or to the page(s) they have marked in their reading book. Consider how the punctuation marks help the reader understand the text. Invite students to offer their explanations to a partner or a small group while you circulate and listen in. Recopy some of these conversations on chart paper and discuss the purpose of the quotation marks. Use a highlighter to mark the quotation marks. Then note the placement of question marks, exclamation marks, and commas when the explanatory words come at the end of the sentence. Finally, share examples where the explanatory words come at the beginning of the sentence. Do this with older students (fourth graders and up). In *Elinor and Violet* by Patti Beling Murphy, the explanatory words always appear at the end of the sentence. It is much easier to teach students this construction first. Consider this sentence, for example: *"Are we going out to tea?" Elinor asked*. Notice that the explanatory words, *Elinor asked*, follow the exact words of the speaker. A period is needed at the very end of the entire sentence, even though the direct quote ends in a question mark. Together with your students, create an anchor chart for using direct quotation marks.

Independent Practice: Ask students to continue to revise their narratives or a notebook entry by adding meaningful conversation. Students may also wish to start a new narrative (fiction or personal narrative) by beginning with an engaging lead, such as in E. B. White's *Charlotte's Web*: "'Where's Papa going with that axe?' said Fern to her mother as they were setting the table for breakfast."

Reflection: After students have the opportunity to revise their writing with conversation added or to write a new piece with some conversation, ask them to share in whole group or small group. Their writing should be displayed on a document imager or whiteboard so everyone can see the punctuation and paragraphing. The following questions can help guide their thinking:

How did your story change when you added some dialogue¿
How is it satisfying¿
Does the conversation you wrote fit the story¿
What kinds of things should you think about as you write conversation¿
Is conversation easy or difficult for you to write¿ Explain.

Your Turn Lesson

Adjective Interrupters

The normal position of an adjective is just before the word it describes. Sometimes, for stylistic reasons, writers use adjectives after the words they modify or as interrupters. Showing students how to manipulate adjectives is both a grammar lesson and a lesson in stylistic devices.

Hook: Read a book that students have already heard read aloud, perhaps more than once, so they know the story. For the purpose of this lesson, concentrate on descriptive words. A good example to use is *Georgia's Bones* by Jen Bryant.

Purpose: *Writers, today we're going to talk about how to use adjectives to add variety to our sentences. I've noticed when I read your writing that most of the time we are using adjectives in the most usual way—just before the word we are describing. There's nothing wrong with doing that, but sometimes it would make our writing more interesting to read if we changed it up a bit. Let's explore how to do this.*

Brainstorm: Adjectives tell which ones, what kind, and how many. Think of as many nouns as you can. Then add two adjectives to describe each noun. For example, *pretty, little girl*; *big, snarling dog*; *happy, contented baby*; *rosy-cheeked, healthy infant*. List the student examples on an anchor chart. (Revisit this lesson later to revise for adjective specificity or for alliteration or even for including similes.)

Model: Using the anchor chart, write sentences in front of the students in which the adjective pairs are placed after the noun or pronoun they modify and are used as interrupters. For example, *We smiled at the infant, rosy-cheeked and healthy, sitting on his mother's lap.* Point out to students how the adjective interrupters slow down the reading of the sentence calling attention to the description. Offer several examples of your own, and also point out examples from other authors. Jen Bryant's *Georgia's Bones* contains several. J. K. Rowling's *Harry Potter and the Chamber of Secrets* also contains some gems: *Not only were there a dozen frost-covered Christmas trees and thick streamers of holly and mistletoe, but enchanted snow was falling,* warm and dry, *from the ceiling.*

Guided Practice: Ask students to go back to their drafts or their writer's notebooks to find examples of adjectives that can be paired with other adjectives or adjective pairs that they have already used. Working with a partner or individually they can manipulate these pairs, placing them in sentences as interrupters.

Ask students to write their examples on sentence strips to share with the class. These can be displayed in the classroom as reminders for use in future written pieces.

Independent Practice: Ask students to designate a page in their writer's notebooks for specific adjective pairs they discover in their independent reading. For each pair of adjectives, write a sentence in which they are used as adjective interrupters. Encourage students to try out this stylistic strategy in their drafts.

Reflection: Ask students to think about how adjectives can be used most effectively in their writing.

> *What do you now know about using adjectives in your writing?*
> *How do adjective interrupters affect the flow of the sentences you write?*
> *What other pieces of writing have you written that you can now revise for adjective interrupters?*

The Apostrophe to Show Possession

Of all the marks of punctuation we teach, the apostrophe often proves to be the most problematic. For one thing, once we teach it, students start placing apostrophes everywhere they see the letter *s*. The apostrophe lesson is one you may need to revisit more than once during the school year.

Hook: Read the book *If You Were an Apostrophe* by Shelly Lyons to the class. In this book, the author immerses the reader in multiple examples of apostrophe use. Ask students to pay attention to the use of the apostrophe to show possession.

Purpose: *Writers, today we're going to look at a mark of punctuation that shows belonging or possession. The apostrophe is a useful tool for making meaning clear. In fact, the only way to know whether it is a "girl's scarf" or a "girls' scarf" is to see it in writing and to notice the apostrophe. So we need to be very careful to put apostrophes in the right place to show possession.*

Brainstorm: Individually in your writer's notebooks jot down all the naming words (nouns) you can think of that end with the letter s in one minute. Have students share these words with a partner and to make a mark next to all of the words that are plural (more than one thing). Make a chart with two columns labeled Singular Nouns and Plural Nouns. In the plural noun column, list the words students volunteer; for example, *girls, boys, schools, teachers, books, trees, birds, clouds,* and *stars.* For each, write its singular form in the singular noun column. If students volunteer words like "happiness" as a plural noun because it ends in *s*, they will quickly realize that happiness does not have a singular and plural form. This may take a little explaining, but it is important for students to recognize that all words ending in *s* are not plural.

Model: Choose sentences from mentor texts that show the apostrophe used for possession, such as Seymour Simon's *Big Cats.*

A cat's senses are very keen, and it can detect its prey at a distance or at night.
Sensitive hairs in this jaguar's ears can pick up the sound of an animal's movements even before the animal can be seen.
The snow leopard's handsome fur has caused it to be much in demand.

Gorillas, also by Seymour Simon, contains an example of apostrophe use with a plural noun:

> The silverback may beat his chest to move family members along, to stop fights that may arise between them, or to attract females' attention.

Here's another example of plural noun with apostrophe in Simon's *Crocodiles and Alligators*:

> Crocodilians' legs are short and not as strong as their tails.

Send students on an apostrophe hunt in their independent reading books and in the mentor text library. Remind them that they are looking for apostrophes that show possession and not apostrophes in contractions. (See the Your Turn Lesson "Contractions Using Pronouns" in Part 2.) Have them write these examples in their writer's notebook in the reference section.

Model: Return to the anchor chart of singular and plural nouns. For each of the nouns listed, demonstrate for students how the possessive is formed. For singular nouns, we add an apostrophe and an *s*. For plural nouns ending in *s,* we simply add the apostrophe. For example, "boy's shirt" is a shirt belonging to one boy, but "boys' shirt" means that the shirt is made for boys, not men. (Note that when a singular noun ends in *s*, as in the name Keats, it is up to the writer whether to add *'s* or just an apostrophe. However, to avoid confusion among young writers, we suggest that if the noun is singular, they be instructed to always add the *'s*. It's not incorrect to do so, and getting into the habit of always using *'s* for singular possessives is good practice.) Be aware that not all the plural nouns on the student-generated list will easily lend themselves to possessive form. Sometimes it is better stylistically to write *the leaves of the trees* than *the trees' leaves*. If the possessive form is awkward, you might point that out to older students. However, for instructional purposes, show how to use the apostrophe in both singular and plural noun forms.

Guided Practice: Working with partners, ask students to go back to the writer's notebook examples gleaned from mentor texts and to place words with apostrophes in the appropriate column: singular possessives or plural possessives. After they have worked on these lists, post the lists around the room and share results. Correct any mistakes before the lists are posted as you circulate around the room guiding students in their work.

Independent Practice: Ask students to return to their writer's notebooks, drafts, or current piece of writing to check for the proper use of apostrophes. During sharing time, ask for volunteers to share any possessive nouns they noticed in their writing and how they punctuated them with the apostrophe.

Reflection: Ask students to jot in the reference section of their writer's notebooks why the apostrophe is important and how the apostrophe in singular and plural nouns helps to clarify meaning.

Why is an apostrophe not used every time you see an s *at the end of a word?*
How do you show possession with nouns that already end in s?

One More Thing about Apostrophes: Many English words form their plural by changing the spelling completely, not just adding *-s, -es,* or *-ies.* Some examples are *child* becomes *children; woman* becomes *women, mouse* becomes *mice,* and so on. Even though *children* is plural, it will still need an *s,* as in *The children's section of the theater was full.* You may need a separate lesson to address these issues.

The Job of a Verb Is to Show Action

Many young writers are still developing their understanding of basic parts of speech. For first and second graders, it is important to know the difference between a noun and a verb and what their jobs are in a sentence.

Hook: Read "The Vacuum Cleaner" by Patricia Hubbell, written in the voice of the cleaning machine, in *Dirty Laundry Pile: Poems in Different Voices* edited by Paul B. Janeczko. Younger students will delight in the personification evident in this piece. While you read the poem aloud, ask the students to close their eyes and imagine what the vacuum cleaner is doing. Read the poem again, sharing the text on a document imager or overhead copy.

Purpose: *Writers, today I'm going to show you how you can find verbs in the sentences you write to make sure that you are writing complete sentences. Every sentence has a "who" and a "what." The who tells us who the sentence is about, and the what tells us what is happening in the sentence or what the who is doing. The who is called the subject. The what is called the predicate. The predicate starts with the verb. Today we're going to practice writing sentences with strong verbs that describe an action.*

Brainstorm: Show a picture of a little boy and a little girl. Ask students to talk about what they do. Make a list to complete this sentence: I _____.

   (You can give them a model here such as *I dance* or *I laugh*.) Be sure to add some of your own thinking here.

Model: Ask students to share some of the ideas from their list of sentences. Create a T-chart with "who" and "what." Write the sentences in the chart. Use picture clues if necessary. After you write, students turn and talk about what they notice. Ask: What words show action?

> *I ride.*
> *I dance.*
> *I climb.*
> *I play.*
> *I bake.*

Ask students to come to the board and underline a verb in each sentence or circle a picture that shows the action if students can't read the verb. Ask this question each time: "What do I do?" What one word answers the question?

Guided Practice: Invite students to find the verbs in Patricia Hubbell's "The Vacuum Cleaner." Make a list of these verbs and/or illustrate the action. Then invite the students to return to their writer's notebook or daily journal and find some verbs to share with a partner. Ask the students to listen carefully and choose the best verb they heard to add to the class list. If possible, add a kinesthetic touch by asking students to act out the action word and let their classmates guess what it is.

Independent Practice: Ask students to make a page in their notebook and give it a title such as "Verbs I Would Like to Use in My Writing" and add words they think show action. It may be a good idea to provide them with a noun and ask them to think of as many verbs as they can to complete the sentence. They should only write or draw one word—the verb. For example, *Snow* _____ (*melts, sparkles, falls, twirls, dances, shines, stings, blankets, flies, floats*).

Note: If some students need more practice, gather them on the rug and use another poem from Janeczko's collection such as "Job Satisfaction" by John Collis (great verb choices; just explain that the first line uses a different kind of verb and that it is *am*, which is not an action verb. Then keep going (verbs in this poem are *enjoy, snuggle, lie, lurk, chomp, chew, say, groan, moan, wish*).

Reflection: After students share some of their favorite verbs from their collection, ask them these questions:

What do you now know for sure about verbs?
How would your verbs help the reader to see the action?
What is the difference between a noun and a verb? (Use this question if you have already worked with nouns.)

When to Make a New Paragraph in a Narrative

Learning to make new paragraphs is an important but sometimes confusing job for young writers. Often students will tell their stories from beginning to end without providing paragraph breaks. Even though these narratives may provide all the elements of story grammar, they are difficult to read and ultimately unsatisfying for that reason. Teaching writers to use paragraphs provides rewards for both the writer and the reader.

Paragraphing for informational and opinion writing is rather straightforward. Each new topic or reason becomes a new paragraph. Help students to recognize the need for new paragraphs by providing many opportunities for shared writing experiences with them.

Hook: On a document imager, show students a chapter (preferably one they have heard before) from your current read-aloud or current selection from the reader anthology. Find a chapter that contains paragraph breaks for several different reasons: speaker changes, new time, new place, new topic, or for dramatic effect, for example. As you read the chapter or section of the chapter, point out the paragraph breaks to the class and lead them to discover the reason (purpose) for each new paragraph. Initially, you may have to *tell* them the reasons.

Purpose: *Writers, sometimes when I'm reading your pieces I get confused because I see a solid block of writing with no paragraphs. I do that sometimes, too, when I'm writing a draft quickly. But I've found that the best time to break a piece into paragraphs is as I draft. Today we're going to talk about how to break up a narrative (story) into paragraphs.*

Brainstorm: Remind students that in the chapter read on the document imager we noticed that the author broke up her story into paragraphs when she changed time, when she changed speaker, and when she changed the setting. In stories, our characters also do things (action), and when the action changes, that might be a time for a new paragraph as well. We might also make a paragraph for dramatic effect, when we want something to really stand out. Make an anchor chart entitled "When to start a new paragraph in a narrative" with each of these items listed. With students, brainstorm phrases or sentences that indicate changing time and place and add those in the appropriate column. Time change could include *later, the next day, in the evening, afterward, by this time, during lunch, at recess*, and *when night came*. Setting could include such examples as *meanwhile in the classroom, on the other side of the pond, in the front of the line, at the back of the bus.* List speaker changes on the chart also and dramatic effect examples that you and the students brainstorm together.

Model: In front of the students, use one of your narratives or a narrative from a student in last year's class to demonstrate paragraph breaks. Ask the students to identify the author's purpose for the start of each new paragraph.

Shared Practice: Ask students to participate in writing a shared narrative piece on a topic in which they all have had an experience: building a snowman with friends, sledding on a day off, riding a roller coaster, or celebrating a special birthday. As the class writes with you, point out the paragraph breaks and ask the students to give you the reasons for each. Label them too.

Guided Practice: Send students on a paragraph hunt in their independent reading and in the classroom library. Ask them to write examples of each of the ways paragraphs are begun in their writer's notebooks. Make sure that they label each of the examples. Share with the whole class what they have found.

Independent Practice: Ask students to revisit their own narratives and to make paragraph breaks where needed. Give them the opportunity to share the changes they have made with a peer or in whole group and to explain why they made them.

Reflection: Ask the class to reflect in their writer's notebooks why it is important to use paragraphs. Give them one or two questions they can reflect on.

> *Why do authors use paragraphs?*
> *How do paragraphs help the reader?*
> *Do all pieces of writing have five paragraphs?*
> *How many sentences must a paragraph include? Is there a correct number?*

Be sure students understand that real-world writing does not adhere to a five-paragraph formula, although it may be helpful for students to be able to imitate that structure when necessary, for example, for test-taking purposes or to help them organize a piece of writing. It may be unusual to write a one-sentence paragraph; however, master writers often do so for dramatic effect. Consider E. B. White's opening paragraph in the chapter "Ames' Crossing" in *Stuart Little*:

In the loveliest town of all, where the houses were white and high and the elm trees were green and higher than the houses, where the front yards were wide and pleasant and the back yards were bushy and worth finding out about, where the streets sloped down to the stream and the stream flowed quietly under the bridge, where the lawns ended in orchards and the orchards ended in fields and the fields ended in pastures and the pastures climbed the hill and disappeared over the top toward the wonderful wide sky, in this loveliest of all towns Stuart stopped to get a drink of sarsaparilla.

Or consider Gary Paulsen's one sentence paragraphs in *The Winter Room*:

In the spring everything is soft.

Father didn't know how old the farm was either, and when I asked Uncle David he just smiled and nodded and Nels didn't seem to hear me.

And one more from *Jelly Belly* by Robert Kimmel Smith:

I, on the other hand, would never have to go back there again [to fat camp].

Part 2

Informational Units of Study

Chapter 5

Introduction to Informational Writing

Think about the types of writing most of us encounter on a daily basis: newspapers, magazines, nonfiction books, blogs, instruction manuals, and so on. Think about the types of writing we produce in the workplace: reports, memos, letters, and journals among other things. Additionally, we listen to speeches, lectures, and news reports. In our daily lives, we are surrounded by informational text. Informational writing, also known as expository writing, is used to explain, describe, clarify, instruct, or otherwise give information to the reader. Good informational writing gives facts and details about a specific topic either by summarizing research from a variety of sources or by drawing conclusions based on facts and information at hand. The benefits of writing (and reading) informational text are many. For one thing, expository text is the kind of writing students are required to produce in every subject area. Furthermore, expository writing requires a level of planning and organization not necessarily needed in other types of writing.

Our students benefit from understanding the various types and styles of informational text. In our lessons with K–6 students, we focused on description of character, description of setting, compare/contrast, and procedural (how-to) text. Among the things students must understand is that in this type of writing the author cannot assume that the reader has any prior knowledge of the topic. Explanations need to be complete and thorough without being redundant. This requirement is a daunting task for young writers as, indeed, it can be for experienced writers as well. The writer must provide facts, statistics, descriptive details, definition, and analysis. She must make observations, draw conclusions, predict, and reflect. Above all, she must engage the reader's interest, convincing him that the topic is important enough to take the time to read about.

Informational writing, then, is a complicated skill. Most young writers have some background in storytelling. They have heard or made up stories themselves. The same is not true of explanations. It is not uncommon for a child to begin to explain a process, for example, how to wash your hands, and forget to mention using soap!

Clearly, as teachers of writing we need to help our students organize their information in such a way that everything necessary is included. Providing graphic organizers and teaching transitional words and phrases are important ways to achieve this end. Besides knowing how to write a good summary, other skills required to write good expository text include knowledge of grammatical constructions. As in all writing, these include, but are not limited to, issues of organization: sentence structure (complete sentences), subject-verb agreement, pronoun-antecedent agreement, use of transitional words and phrases, and consistency in use of verb tenses. As we think about the grammar and punctuation that may be embedded in expository units of study, we recognize that these issues may arise, but we are always aware of the needs of the students in the writing workshop, allowing the drafts of their writing to guide us in planning appropriate grammar lessons.

Chapter 6

Writing Descriptions
in the Primary Grades

Writing descriptions of people, places, objects, and events is a great way to help writers of all ages develop quality ideas and add style to their piece of writing. The wonderful thing about teaching students how to write descriptions is the application of this instruction across all the modes of writing: narrative, informational, and opinion writing. Although it seems as though students should be able to do this without much instruction, guidance, and practice, years of experience in the classroom have taught us that our students cannot, for the most part, naturally write good descriptions.

Lynne decided to work on description with several classrooms in the Upper Moreland Primary School to help them build content in informational writing. She thought about which grammar and convention lessons she wanted to embed within each grade-level experience but kept an open mind to problems, concerns, and "Aha!" moments that arose on a daily basis. Cathy McParland's pull-out ESL kindergarten class wrote descriptions of summer activities using the outside-inside scaffold of Carolyn Crimi's book *Outside, Inside*. Lynne used the book again in Alison Navarrete's kindergarten class, while Shelly Keller's kindergarten class wrote descriptions of a person they knew very well. Chris Flaherty's first graders and Maribeth Batcho's second graders composed descriptions of their favorite places.

In Cathy McParland's ESL class for kindergarten students, Lynne worked with the mentor text *Over and Under the Snow* by Kate Messner, a recount of a day a child spends in the winter woods with her father. The child discovers the worlds above and below the snow. The book is reminiscent of Jane Yolen's *Owl Moon*. It is filled with specific language and words that help readers imagine and visualize. Lynne focused on nouns and verbs. The naming words were a good starting point for English language learners. Lynne chose several pages of text to examine and had students help find all the naming words. Then she reread the page and asked students to find a word that helped them see what the animal or narrator was doing. Students tried to act out the verbs, becoming dancing shadows or licking their lips (she actually used marshmallows so that students could act out Kate Messner's sentence "I lick sticky marshmallows from my lips and lean back with heavy eyes."). From just two pages of text, she made this chart:

Naming Words Nouns	Action Words Verbs
Beavers	gnaw
I (pronoun)	stand
I (pronoun)	stare
I (pronoun)	lick
I (pronoun)	lean (back)
fire	crackles
shadows	dance
sparks	shoot (up)

Using a simple scaffold, Lynne created an opportunity for the students to play with nouns and verbs. She modeled with her poem, "White,

Wonderful Winter." Her poem made use of noun-verb sentences, but care-ful attention was paid to the pairs of words so that they could create a strong image:

> *Adults cuddle,*
> *Children huddle,*
> *White, wonderful winter!*
> *Mice scurry,*
> *Snowflakes flurry,*
> *White, wonderful winter!*

The kindergartners tried several shared writing experiences using the poem title "Wild, Wonderful Summer" and did not worry about rhyme. First, they made a list of some things that reminded them of summer: lady-bugs, bees, flowers, swimmers, baseball players, ice cream, grass, lawn-mowers, and birds. Lynne referred to these words as nouns but emphasized the job they do: nouns give everything a name. Mrs. McParland pointed to objects and people in the classroom as examples. Basically, the students were told that if you could point to someone or something, if you named it, him, or her, you needed a noun. Then students talked with a partner about what some of the people, animals, plants, or food items could be doing in summer. Cathy told her students that they should think of an action or doing word. The class shared their thinking, and Lynne and Cathy, their teachers, wrote them on the board as poems. Here are two kindergarten shared experiences:

> Bees sting,
> Ladybugs tickle.
> Wild, wonderful summer!

> Flowers tower,
> Swimmers dive,
> Wild, wonderful summer!

Finally, Lynne and Cathy asked the students to read over the list again aloud with them and find some noun-verb pairs that might belong together in the same stanza. In order to help the students, Cathy read only one noun, "children." Then Lynne read the list of verbs and asked the students to give a thumbs up for any action word that would be something children might do. When students' thumbs went up, Lynne stopped so they could read the noun-verb pair as a sentence. The verbs the students chose to pair with the noun *children* included *swim, dive, lick, jump, run, climb,* and *grow.* The students were quick to orally write again while Lynne recorded their thinking:

Lawnmowers chop,   Children lick,
Grass grows,   Ice cream melts,
Wild, wonderful summer!   Wild, wonderful summer!

Lynne and Cathy were able to use these poems to look at uppercase and lowercase letters as well as the use of the exclamation mark at the end of the final line. Students talked about how an exclamation mark was different from a period and how the reader should read a sentence ending with an exclamation mark. Students returned to their lists and found two ideas they wanted to use independently in their summer poem. Some students used the -ing form of the verb such as Jana's example, for instance (spelling was edited here but not in her journal).

Children running,
Swimmers diving,
Wild, wonderful summer!

The next week Lynne read *Outside, Inside* by Carolyn Crimi. The book follows a seesaw text structure, alternating between things that are happening outside and inside. After she read the book aloud to the students, they went back to find the naming words and action words and placed them on an anchor chart. The children talked about the things they liked to do outside in any season. On the board, Lynne charted another list for "Things I Like to Do Outside." She modeled with her list. Then she wrote some sentences using the chart to help her:

Outside, I walk my dogs through the woods. The dogs bark. They tug on the leash. A squirrel climbs up, up, up a tall tree. He is very scared!

She asked the group for their ideas and focused on nouns and verbs but included other words that the students used to create their description. Before they wrote in their journals, each student took a turn to share what he likes to do outside. The students had time to think before they shared. Sometimes, Cathy or Lynne asked a question as a gentle nudge to think again, and possibly write more. When the students composed, Cathy and Lynne helped them stretch the words to hear their sounds and write down the letters for those sounds. It is no surprise that most students used only the consonant letters, although some students were able to get their words down quickly.

The next day Cathy repeated the process, this time, asking students to think about the things they like to do inside and charted their responses. The students orally wrote. Again, Cathy asked questions to get students to elaborate when their thinking was unclear. She tried to keep their thinking focused on their topic and asked them to act out their sentence whenever it was appropriate to do so.

In the next several days, Lynne and Cathy continued to work on descriptions of summer activities with students. It seemed so appropriate since it was early May and students were starting to think about summer vacation. Lynne shared *Looking for Crabs* by Bruce Whatley, a very funny book about a family on vacation at the seashore. The book focuses on the one way the family spent their time at the beach looking for crabs. Lynne chose going to watch the Fourth of July fireworks as a topic for her description. She wrote on the board in front of her students:

I love summer. On the Fourth of July we go to Roslyn School after dark. We take beach chairs and sit outside in the parking lot. All of a sudden, bright patterns explode in the inky sky. My favorite ones are the golden sunbursts that light up the sky. Streamers rain down in all directions. Sometimes, loud booms and cracks echo through the night. I whistle and clap at the end of the show!

The students were asked to think about activities they enjoyed doing in the summer months. They shared them orally. Then Lynne and Cathy asked them to choose one activity and together they wrote a description as a shared experience on chart paper. Each student first drew a picture about playing tag. Lynne recorded their thoughts:

We love to run and play tag. It is fun to run away and hide. It is not fun if you are "IT." Everyone screams and runs away from you. When you tag someone, you are not "It" and can run and run. You can scream and scream!

After they read and reread their shared piece, they chose another activity and drew a picture. Then they used their drawing to talk about their summer activity and wrote about it in their journals. After they wrote about their activities, they read them aloud to the group several times to decide where a period might be placed. They looked at Lynne's sample again to examine the only sentence ending with an exclamation mark. Cathy asked them to read the sentence chorally with her. She asked them what they noticed about the way that sentence was read aloud. Alan said that a sentence with an exclamation mark is louder. Nathaniel added that you are excited and that's why you use it. The students were asked to choose one sentence that needed an exclamation mark to close the thought. Jana wrote about going to the swim club and included an important detail—"I like to lie on my back." Although she told us she was lying on her back in the water, and we finally supplied the word *floating* for her to use, Jana did not add it to her final draft. She did, however, decide not to use the exclamation after her first sentence, and tried to erase it when she decided to put one at the end of her last sentence, "I don't want to go home!" In Figure 6.1, Jana, an ESL student, describes a summer activity.

Kishan could not give up the exclamation mark at the end of his first or last sentence. Cathy and Lynne loved his involvement with this piece and marveled at his sense of sentence. His last sentence was originally written: Whn it is sune, I! cn play. (When it is sunny, I! can play.) He decided on his own to move his exclamation mark to take the place of final period after listening to the group's discussion. See Figure 6.2.

Alan knew how to use end punctuation and made only one mistake with it in a sentence that really could have been written using commas for listing. At first glance, you may think his problem is more with focus. Alan's

Figure 6.1
Jana writes about swimming as a summer activity:
"I love summer.
Because it is fun and I go to the swimming pool.
I like to lie on my back.
I don't want to go home!"

Figure 6.2
Kishan writes about
playing cricket:
"I love summer!
I like to play
cricket. I hit
the ball far
and high. When
it is sunny I
can play!"

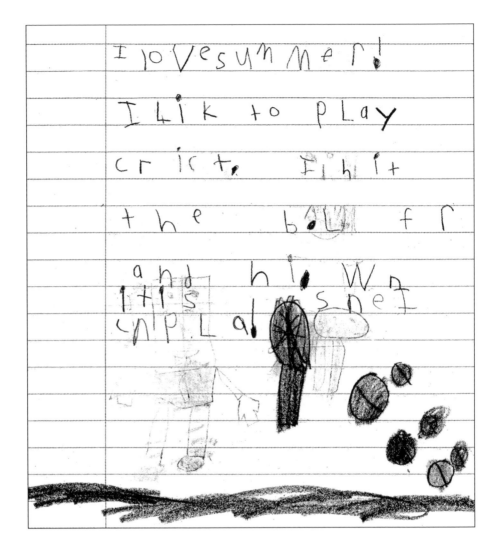

piece is really all about swimming at the swim club. He writes about going down the slide (into the water), getting snacks, and playing with his friend Eric and his baby brother. His periods are rather large, but Lynne and Cathy did not comment on this. Alan was proud of his use of end punctuation, especially his final exclamation mark. See Figure 6.3.

Next, Lynne and Cathy urged the young writers to describe a favorite place or the things they liked to do there. They modeled with descriptions of the classroom and asked the students to suggest another place everyone could write about. The children chose the playground. They orally rehearsed what they wanted to say before writing it in their journals. Lynne reminded them to use uppercase letters to begin each new sentence and a

Figure 6.3
Alan writes about going to the swim club:
"I love summer.
I like to swim.
And I like to slide.
And I eat. And I play.
Eric and my baby [brother] swim with me!"

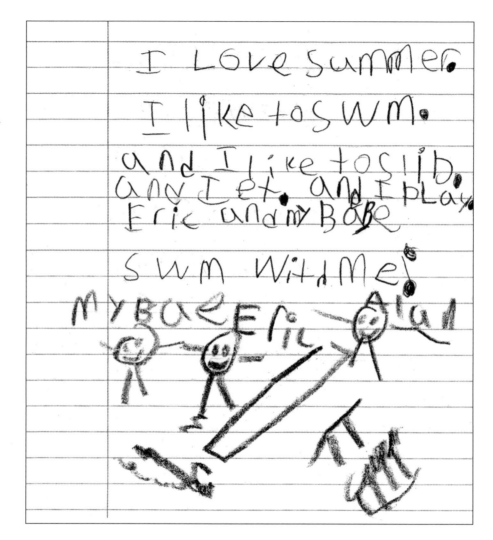

period or exclamation mark to end each sentence. Jana decided to end each sentence with an exclamation mark even though Lynne and Cathy advised the students to find one special sentence that needed the exclamation mark to show excitement or to let the reader know it should be read in a louder voice. Sometimes, we have to decide what battles we choose to fight. Since Jana was able to write in sentences beginning with a capital and ending with a mark of punctuation, Lynne did not ask her to change three of her exclamation marks to periods. During a quick conference, Jana told Lynne that all of her sentences showed that she was excited so they all needed the exclamation mark. Lynne felt she had a clear rationale, and insisting on the change would have taken ownership away from Jana. In the end, Jana decided to make the change.

Teaching Point: Students need gentle nudges to try new things. A teacher learns the difference between a nudge and a shove through myriad experiences, especially in one-on-one conferences. The "shove" makes the piece the teacher's writing, not the student's writing. Young writers cannot make multiple changes or remember different pieces of advice. Decide what you think might be a doable revision or edit for the student writer and ask him to try it out.

 Grammar Reference: An exclamation mark is used to show strong feeling. It can be used at the end of a command such as "Help!" and is used after most interjections such as "Goodness gracious!" It may be used at the end of a sentence that could also be written as a question. When a writer chooses to do that, the writer is trying to show heightened or extreme emotion. "What are you doing!" I still remember my grandmother's tone when she found me using the ivory-white walls of her dining room as my canvas for a picture drawn with my crayons. The exclamation point is rarely found in formal compositions and has virtually disappeared from newspaper articles. It didn't even appear as a standard feature on keyboards until the 1970s (ask.com).

With the help of Charlotte Zolotow's picture book *The Moon Was the Best*, Lynne began a study of description in first and second grades. Zolotow's book describes Paris with incredible snapshots, all beginning with the phrase, "She remembered . . ." The students discussed her use of well-placed adjectives such as "silvery" to describe pigeons, "unwrapped" to describe bread, and "outdoor" to describe cafés. They discussed the importance of knowing that, even in a butcher shop, flowers appeared in the window. The students decided that the describing word *butcher* was important here because you simply would not expect to see flowers in a shop where you went to buy meat. The first graders' discussion led to this conclusion: adjectives don't always have to be fancy. Sometimes they are just the perfect word in the perfect place. The children looked at the story for proper nouns—Paris and the Seine—and also found specific nouns like "carousel," "fountains," and "loaves." They decided that exact nouns and adjectives play a big part in writing good descriptions. After the students individually brainstormed a list of places they knew and loved, they shared in whole group while their teacher, Chris Flaherty, charted them on the whiteboard. Lynne and Chris decided that a mini-lesson on proper nouns would fit nicely here. Many students named places that needed a capital letter such as Great Wolf Lodge, Wildwood, Willow Grove, and Masons Mill Park. The students decided whether their place needed any capital letters after Lynne modeled with this example:

I remember the playground at the Upper Moreland Primary School in Hatboro, Pennsylvania. I remember its colorful swings and a wide, curving sliding board. I remember the enormous sandbox full of white sand. I remember the wood chips that cover the ground under the monkey bars and make a soft landing for children who sometimes slip and tumble from the bars. The playground is surrounded by a high fence so small children cannot wander out into the driveway. Best of all, the playground is behind the school and gets plenty of afternoon sunlight.

The students noted the words that Lynne capitalized. First, she asked them what kinds of words started with a capital letter. As they highlighted these words, Lynne asked them to think about the job each word or group of words did. Makenzie decided their job was to give something a name. Lynne asked the class to think about what kinds of words do this job. On the count of three, the class whispered, "Nouns!" Then she asked them to hunt for other nouns in her description. Patricia noticed that sometimes the word *school* was capitalized and sometimes it was not. This observation led to a rich discussion. Students discovered that some nouns get very specific, naming only one person, place, or object. Other nouns can be used to give a general name to a person, a place, or an object. Students looked at other examples such as road or Byberry Road, park or Willow Grove Park, school or Upper Moreland Intermediate School. Lynne and Chris asked them to go on a proper noun hunt in their reading books and in signs posted in their school. Some of their finds included Clifford (name of a dog and a book), Paris, Empire State Building, Oreo, Snoopy, Wii, Jupiter, North Pole, Valentine's Day, Christmas, Thanksgiving, Halloween, and Santa Claus. They spent the next several days hunting for proper nouns and charting them with Chris and Lynne. The children asked their parents, siblings, and friends for help. Here is one anchor chart they started to create:

Holidays: Christmas, New Year's Day, Hanukkah, Thanksgiving, Halloween, Mother's Day, Father's Day

Cities, States, Countries, Continents: San Francisco, Philadelphia, California, Maine, France, Europe, Africa

People and Pets: Ms. Frizzle, Rip Van Winkle, Charlotte, Wilbur

Books, Newspapers, Magazines: *One Tiny Turtle, New York Times, Weekly Reader, Highlights for Children*

Companies and organizations: Google, Boy Scouts of America, Toys R Us, Toyota, Ford

Places, Buildings, Restaurants: Yellowstone National Park, Empire
    State Building, Delaware River, Olive Garden
Titles: President Obama, Prince William, Queen Elizabeth, Judge Judy
Brand names: Apple, Dell, Sony, Pepsi, Nike

As the students turned their attention back to the work of writing a
description that used the scaffold from *The Moon Was the Best,* they used their
senses to explore their setting and began their sentences with "I remember
. . ." to imitate Charlotte Zolotow's craft. Lynne modeled with a piece about
her own grandparents' home. She wrote on the board in front of the students in the first- and second-grade classes. Here is Lynne's model:

*I remember spending long summer vacations at my grandparents' ranch house in
Coopersburg. I remember the cozy kitchen was filled with different smells: turkey
roasting, brownies baking, and chicken frying, crisp and crunchy. I remember the big
screened-in porch and looking out at the dark woods where fireflies blinked on and off
like Christmas lights. But the best thing of all was curling up in the hammock with
my dog Pixie nestled on the floor below and falling asleep on the porch with the cool
night breezes brushing my cheeks.*

Teaching Point: As often as possible, model with your own writing. Students will
learn to trust you and your advice if they see you as a writer, too. You will grow
in confidence as a writer and be able to offer sage advice during conferences. You will understand your students' struggles and help them cultivate
their problem-solving skills.

Lynne read her piece aloud to the first graders. She asked them to notice
her use of the colon and how it helped her include a list in that particular sentence. She asked them to find nouns, naming words, that they felt were specific and helped them to form pictures in their minds. The students' lists
included "fireflies," "kitchen," "ranch," "porch," "hammock," "chicken," and
"brownies." They talked about the words *ranch house* and how that kind of
home looks different from a colonial, an apartment, or a castle. She pointed to
her apostrophe and talked about its use to show ownership but did not dwell
on placement with the first graders. The first graders found adjectives they
thought were interesting and important such as "cozy," "cool," "crunchy,"
"crispy," and "screened-in." Lynne told them that adjectives help make a
description even more specific by describing the nouns and telling "what kind."
She had them try it out by asking, "What kind of kitchen?" or "What kind of
porch?" or "What kind of breeze?" Students responded chorally.

Grammar Reference: Adjectives are describing words and usually come right before the noun they describe. They often answer the question, "What kind?" and can also include number words such as *few, many, some, two, ten*, and all color words. Sometimes an adjective stands alone at the end of a sentence such as *The sunset was beautiful.* Sometimes one or two adjectives come after the noun they describe as in this sentence: *The father, proud and loving, held his first child in his arms.*

Lynne and Chris allowed time for drawing and labeling first, followed by time to write a draft. As they conferred, they noticed how the students handled proper nouns and exact nouns, adjectives to describe nouns, end punctuation, the use of exclamation marks, and the apostrophe to show ownership. These grammar and mechanics issues were common to many writing pieces. Spacing between words may still be an issue for some students. First grade is a good place to master this skill. Lynne shared the correct apostrophe placement for both singular and plural nouns since this knowledge seemed important for Patricia's piece (see Figure 6.4). Patricia

Figure 6.4
Patricia's description of her grandparents' house:
"I remember my pop-pop's house. He lives in Willow Grove. I remember his birthday party where I had chocolate cake. I remember playing games with a huge exercise ball at my grandparents' house. I remember my grandparents' basement. I played in it all the time!"

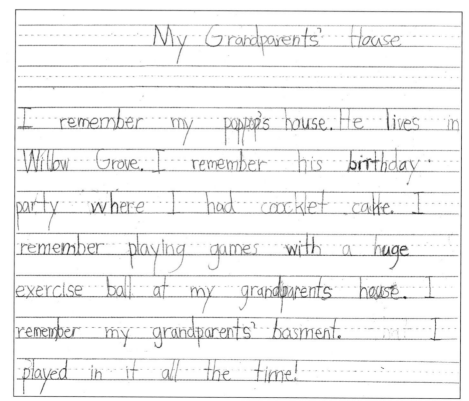

seemed to understand which nouns needed a capital letter and ended her sentences with periods, reserving a spot for an exclamation point to end her final sentence. Sometimes, a teacher must make decisions on an individual basis for matters of revision or editing. Spelling errors were not corrected unless the student asked for help. Certain words such as *remember, with, where,* and *when* appeared on the board, anchor chart, or alphabetized word wall. All students were expected to check their work and "read the environment" to help them correct spelling.

Patricia chose a few important adjectives in her piece, such as *birthday* to describe what kind of party, *chocolate* to describe the cake, and *huge* and *exercise* to describe the ball. She knew how to capitalize the city and all the words in her title. Patricia also understood how to use the apostrophe for singular possessive, but Lynne showed her where to place the apostrophe in the plural possessive form for *grandparents'*—used in both the title and within the piece. Of course, there was no expectation to master forms of the apostrophe at this level, but showing Patricia the correct placement in this particular piece seemed timely. She chose to use an exclamation mark to end her last sentence because she said the basement was her favorite room in the house because her toys and games were kept there on shelves. Lynne asked her if she wanted to add that explanation to her description, but Patricia decided not to add it.

Indy wrote about Great Wolf Lodge (see Figure 6.5). During the conference, Lynne and Indy discussed the use of precise nouns such as *sprinkler* and how he helped the reader feel his fear and excitement, especially his choice of words to describe the experience—"a night of terror!" They also talked

Figure 6.5

Indy remembers Great Wolf Lodge: "I remember the water park at Great Wolf Lodge. The huge slides go super fast. In wave pool the waves are super scary! And a hot tub was there, too. And in a basketball pool, I can slam duck it. I remember the sprinkler that I pretended was a shower. The best thing of all was the even bigger water slide. It was like the night of terror! I was almost going to cry! I love the water park at Great Wolf Lodge."

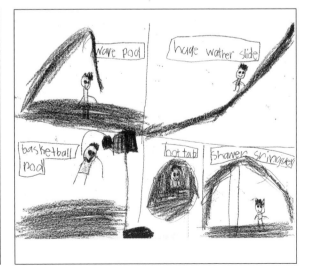

about the use of exclamation marks and whether Indy could eliminate any. He decided against it because he said those sentences showed how he felt about the water rides. Lynne talked about spacing between ending punctuation and the next sentence. She showed him how two of his sentences could be easily rewritten by eliminating the word *and*, such as *In the basketball pool I can slam dunk it.* Lynne noticed how Indy used the comparative form of *big* (bigger) in his piece but did not know how to spell it. She talked with Chris about a possible mini-lesson or Your Turn Lesson on comparatives and superlatives.

Grammar Reference: Adjectives have special forms called comparatives and superlatives that are used to compare things. You simply add the suffix -er to compare two people, objects, animals, or places. For example, *Cindy is taller than Susan.* The superlative form ends in the suffix -est and is used to show that one thing stands out above all the rest, such as, *Andrew is the brightest boy in his graduating class.* Sometimes you form the comparative form by adding the word *more* in front of the adjective. *Bob was more careful completing his math assignment than his twin brother.* You may need to place the word *most* in front of some adjectives to form the superlative. *Jill was the most happy that her family was going to Florida to visit their cousins.* However, it is important to note that you never use -er with *more* or -est with *most*. It is one or the other!

During Aidan's conference, Lynne talked about his use of strong verbs and well-placed adjectives. His sentences conveyed all the energy and joy that Aidan felt while he was at the shore and created a good snapshot for his readers. Aidan reserved his use of the exclamation point to the last sentence in his piece about the shore (see Figure 6.6).

The next day Lynne and Chris asked the class to look through their final drafts of descriptions to find adjectives that ended in *-er* or *-est*. They borrowed some sentences from Seymour Simon's *Gorillas* to use as models.

"Gorillas have bigger and more powerful muscles in their arms than in their legs."

"But the arms are much longer, and the chest, shoulders, neck, and head are much larger and heavier than yours."

"Of course, gorillas are much hairier than humans."

"Mountain gorillas are the rarest of all gorillas."

"Around midday, when the sun is at its highest point, the group stops for a rest."

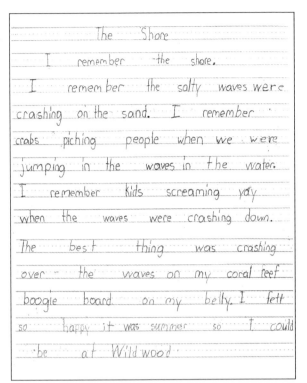

Figure 6.6
Aidan remembers the shore:
"I remember the shore. I remember the salty waves were crashing on the sand. I remember crabs pinching people when we were jumping in the waves in the water. I remember kids screaming yay when the waves were crashing down. The best thing was crashing over the waves on my coral reef boogie board on my belly. I felt so happy it was summer so I could be at Wildwood!"

Lynne and Chris wanted to show their students how adjectives are used to offer comparisons as well as to create an understanding of their forms to show degrees of comparisons. Students came to the board in pairs to find the adjectives, and the group discussed how they helped the reader understand the meaning of the sentence. They talked about the difference between using the *-er* form and the *-est* form. For example, Chris asked about the use of "rarest" to describe the mountain gorilla. Olivia said that it helped you to know that, out of all the gorillas in the world, the mountain gorillas were hard to find because there weren't many left. Makenzie offered that "rarest" was the most important word in the whole sentence. After discussing the sentences on the board, Lynne and Chris asked the students to help them chart some examples and to choose one adjective to create a flipbook with an illustration to accompany each adjective form (see the chart on the following page).

This chart was only a beginning. Students in first grade often need to compare things and will use the *-er* and *-est* forms of adjectives fairly often. A formal introduction to these forms will raise awareness and help students make good decisions. Of course, this concept will also be addressed in second and third grades to help students master the art of comparing things. At

Adjective	*-er* (Comparative)	*-est* (Superlative)
one-syllable words		
hard	harder	hardest
soft	softer	softest
small	smaller	smallest
one-syllable ending in silent −e		
white	whiter	whitest
rude	ruder	rudest
rare	rarer	rarest
one-syllable words ending in b, d, g, m, n, p, t		
big	bigger	biggest
fit	fitter	fittest
sad	sadder	saddest
thin	thinner	thinnest
two- or more syllable words		
polite	more polite	most polite
careful	more careful	most careful
skillful	more skillful	most skillful
two-syllable words ending in y		
silly	sillier	silliest
heavy	heavier	heaviest
funny	funnier	funniest

that point in time, teachers can also address the troublemakers—irregular forms such as *good, better, best* and *bad, worse, worst.*

In second grade, Maribeth Batcho's class also used *The Moon Was the Best* as their mentor text to write a good description along with *When I Was Young in the Mountains* by Cynthia Rylant. The students were enthralled with the description of the walk to the outhouse and the chore of pumping water from the well and heating the water to fill the round tin tubs for baths, or going to church in the schoolhouse and walking down to the river for a baptism. The students could see how Rylant created mind pictures—like turning the pages in a photo album—for her readers to engage with and how she helped them experience her childhood through all the senses. They talked about many scenes, but they all seemed attached to her first image:

> When I was young in the mountains, Grandfather came home in the evening covered with the black dust of a coal mine. Only his lips were clean, and he used them to kiss the top of my head.

The students found adjectives that offered strong images. Jake said he could picture the clean lips while her grandfather's arms, hands, and face were covered in the black dust. There was some confusion about the word *coal*. Some students thought it was a naming word while others called it an adjective. Maribeth and Lynne took this opportunity to explain that sometimes words can do several jobs and here the word *coal* was being used to describe what kind of mine. Lynne showed how the word could be replaced by *silver, gold, emerald,* or *diamond,* to name a few that could describe what kind of mine. All of these words could also be used as nouns instead of adjectives. Lynne offered two examples: *Everything King Midas touched turned to gold.* She also wrote this sentence on the board: *An emerald is a valuable gem stone that is used in rings, bracelets, and necklaces.* Students were encouraged to create sentences with a partner that used a noun as an adjective and share in whole group. Max and Julia shared, "The <u>rainbow</u> sunset was beautiful." Ryan and Stephen offered, "The cat's <u>chocolate</u> eyes stared at me." Stephanie and Aidan wrote, "I swing from the <u>monkey</u> bars every day at recess."

The next day they looked at prepositional phrases in some of Cynthia Rylant's descriptions. "When I was young in the mountains, we went to church in the schoolhouse on Sundays, and sometimes walked with the congregation through the cow pasture to the dark swimming hole, for baptisms." Lynne and Maribeth talked about the job of a preposition—to tell you how one thing is related to another. They showed the young writers how prepositions are attached to a noun or pronoun. In Rylant's snapshot, many prepositional phrases are used:

- in the mountains
- in the schoolhouse
- to church
- on Sundays
- with the congregation
- through the cow pasture
- to the dark swimming hole
- for baptism

Lynne shared that prepositions link nouns, pronouns, and sometimes adjectives to other words in a sentence. She demonstrated by using the noun *book* in several different sentences with a different preposition each time to show how the preposition locates the noun *book* in space or in time (see the Your Turn Lesson "Prepositions and the Prepositional Phrase" at the end of Part 2):

- The book is on the table.
- The book is beneath the table.
- The book is leaning against the table.
- The book is beside the table.
- She held the book over the table.
- She read the book during class.
- She read the book before recess.

She continued to use prepositions to show where one thing is in relation to another. Each of the italicized words in the following sentences is a preposition:

- The spider crawled slowly *along* the banister.
- The dog is hiding *under* the porch because it knows it will be punished for chewing up a new pair of shoes.
- The rain was beating hard *against* the window.
- Long ago people skated only *on* frozen lakes or ponds *in* winter.
- The ice-cream truck meanders *down* the quiet street and pulls the children *from* their houses like a powerful magnet.

Grammar Reference: Many verbs look like they are followed by a preposition. For example, "The beagle chewed up the newspaper." Another example is "I went to the hospital to cheer up my friend." Common constructions are *to break down, to cheer up, to break in, to loosen up, to break out.* In these instances, these words are thought of as part of the verb and not as prepositions.

Together with the students, the teachers created an ongoing list of prepositions as an anchor chart, including *in, out, on, to, before, after, under, from, around, between, over, along, beside, above, below, up, down, across, by, beyond, into, near, off, among, underneath, atop, at, about, amid, aboard.* They encouraged the students to build and expand their sentences by using prepositions that showed where one thing is in relation to another or when something happened in relation to something else.

Maribeth and Lynne talked about how good description often evokes a feeling. A setting can be scary, peaceful, exciting, or busy. Marcus tried to capture the feelings and engage his readers' senses with his piece about his home. He tried out a colon twice in this piece to help him announce that a list was following and knew he needed commas. Here is his description of his home:

I remember the backyard so big, flat, no fences, and so wonderful for a great big soccer
    game.
I remember my great neighbor Bo Meakim. We play: Minecraft, soccer, and basketball.
I remember my room with all my soccer posters and trophies all over my ceiling and wall.
I remember my kitchen fridge where all the sweet food I steel comes from: applesauce, ice
    cream, raspberry water ice.
I remember the awesome basement where all the Wii and games start.
I remember the screened-in-porch where all the wind and air come in.
I remember the porch where baby Red-Headed Finches hatched.
I remember the living room made the love grow to the warm heart of the house.
The living room was the best.

Jake's piece about New York City was delightful. He also used a colon, highlighted a verb by repeating it in the plain form before the *-ing* form, and capitalized his proper nouns. He understands how to use an apostrophe to show ownership, and he uses the exclamation mark appropriately. The reader gains a sense of the business of Times Square and all that it has to offer:

New York City
by Jake, grade two

I remember Times Square. I remember loud, colorful parades. I remember the smell of yummy hotdogs on the hotdog cart's grill. I remember big, bright video screens blinding my eyes. I remember wonderful street dancers and a special candy store: big, flavorful lollypops ready to lick and eating all the candy you can when your parants aren't looking! I remember desplase (displays) made of colerful jellybeans. I remember when I was walking out of Times Square. I saw peaple trying to scrub off gsrffiti (graffiti) and silver and black pigeons peck, peck, pecking scraps of food on the ground. But the best thing of all was the neon sinhgns (signs) and the blazing lights on the inly black sky!

In Shelly Keller's kindergarten class, Lynne and Shelly decided to write descriptions of familiar people. They felt it was a good time to do this since Mother's Day was looming in the near future and the students could write descriptions of their mom, grandmother, or godmother if they wanted to offer their writing pieces as a gift. Lynne wanted to provide a model that the students could all relate to so she read *Georgia's Bones*, a picture book by Jen Bryant. Lynne had photos of Georgia O'Keeffe's work from a display she had visited at the Art Institute in Chicago. The students watched Lynne compose her description:

Georgia O'Keeffe was an artist. She lived in New York City. She collected seashells and bones. When she was visiting New Mexico, she found the beautiful white bones

on the desert, picked them up, and took them home. She found and painted skulls of
cattle and horses. Later, she painted the sun-bleached skulls. She thought they were
as beautiful as anything she had ever known!

Lynne asked the students to help her revise the piece. She asked if someone could turn the lead sentence into a question. Hannah volunteered: *Did*
you know that Georgia O'Keeffe was an artist? Lynne asked the students to help
her find the word *she* and highlight it in yellow on the chart paper. Lynne
said that this word acted like a substitute teacher and stood in for the name
Georgia. She asked if they could change one or two of the pronouns *she* back
to the proper noun *Georgia*. In the final sentence, she asked for another word
to rename the pronoun *she* without using *Georgia*. Jadyn offered *painter*.
Kelly said we should use *artist*. Julianne offered *lady*. Here is the revised
piece:

<u>*Did you know Georgia O'Keeffe was an artist?*</u> *She lived in New York City. Georgia*
collected seashells and bones. When she was visiting New Mexico, <u>*Georgia*</u> *found*
the beautiful white bones on the desert, picked them up, and took them home. She
found and painted skulls of cattle and horses. Later, <u>*Georgia*</u> *painted the sun-bleached*
skulls. <u>*The artist*</u> *thought they were as beautiful as anything she had ever known!*

Lynne and Shelly placed the paragraphs side by side and asked the students to read them aloud several times with the help of the teachers. Since
language is an oral imprint first and foremost, Lynne and Shelly wanted the
students to understand the importance of training and listening to the sound
of language. Often, young writers can decide on what is best simply by the
way a sentence sounds when it is read aloud.

Teaching Point: From the youngest grades, get your students in the habit of
reading their work aloud. Take time to demonstrate how the sounds of language can help the writer make a good decision about word order or word
choice. When students read, "Charlotte wrote a word into her web to save
Wilbur in an instant" they might decide to rewrite it as, "In an instant, Charlotte
wrote a word into her web to save Wilbur." Moving a phrase sometimes helps
to make the meaning clearer. For example, "Jim and me went to the store"
can be read aloud without the other person named to decide what sounds
best—"Me went to the store" or "I went to the store."

Together with the students, Lynne and Shelly composed a descriptive
paragraph about Mrs. Keller. Before they began the shared writing experi-

ence, Lynne created an anchor chart with them to help the young writers think about renaming their nouns—especially the noun that named the topic or subject of the piece of writing—instead of using the same one over and over again. She asked for volunteers and called Anthony to stand beside the chart. Lynne wrote his name on the chart, asking students to tell her what kind of letter she needed to start his name. On the count of three, the class whispered, "Uppercase *A*." After she received an abundance of substitute nouns by sometimes asking for a synonym for a word on the chart (such as *pal* for *friend*), she asked Mrs. Keller to stand by the chart. The class repeated the process sometimes finding a useful noun from the list they had already created to rename Anthony. Lynne and Shelly were surprised by the great choices the kindergartners came up with after allowing them to talk with a partner. Suggesting that they think of synonyms for some of the words on the chart and giving them the time they needed to think and think some more definitely helped. (See the table that follows.)

Anthony	**Mrs. Keller**
he	she
boy	adult
friend	friend
pal	teacher
buddy	woman
student	writer
classmate	poet
child	reader
author	author
kid	lady
artist	poem-maker
illustrator	grownup
athlete	dog lover

When they were finished, Lynne reread the choices to rename their classroom teacher. They drafted the description of Shelly as a shared experience and revised to rename the subject of their paragraph, Mrs. Keller.

In our classroom Mrs. Keller teaches math and writing. She writes in her writer's notebook and shares it with the class. Our <u>teacher</u> (changed during revision from the noun "Mrs. Keller") reads books so we can make books. Our <u>guide</u> (changed during revision from the word "she") is very smart and makes us feel happy. This <u>dog lover's</u> (changed from Mrs. Keller's) eyes sparkle when she talks about her Ginger. Mrs. Keller is an <u>author</u> and reads us stories from her writer's notebook. Our <u>friend</u> (changed from the noun "teacher") is beautiful on the inside and outside, too!

The students tried out two more shared experiences as oral rehearsals with their principal, Mrs. Smith, and their music teacher, Mrs. Meinhart. Shelly and Lynne asked them to make a list of three or four people they could describe. They chose one person and drew a picture with labels. Then they were ready to do an oral rehearsal, talking about their person with a partner and using their labeled picture. Finally, they were ready to write the next day. Lynne and Shelly reminded them to begin each sentence with a capital letter and use end punctuation. They could describe what their person looked like, what their person liked to do, and how they felt about the person they chose. The students were asked to share their piece with at least three different classmates so they could hear how their piece sounded. Here are several samples. Although their ideas are not grouped in a meaningful order, the kindergartners were able to describe what their favorite people like to do, what they are good at, and sometimes, what they look like. For the most part, the students tried to keep spaces between their words, use periods or exclamation marks, and begin each new thought with an upper-case letter. Looking through the entire class set, these young writers must continue to work on when to use uppercase and lowercase letters. Particular offenders are the letters *b, K, M, S,* and *P.* Figures 6.7–6.9 show a few student drafts:

Figure 6.7
Allie, a kindergarten student, describes her mom:
"My mom dances with me when the music is on! She has light color skin. Mom is the best mom ever. She plays with me. My mom is a parent. She is a teacher and she teaches babies."

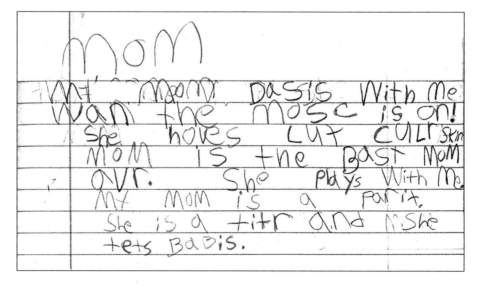

Figure 6.8
Hannah, a kindergartner, describes her mom:
"Mom's favorite place is the mall. My mom loves me. She makes good pancakes. She is fancy. She is very loving. She is going out all the time. My mom plants flowers. My mom is pretty. She knows I am hers. She plays with me. Mother makes dinner. Mom keeps the home clean."

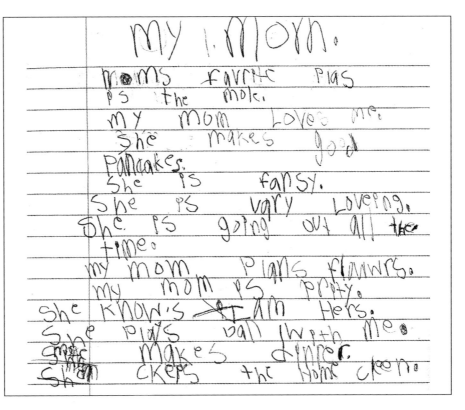

Figure 6.9
Mikel describes her father for a Father's Day gift:
"Daddy works on the computer every day. Daddy cooks and he plays with me. Daddy cuts the grass and he loves me very much. He does math with me. Daddy takes me to restaurants and he lies [down for a nap] with me. Daddy takes me to my soccer games. Thank you, Daddy!"

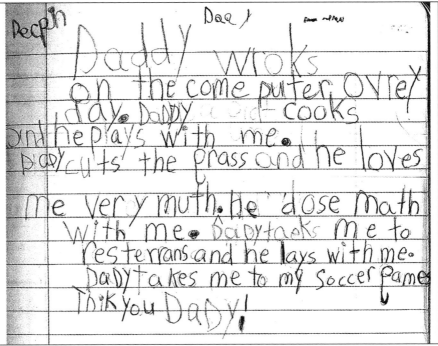

Starting in kindergarten, teachers of writers try to convey a sense of sentence. For young children, the best way to describe a sentence is to tell them it is a group of words that can stand alone and still make sense. It starts with a capital letter and usually ends with a period unless you are asking a question or saying something with lots of feeling. In Shelly's kindergarten class, the children read and reread the shared writing experiences to listen for a drop in tone and a clear stop. Then they all raised an index finger and punctuated the air with a period for emphasis. Students also read questions to hear how their voice went up at the end of this kind of sentence and practiced reading some sentences that ended with an exclamation mark to hear the difference in tone.

Writing good description is hard work! Younger writers need myriad experiences, writing down telling details and trying to stay on topic with a clear focus. By the time students reach third grade, they can begin to think about their organization as they draft or during the revision process. They will learn to choose a pattern that seems to best suit their topic. A topic sentence and four or five supporting details can evoke the senses, the emotions, and clearly help the reader visualize a place, a person, an event, or an object. For example, here is a descriptive paragraph about the Statue of Liberty. After Billy returned from a weekend visit to New York City, he spilled this paragraph into his writer's notebook. The mentor text he used to help him think about how to focus his description was Ben Hillman's *How Big Is It? A Book About Bigness*. For this third grader, it was all about size. The reader can understand something about the enormity of this national treasure from Billy's description:

The Statue of Liberty looks tiny when you see it from the ferry, but when you see her up close, she is colossal! The statue is about 305 feet. Her face is more than 8 feet tall. That's taller than the players in the NBA! There are over 100 steps from the pedestal to the head. Seven rays on her crown point to the seven continents. Each ray is about 150 pounds and is about 9 feet long. This 225 ton statue stands on Liberty Island in the New York Harbor.

Of course, well-chosen adjectives deliver clear, accurate pictures and help to create a certain mood. Students should begin to notice good descriptions in nonfiction text and not reserve descriptions only for writing narrative pieces, memoir, and poems. For younger students, learning to use strong adjectives, proper nouns and specific nouns, and prepositional phrases can help them begin to write good descriptions. Other effective grammar lessons for descriptive writing might involve replacing a recurring noun with effective substitutes. For example, if a student is writing about a tiger, he might rename the tiger with synonyms, including *cat, hunter, animal, creature*, and *predator*. Another lesson might be comparative and superlative forms of adjectives. For older students, lessons could include the comparative and superlative forms of adverbs.

Grammar Reference: Students often confuse the words *quiet* and *quite*, usually a spelling mistake. It might help if they knew how to use *quite* so they really understand the difference in meaning between these two words. Students know that *quiet* is the antonym for *noisy*. They probably need help with *quite*. This word usually means "very," as in the sentence, "I am quite pleased with my art project." It also can mean "completely," as in these sentences: "I am quite through with your tantrums!" Mom said firmly. Or "I am quite sure you need to make a right turn at the next intersection."

Chapter 7

Description and Compare/Contrast

Writers of nonfiction use description in many ways, from lead paragraphs through satisfying conclusions. Though the Common Core State Standards (CCSS) mention descriptive details only in regard to narrative writing, we believe that providing the "details" and "precise language" that CCSS calls for in informational and opinion writing is often accomplished by providing vivid description. In upper elementary grades, Diane worked with fourth graders in the Bristol Township School District in suburban Philadelphia to develop their descriptive writing skills in preparation for writing compare/contrast pieces.

Description

Diane began by reading examples of description from several mentor texts: the opening paragraphs of *Thunder Cake* by Patricia Polacco; the opening pages of *Barn Savers* by Linda Oatman High; several pages that describe the coming of winter from *In November* by Cynthia Rylant paired with a similar description from *The Snow Speaks* by Nancy White Carlstrom, and the opening of *Owl Moon* by Jane Yolen. Additionally, Diane used two Seymour Simon nonfiction books, *Volcanoes* and *Spiders*. Students underlined appeals to the senses, which were listed on an anchor chart in sentences or parts of sentences that were pulled from these mentor texts when the children noticed them.

Appeals to the sense of sight

The moon was so bright the sky seemed to shine. (*Owl Moon*)
Storm clouds drift low over the fields. (*Thunder Cake*)
Birds fly close to the ground. (*Thunder Cake*)
The moon is a sliver of ice melting in the sky . . . (*Barn Savers*)
The bed is white . . . (*In November*)
 . . . the trees are standing all sticks and bones. Without their leaves, how
    lovely they are, spreading their arms like dancers. (*In November*)
The darkness fades to dawn . . . (*Barn Savers*)
A male wolf spider waves his pedipalps like signal flags when he spots
    a female. (*Spiders*)
 . . . striking sparks as he made swords and armor . . . (*Volcanoes*)

Appeals to the sense of touch

 . . . the stars are brittle. (*In November*)
 . . . with a kiss on their heads. (*In November*)
 . . . the air gets damp and heavy. (*Thunder Cake*)
When words freeze in the thin, brittle air . . . (*The Snow Speaks*)
It is light as feathers. (*The Snow Speaks*)
 . . . slick from the melting moon (*Barn Savers*)
Due to their small poison glands, their bite (tarantulas) is about as
    painful as a hornet or bee sting. (*Spiders*)
Vulcan worked at a hot forge. (*Volcanoes*)

Appeals to the sense of hearing

 . . . the earth is growing quiet. (*In November*)
The bed is . . . silent. (*In November*)

. . . a train whistle blew, long and low, like a sad, sad song. (*Owl Moon*)

A farm dog answered the train . . . (*Owl Moon*)

They sang out (*Owl Moon*)

. . . when their voices faded away it was quiet as a dream. (*Owl Moon*)

. . . a roaring, low, rumbling sound of thunder makes the windows shudder in their panes. (*Thunder Cake*)

. . . the mountain seemed quiet and peaceful. (*Volcanoes*)

As students began to draft their descriptions, they added appeals to the senses in their writer's notebooks.

Teaching Point: Diane purposely did not select passages with examples for sense of taste and smell for this lesson. When young writers try to appeal to ALL the senses, their writing becomes contrived. We recommend that teachers limit examples to three senses at a time.

Using the same mentor samples, students listed exact adjectives, nouns, and verbs that communicated specific descriptions. This activity provided the perfect opportunity to teach/revisit these parts of speech. The students noticed the following descriptive words and phrases from *In November*: "quiet"; "white and silent"; "hide beneath its blankets"; "standing all sticks and bones"; "lovely, spreading, arms like dancers"; "time to be still"; "brittle"; "tucked." Diane asked students to think about the jobs of these words. Which words are naming words (nouns)? The students came up with *sticks, bones, arms*, and *dancers*. Which words are describing words (adjectives)? The students came up with *quiet, white, silent*, and *brittle*. Which words are action words? The students said *hide, standing, spreading*, and *tucked*. These examples were listed on anchor charts for nouns, adjectives, and verbs. Then students returned to the mentor sentences from *Owl Moon, Thunder Cake, The Snow Speaks*, and *Barn Savers* to identify exact nouns, adjectives, and verbs. Diane reminded her writers to use exact nouns, adjectives, and verbs in their own descriptions.

The following day the fourth graders brainstormed lists of their favorite places. They shared their lists (to give students the opportunity to borrow from their classmates), chose a place, and then talked with a partner about how they intended to describe the place. Then they began to draft. As Diane circulated around the room to peek over the writers' shoulders, she noticed that many students were writing narratives, not descriptions. In order to refocus the students on description, Diane wrote about her backyard.

I woke up and ate breakfast. It was a sunny morning. I looked out the window at my backyard. Our backyard is covered by a blanket of green grass and wild moss. Violets peek up through the greenery in the spring. Oak trees and tulip poplars, tall and stately, shade our patio. Families of squirrels make their nests in the tallest branches. Wrens, robins, and sparrows live in the lower branches and serenade us during the day. I have three children and seven grandchildren and they love the back-yard. One time we had a barbecue and one of the neighborhood dogs tried to steal a hot dog from the grill. Everybody laughed. The dog ran right to the shed to bury his food. The shed, painted red with white shutters, sits on the right side of the yard behind the patio. In the summer I plant pink and white impatiens in the shed's window boxes. Everybody likes impatiens. This year a disease is attacking impatiens so we won't plant them. On a shepherd's hook next to the patio hangs a hummingbird feeder, filled with sweet-smelling liquid. The tiny red-throated hummingbirds come to sip this nectar throughout the day. As I sit at the picnic table, I gaze around me and think about how much I love my backyard.

She provided each student with a copy and asked the class to look at what she wrote and to help her by removing any detail that was not descrip-tion. They worked in partners to cross out sentences that did not describe the backyard. They agreed to eliminate the first three sentences, the four sen-tences beginning with *I have three children*, and the two sentences beginning with *Everybody likes impatiens*. These details might be interesting in a narrative (story) about my backyard, but they don't add anything to a description.

Diane asked students to go back to their drafts and cross out any details that were not descriptive. Diane's purpose for doing this was to emphasize how important it is for students to take a second look at their writing. Before we can instruct students on the finer points of grammar, students need to be amenable to looking at their work with a fresh point of view. Brandon dis-covered that most of what he wrote told the story about his trip to a Phillies game.

In a conference with Brandon, Diane pointed out that his original entry had many references to food. Brandon agreed that he enjoyed eating at the Phillies game. His description then refocused on his visits to the food stands at the stadium. Once Brandon had focused his description, Diane pointed out that his draft used both present and past tense. Brandon decided to write his description using the present tense. The first paragraph of his description follows:

The Phillies games are awesomely awesome to go to. Half the game I am at the food stands. The worst part is when I have to wait in the lines that wrap around Citizens Bank Park. The buttery popcorn smell makes my mouth water. I can hear the crowd yelling. The line is not moving. I'm starving and I'm missing the most exciting part of the game. I finally get my french fries and I rush back to my seat in the hot sun to watch the game with my Mom. I love the ball park!

Ariana looked at her description of her Mom-Mom and Pop-Pop's house and eliminated sentences that did not describe.

The first thing a visitor notices when driving up to my Mom—Mom and Pop—Pop's house is a huge blue house and a huge front and back yard with a pond full of fish and frogs in the pond. There are lots of trees. Inside are stairs that lead to the second floor. On the first floor are two living rooms and a dining room and a kitchen. Both owners have dogs. One dog's name is Ryan and the other dog's name is Rocky. Ryan's owner is Mom—Mom and Rocky's owner is Pop—Pop.

Diane agreed with Ariana that the information about the dogs was not necessary to describe her Mom-Mom and Pop-Pop's house. In conference, Diane asked Ariana to think about why this place is her favorite place to be. Ariana revised her description, eliminating the information about the dogs and organizing the description to include the ways this place is special to her. Here is her first paragraph:

The first thing a visitor notices when driving up to my Mom—Mom and Pop—Pop's house is its color. It is a cheerful bright blue. The front yard welcomes you with shaded trees. The back yard stretches a long way and has a pond filled with fish and some frogs. I spend lots of afternoons at the pond.

As students worked on their drafts and revisions, Diane presented revision mini-lessons. One of these lessons involved varying sentence structure by focusing on sentence patterns. Diane introduced two sentence patterns: N-V (noun-verb) and N-V-N (noun-verb-noun). Using student work as mentor text, Diane showed students two of Dominic's sentences with the N-V sentence pattern (The sun shines. Plants grow.) and Bryce's two sentences using the N-V-N pattern: (Grundy arena is an exciting place for me. We grab a black hockey puck.) Students offered their own examples from their drafts, which Diane wrote on the board. Together the class revised their sentences for variety.

There were disco lights there that were as colorful as a rainbow. (original)

Colorful as a rainbow the disco lights shined. (class revision)

I sat in the back of the car with my brother Colton and my sister Cassidy. (Connor's original)

Sitting in the back with my brother Colton and my sassy sister Cassidy felt really cramped. (Connor's revision)

Grammar Reference: Every sentence has two basic parts—subject and predicate. Within the subject is a simple subject, a noun or a pronoun, and within the predicate is a simple predicate, a verb. Some sentences consist of subject and verb only, as in "Athletes practice." Modifiers added to the subject and verb do not change the sentence pattern. "Olympic athletes practice for many hours each day." The second sentence has the same sentence pattern as the first despite the addition of the modifiers. Other sentence patterns are created by the addition of complements (DO, direct objects; IO, indirect objects; PN, predicate nominatives; and PA, predicate adjectives). Examples: Olympic athletes encourage their teammates. (The sentence pattern is S-V-DO.) Olympic athletes give their teammates encouragement. (The sentence pattern is S-V-IO-DO.) Olympic athletes are world-class performers. (The sentence pattern is S-V-PN.) Olympic athletes are determined. (The sentence pattern is S-V-PA.)

Diane also talked with students about using prepositional phrases as a way to change the pattern of their sentences. Here is one of their revisions made during the shared writing portion of the lesson:

I went to the food court for a hot dog. (original)

At the food court I selected a hot dog. (class revision)

When students returned to their drafts, they made the following changes: Ashley changed "The boardwalks are over the sand and over the water" to "Over the sand and the water the boardwalk sits." Bobby changed "After you walk out of the living room in the back is Tyler's room it's small and messy" to "In the back of the house behind the living room is Tyler's room. It's small and messy." Notice that Bobby also fixed the run-on sentence. Pointing out the S-V pattern to Bobby helped him to recognize the fact that he had combined two complete thoughts without using any mark of punctuation.

Grammar Reference: A word about unnecessary prepositions is in order. In conversation, we often hear speakers say things like, "I saw him throw the trash <u>out of</u> the car window," or "I met <u>up with</u> him at the restaurant." Perhaps the most common misuse is the phrase "off of" as in "She fell <u>off of</u> her bike." These constructions are incorrect and should not be used in writing. The sentences should read: "I saw him throw the trash out the window," "I met him at the restaurant," and "She fell off her bike." Point out to students that prepositions are single words that introduce the prepositional phrase. Sometimes speakers add a preposition where none is needed at the end of a sentence. For example, "Where is your school <u>at</u>?" or "Where did he go <u>to</u>?" The proper expressions are "Where is your school [located]?" and "Where did he go?" Encourage students to be grammatically correct in speaking as well as writing.

Another opportunity for grammar embedding occurred with Tyler's piece, reproduced here.

Messy, messy, messy! A mess everywhere! Toys in every corner! You can't see the floor. Shelves and shelves! Toys and toys! In one corner shelves with bins stuffed with toy cars and super heroes and kid movies. Next to the shelves an open space with toy swords in arm's reach. A bin of all sorts and sizes. A TV, a small one that you can see anywhere in the room, sits in a corner. There are four chairs. Two have Tyler and Jack printed on the front. A hall leads you to my bedroom. Whoever sees this place the first thing they think of is a pig pen. The rarest thing to see is a clean room. The messy very messy place is my playroom.

Does Tyler have a sense of sentence? He uses fragments effectively, but does he understand the sentence unit? In Diane's conference with him, Tyler read the piece aloud, adding verbs in his reading that were not present on the page. Diane asked Tyler to insert the verbs he read aloud into his written piece. Tyler did not notice the fragment "A bin of all sorts and sizes." By asking Tyler about the bin, Diane discovered that the bin contained more "toys of all shapes and sizes." Tyler then revised the sentence to say, "Under the toy swords an open bin is filled with more toys of all shapes and sizes." Here is Tyler's description of the messy playroom with the added verbs.

Messy, messy, messy! A mess everywhere! Toys in every corner! You can't see the floor. Shelves and shelves! Toys and toys! In one corner are shelves with bins stuffed with toy cars and super heroes and kid movies. Next to the shelves is an open space with toy swords in arm's reach. Under the toy swords an open bin is filled with more toys of all shapes and sizes. A TV, a small one that you can see anywhere in the room, sits in a corner. There are four chairs. Two have

Tyler and Jack printed on the front. A hall leads you to my bedroom. Whoever sees this place the first thing they think of is a pig pen. The rarest thing to see is a clean room. The messy very messy place is my playroom.

In sharing Tyler's piece with the class, Diane spoke about effective use of fragments to create a rhythm or mood, convey sensations, emphasize an idea, or draw the reader's attention to a particular place in a paragraph.

 Teaching Point: Be judicious about introducing the idea of sentence fragments to your students. Even though people speak in fragments frequently, and we become accustomed to hearing them, fragments in writing often don't work because they confuse the reader. Students must first have a sense of sentence, which includes the subject (what the sentence is about) and the verb (what is happening or has happened). Students must first know the rules before they can break them. When fragments are not used purposefully or are overdone to the point of boring the reader, they are ineffective and should be eliminated. If a fragment makes sense in its position in the text and serves a useful purpose, then student writers should use the fragment. When fragments occur naturally in the flow of writing, they may add to the writer's voice and overall style.

 Grammar Reference: We know that a sentence expresses a complete thought and contains a subject and a predicate. Sometimes students mistake a predicate for any verb in a sentence. For example, "After we ran" is not a sentence because even though it contains a subject (*we*) and a predicate verb (*ran*), it is not a complete thought. Teach students how to recognize independent and dependent clauses to help them understand this concept. (See Your Turn Lessons "Expanding a Sentence Using Compound Elements" following Part 2 and "Expanding a Sentence Using Complex Elements" following Part 3).

In the following excerpt from *A Wrinkle in Time* by Madeleine L'Engle, notice that only the first and last sentences are complete sentences; the rest are sentence fragments.

IT was a brain. A disembodied brain. An oversized brain, just enough larger than normal to be completely revolting and terrifying. A living brain. A brain that pulsed and quivered, that seized and commanded. No wonder the brain was called IT.

An example like this is appropriate for "tweeners" and "teeners" to demonstrate how effective well-placed sentence fragments can be in a piece of writing. Surely, L'Engle knows the difference between a complete thought and a fragment. However, she purposely chose to break the rules here. Each fragment adds a striking detail that is emphasized by standing alone instead of stringing the details together in one long sentence. The fragments, of varying lengths, force the reader to slow down and notice each one individually. Powerful! Further grammar lessons for Tyler and for the class could focus on verb choice, eliminating the *to be* verbs for more descriptive and expressive ones.

Compare/Contrast

After students in the fourth grade had written their descriptions, Diane worked with them to use their descriptions to write compare/contrast pieces. First, she read *Elinor and Violet: The Story of Two Naughty Chickens* by Patti Murphy. The children enjoyed the story of Elinor, who is just a little bit naughty, and her friend Violet, who delights in being very naughty. Using a Venn diagram, Diane led the students to list the ways that Elinor and Violet were alike and the ways that they were different. Diane then wrote in front of the class a short compare/contrast piece describing Elinor and Violet.

Have you ever wondered if chickens make friends? Patti Murphy's picture book supposes that chickens do have friends. Elinor and Violet are two naughty chickens who become friends one summer when Violet is visiting her grandmother. The story of their friendship and how it changes each of them is called Elinor and Violet: The Story of Two Naughty Chickens.

Both Elinor and Violet are naughty. Elinor's sisters are annoyed by Elinor's behavior. Elinor says bad words, writes on the walls, and talks back to her mother. Violet is naughty too. She also says bad words, writes on the walls, and talks back to everyone.

Elinor, however, is only a little bit naughty. When she says bad words, she says them softly under her breath. When she writes on the walls, she does it in tiny letters where no one can see it. When she talks back to her mother, she never does it out loud. Elinor tries to be good some of the time, but she enjoys being a little naughty.

Violet, on the other hand, is very naughty. When she says bad words, she sings them very loudly while walking down the street. When she writes on walls, she uses indelible markers. She even talks back to the librarian! Violet likes being naughty all the time, and she wants her friend to be as naughty as she is.

When Elinor and Violet cause trouble with Elinor's Aunt Lucy, they each learn a lesson about friendship. Even though they are naughty chickens, both Elinor and Violet learn that being good can be fun too.

Diane demonstrated how she used the information on the Venn diagram to plan her compare/contrast piece. The three body paragraphs are organized to show the similarities first (how are Elinor and Violet the same), then the differences (one paragraph describing Elinor and one paragraph describing Violet). The piece also has an introduction and a conclusion.

Diane and the class composed a shared compare/contrast piece describing Diane (Mrs. Dougherty) and their teacher Mrs. Hawes. First, they listed the similarities and differences in a Venn diagram. Then, they wrote the piece together.

Some fourth-graders don't like to write. Some fourth-graders don't write every day. We do. We are lucky to have two writing teachers in our classroom. One of our teachers is Mrs. Hawes, and the other is Mrs. Dougherty.

Both teachers tell us stories and read to us. The stories help us to get ideas for our writing. Both teachers help us to think about what we want to say and encourage us to do our best. Both teachers prepare writing lessons so that we will get to be better writers. We get to share our writing with the teachers and with our classmates every day.

Mrs. Dougherty visits our classroom in the mornings, and she teaches only writing lessons. She shares her writing with us, and sometimes she asks us to help her revise her writing. She works with other students in other schools too. She even works with college students. Mrs. Dougherty may be in two or three schools in one day.

Mrs. Hawes, on the other hand, stays in our classroom all day. She teaches both reading and writing, and she teaches math too. Mrs. Hawes works only in Washington School. She sets the class rules and expects us to be good students. She gives us report card grades and has conferences with our parents.

We have two teachers who like to teach writing, Mrs. Hawes and Mrs. Dougherty. We are lucky and we like to write!

Again, the class noticed how the piece is structured: an introduction, a paragraph that explains how the two teachers are the same, a paragraph describing Mrs. Dougherty, a paragraph describing Mrs. Hawes, and a conclusion. Though there are other structures that may be used for comparison/contrast, this particular organization is easy for fourth-grade students to follow. Next, Diane asked the class to look at their descriptions to see if they could use them in a compare/contrast piece. Ashley decided that her description of the beach could be used to compare a day visiting the seashore to a day visiting the lake. Jordan used her description of a busy New York City street to compare with a visit to Peddler's Village. Tyler compared his messy playroom to the living room of his house. Matt compared his friends Tyler and Bobby. Students who couldn't use their descriptions brainstormed for other compare/contrast topics.

As they wrote, Diane conferred with the writers and made notes on the grammar instruction that would follow. She noticed that a number of students were writing run-on and run-together sentences. For example, Laura's draft contained this structure:

Cherrystone campground and the beach at Wildwood are alike because they both have smelly salt water, also they both have burning sand that you run on to get to the water. Your surrounded by smelly water, your in your swimming clothes.

Teaching Point: "Your" in the previous sentence needs to be the contraction "You're." Since the lesson of the day is sentence structure, Diane made the "your" to "you're" correction, saving the lesson on the use of apostrophes in contractions for another time. It is important not to overload the instruction and to focus on one thing at a time. Teaching grammatical concepts means more than merely mentioning them, however. It's not enough to tell students that sentences have a subject and a verb and make sense in themselves and then move on. Direct instruction and student practice are necessary even if the instruction takes time away from writing workshop. If students are not writing clearly, there is no point in their continuing to write for the sake of writing. As writing teachers our responsibilities include direct instruction of grammatical concepts.

Grammar Reference: A run-on sentence is a construction that occurs when two complete thoughts are connected without the use of a coordinating conjunction. Often, students make this mistake when they use adverbs like "however" or "therefore" in the place of a coordinating conjunction or without benefit of a semicolon. For example: "We wanted to go to Disneyland however it was closed for repairs that day." Young writers write more run-together sentences where the construction may be correct but where too many independent clauses are strung together. The result is to leave the reader breathless. These run-together sentences often need commas and periods or other marks of punctuation to separate the thoughts. For example: "Jimmy and I arrived at the stable to muck stalls and stack hay so we could earn our riding lesson but the sky turned gray and then it started to pour so we went home without ever getting our lesson that day."

Jacob wrote the following in his draft:

Imagine if there were no more arcades, what would you do to keep occupied and what would entertain you?

Later in the same piece he wrote:

On the other hand, Dave 'n Buster's is more than an arcade, for instance, it is kind of like a mall.

Ashley wrote:

When I hear the seagulls they will not be quiet so I throw a piece of food and they come running after me so I scream so loud the seagulls fly away.

Similar run together sentences in other student drafts pointed Diane to a grammar lesson on complete sentences.

Diane began the next session by showing (with her permission) Laura's description. Together with the class each word group was deconstructed for each "complete thought." For example, Diane revised first for structure.

> *[Cherrystone and the beach are alike because they both have smelly salt water, also they both have burning sand that you run on to get to the water. You're surrounded by smelly water, you're in your swimming clothes]* as follows: *Cherrystone and the beach at Wildwood are alike in some ways.* (Complete thought: predicate verb = are; compound subject = Cherrystone and the beach)
> *Both places smell like the sea and salt water.* (Complete thought: predicate verb = smell; subject = places)
> *Both have sandy beaches.* (Complete thought: predicate verb = have; subject = both)
> *The sand burns your feet as you run to the water.* (Complete thought: predicate verb = burns; subject = sand)

Diane noted that this sentence contains a dependent clause (*as you run to the water*). Though this clause contains a subject and a verb (*you run*), it cannot stand alone and is not a complete thought.

> *At both places you wear a bathing suit.* (Complete thought: predicate verb = wear; subject = you)

At both places you are surrounded by smelly water. (Complete thought: predicate verb = are surrounded; subject = you)

This lesson provided the springboard for revision for content (smelly water, for example) and also revision to avoid the same sentence patterns for a variety of sentence types and lengths. Diane revised the sentences as follows, explaining her revisions as she shared them. She began by organizing the details: sand, water, smells and taste, and attire.

Visitors to both Cherrystone Bay Campground and Wildwood Beach will notice some similarities. Both smell like the sea. Also, both bay water and ocean water taste salty. Dressed in bathing suits, vacationers in both places run across the hot burning sand to the cool water at the shore.

Diane reminded the students of the lesson on prepositions and prepositional phrases and asked them to notice how she used prepositional phrases to add details to the last sentence. She also read each sentence aloud to be sure each one was a complete thought. Finally, the students counted the words in each sentence, noting the variety in length as well as structure. Then, students worked with a partner to revise Jacob's and Ashley's sentences. Finally, the class returned to their drafts looking specifically for run-on or run-together sentences for correction and revision. As they worked, Diane conferred with students to guide them in these revisions.

Reilly revised *What if there was a world without friends who would have your back?* to *Imagine a world without friends. Imagine having no one to be on your side.*

Patrick revised *Both Grundy Arena and Flyers Stadium are hockey rinks both places have scheduled games* to *Both Grundy Arena and Flyers are hockey rinks where you can go to see hockey played.*

Jada revised *A sky blue waterfall was falling on me I was scared to go under* to *A sky blue waterfall tumbled down into the pool. At first, I was scared to go under it.*

Gia revised *The salty waves are refreshing we feel relieved after a hard winter* to *At the beach we feel relieved after a hard winter by the salty, refreshing waves that splash us.*

Students shared their revisions on the document imager explaining why they made the changes they did. Diane reviewed the definition of *sentence* and asked students to check their drafts to be sure they had fixed any run-on sentences.

Teaching Point: Beginning the unit of study for compare/contrast writing with description was a conscious effort to demystify the process. Writing description is comfortable for most young writers. They read lots of description in their independent reading, and they have likely practiced writing description too. Once writers have descriptions ready to go, it is not much of a leap for them to compare/contrast this description with something similar. Using drafts for multiple purposes is an efficient use of writing workshop time.

Another opportunity for grammar and style instruction presented itself in this unit of study. In discussing nouns and verbs and the complete sentence unit, Diane pointed out the inclusion of modifiers (specifically, adjectives) in sentences that the students had written. She began with Ariana's opening paragraph:

The first thing a visitor notices when driving up to my Mom–Mom and Pop–Pop's house is its color. It is a cheerful bright blue. The front yard welcomes you with shaded trees. The back yard stretches a long way and has a pond filled with fish and some frogs. I spend lots of afternoons at the pond.

Diane asked students to look for the naming words (nouns) and for words that describe the nouns (adjectives). Adjectives tell which ones, what kind, or how many. They found "shaded" and "long" but did not point out "cheerful bright blue." Because they had learned that adjectives describe naming words (nouns or pronouns) and "cheerful bright blue" comes at the end of the sentence and doesn't appear right next to "house," students initially overlooked these describing words. Diane asked the class to tell her what "cheerful bright blue" is describing. They immediately could see that these words tell something about the house. Diane noted that the sentence "It is a cheerful, bright blue," is a complete thought that refers to the sentence before it: "The first thing a visitor notices when driving up to my Mom-Mom and Pop-Pop's house is its color." Adjectives, especially specific adjectives, give our descriptions life. They help readers to see, hear, taste, touch, and smell what the writer is describing.

An element of style is sentence variety. Adjectives used as interrupters can provide sentence variety and interest to a piece of description. In Ariana's short paragraph the class, with Diane's help, revised her description to add more specific description. (See the Your Turn Lesson "Adjective Interrupters" following Part 1.)

It is a cheerful bright blue. Diane asked students to think of the color blue and to brainstorm shades of blue: sky blue, cobalt blue, royal blue, baby blue, powder blue, robin's egg blue, dark blue, sapphire blue, and slate were some of the suggestions. Ariana chose robin's egg blue. Then, Diane showed how to combine Ariana's first three sentences by using the adjectives as interrupters instead of as predicate adjectives. She wrote: *The first thing a visitor notices is my Mom-Mom and Pop-Pop's welcoming house, bright and robin's egg blue, shaded among the trees.*

Diane asked students to go back to their drafts to see if there was any place where they could change general adjectives to specific ones and to try using adjectives as interrupters in their sentences. Students shared changes at the end of writing workshop that day.

Teaching Point: During writing workshop conferring time, keep a look out for possible grammar and style lessons that will help students to explore the possibilities in their drafts. Always provide time for sharing student results.

Chapter 8

Procedural Writing

In Shelly Keller's kindergarten class, Lynne and Shelly introduced procedural writing to the kindergartners with several passages from nonfiction books with beautiful photographs. They wanted these young writers to see how authors use paragraphs of explanation to describe a process—how to do something. From Seymour Simon's *Gorillas* they shared this paragraph on a document imager:

> Gorillas are awkward climbers. They use both their hands and feet when they go up a tree. They rarely jump from branch to branch the way monkeys do. Gorillas come down from a tree slowly in reverse, hind feet first, carefully checking branches all the way to the ground.

Shelly asked the students to turn and talk about the tree-climbing process for these giant apes. She encouraged them to collaborate with a partner to draw the pictures they imagined in their mind from the words. (Lynne had planned to take the class to the playground and actually ask a few students to demonstrate the words in the text as she read them aloud by climbing up the ladder to the slide and then slowly climbing down the ladder backward, pausing the way the gorillas do, but there was no time.) Lynne and Shelly then charted the paragraph and numbered the process. They asked the kindergartners for their help to break down this process:

LEAD SENTENCE: "Gorillas are awkward climbers."
PROCESS:
1. They use both their hands and feet to climb up the tree.
2. They come down in reverse and take their time.
3. They check the branches all the way down.
4. Gorillas almost never jump from tree to tree. They weigh too much and could break a branch and fall.

They tried it out again with another passage, this time using *Crocodiles and Alligators* by Seymour Simon. Although the vocabulary in Simon's books is quite challenging for these young readers, the structure and organization of the sentences is not above these young writers. With help from the teacher, these texts model effective writing and are of high interest to five- and six-year-olds.

Alligators build their nests out of leaves, branches, and mud above the ground. The mother shapes them into a mound about 6 feet wide and 3 feet high. She scoops out a hole in the center and lays as many as seventy eggs in the hole, then covers them up. As the leaves and branches decay, they give off heat and help keep the eggs warm.

Again, the students broke down the process:

LEAD SENTENCE: Alligators build their nests above the ground.
PROCESS:
1. They collect leaves, branches, and mud.
2. The mother shapes them into a little hill.
3. She scoops out a hole in the center.

4.   She lays her eggs in the hole.
5.   She covers up the hole with leaves and branches.

Lynne took their information and added a few transition words and phrases. Then she asked the students if they liked the revisions and if it helped the reader in any way:

An alligator mother builds her nest above the ground. First, she collects leaves, branches, and mud. Next, she shapes them into a small hill. Then, the alligator scoops out a hole in the center of the mound. After that, she lays her eggs in the hole. Finally, she covers up her nest with leaves and branches to keep her eggs warm. Alligator mothers know how to build the perfect nest for their eggs.

The students found the transition words and talked about the way they helped the reader follow the order—what happened first, what happened second, what happened third, and so on. Lynne and Shelly pointed to the comma that followed the transition words and asked the students if they knew what job the comma did. Mikel said that a comma asks you to wait for a second or two before you keep going. Yusef added that the period made you stop, but the comma was not a full stop. Hannah said a comma was like the yellow light and the period was the red light for cars. Lynne and Shelly made a list of time order words on the board, including *first, first of all, next, then, finally, last of all, before*, and *after*. They told the writers that they could use this list when they wrote their own procedural piece.

Lynne modeled with a piece titled "How to Make Friends." She talked aloud as she wrote on the chart paper:

It is easy to make new friends. First of all, go up to some kids and say hello. Next, tell them your name and ask them for their names. Ask more questions like, "What do you like about this school?" Share your cookies or pretzels with your new friends. Then, try to find something everybody likes to do at recess. Finally, don't forget to smile! That's how to make new friends.

The students noticed the transition words, commas, and topic sentence. Lynne asked if there were other ways to make new friends. The students talked about their ideas. Each time Lynne asked them if they had to do something first. For example, it makes more sense to introduce yourself and tell someone what your name is before you do something else. Dilan suggested that you should shake hands with your new friend while you are telling him your name. The kids noticed that each new sentence began with a capital letter and ended with a period or exclamation mark. The students talked about when to use an exclamation point and noticed that only one was used in this writing. Lynne also showed them how to turn the lead sentence into a question: "Do you know how to make new friends?"

The next day Shelly conducted a shared writing experience using the topic, "How to Make a Book" since all the kindergartners could participate here. She asked the students for transition words as they went along, using the anchor chart as a guide. Their finished piece, recorded on chart paper while the students sat on the carpet in front of the chart, was a good bit of writing for this age level:

How to Make a Book

First, think about what kind of book you want to make. You can draw pictures or you can write words. It's your choice. Next, go back and check to see if you have enough details. Then, look at your writing to make sure every sentence begins with an uppercase letter and ends with a period, question mark, or exclamation point. Add a cover with a title, picture, and author's name. Finally, share your book with a friend. That's how to make a book!

The students checked the shared writing to make sure they had used capital letters to begin each sentence and end punctuation. As students volunteered their ideas, Shelly asked them for a mark of punctuation. She wrote their ideas down and nudged them to use a transition word from the anchor chart if they did not use one. She made sure they understood that not every sentence needed to start with a transition word and asked them to find three sentences where they decided not to begin with one. The students talked about the apostrophe use in *it's* and *that's* so she could check for understanding. "What two words make up this word *it's*? Lynne and Shelly would return to the idea of contractions the next day and in one-on-one conferences.

Then the students volunteered their ideas for a how-to piece of writing, and Shelly charted their ideas so they could make a good choice:

How to

give a dog a bath	plant a flower
play baseball (hit a ball)	float in the pool
ride a horse	eat watermelon
ride a scooter	do a forward roll
make a snowman	make a bed
jump rope	make a sundae
do a cartwheel	decorate a birthday cake
make books	draw a robot

play Simon Says

teach a dog to sit

lose a tooth

tie a shoe

play leapfrog

put on a sweater

blow up a balloon

get a touchdown

The next day Lynne and Shelly gathered the students on the rug. They shared a small paragraph from *Spiders* by Seymour Simon:

> One type of spider that lives in Europe and Asia spends much of its life underwater inside an air bubble called a diving bell. To make a diving bell, the spider spins a web attached to an underwater plant. Then it swims to the surface, traps a bubble of air, and carries the bubble down to its web.

Again, the students identified the lead sentence that introduces the big idea and listed the steps in order. The students noticed one transition word. Lynne said that more transition words could be used if the three steps were not listed together in one sentence. She challenged the students to help her write this paragraph a different way using a transition word to begin each new thought. Jaylen offered, "First, the spider spins a web." Riya continued, "Next, it attaches the web to a plant in the water." Kelly thought they should keep "Then it swims to the surface." Felicity added, "After that, it traps a bubble of air." Mikel finished the thinking with, "Last of all, the spider takes the air bubble down to the web." Lynne displayed this paragraph on the board and placed Seymour Simon's paragraph next to it on chart paper. Lynne said that both paragraphs worked well. She asked the students to talk with a partner about the most important thing to remember about this kind of writing—writing about a process or trying to offer an explanation. Some of the students talked about beginning sentences with capital letters. Lynne said that was a great idea, but that was true of all kinds of writing. After students shared several other worthwhile responses, Lucy said that you had to write things down in the right order or it wouldn't make any sense. Lynne asked the students what they thought of Lucy's idea, and the students gave the thumbs up signal. Lynne said she agreed. The spider couldn't carry down the water bubble to live in if she hadn't already spun her web and attached it to an underwater plant.

Teaching Point: *Its* and *it's* are confusing word forms for students at many levels. The pronoun *its* shows ownership without the use of an apostrophe and the contraction *it's* always stands for "it is." Ask students to try reading the sentence aloud and substituting "it is" to see if the sentence makes sense. If it does, then they will need to use *it's* with the apostrophe. If it doesn't, then they probably need *its* without the apostrophe. Students could also reread the sentence aloud and substitute "his" or "her" to see if the word in this sentence means "belonging to someone." Then they will be sure to use "its." Students can collect examples of each in their writer's notebook like the sentence from Seymour Simon's book: "One type of spider that lives in Europe and Asia spends much of its life underwater inside an air bubble called a diving bell."

Now the students were ready to share their topic for their how-to piece. Students sat with a partner and talked out their process. Next, they returned to their seats to draw their process in several boxes and label them. Students began to draft their pieces as Lynne and Shelly circulated and encouraged them to slow down, think about each step, and try out some transition words. Lynne and Shelly reminded the students about their work with capitals for words in a title, referring to work they had done while writing their book reviews. Figures 8.1–8.4 are some completed drafts.

Kelly had a good sense of how to embed transition words. She tried to use contractions for "here is" and "that is" and was fairly successful. Kelly

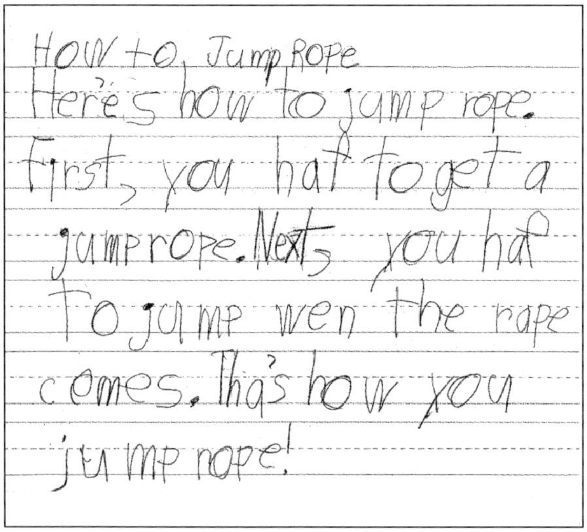

Figure 8.1
Kelly explains how to jump rope:
"Here's how to jump rope. First, you have to get a jump rope. Next, you have to jump when the rope comes. That's how you jump rope!"

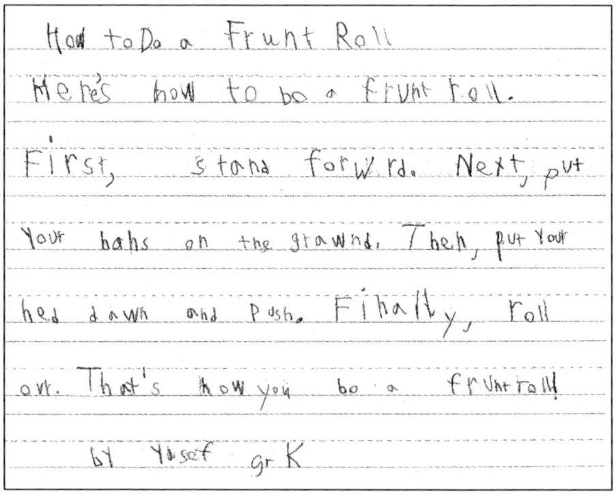

Figure 8.2
Yusef offers instructions for executing the perfect front roll:
"Here's how to do a front roll. First, stand forward. Next, put your hands on the ground. Then, put your head down and push. Finally, roll over. That's how you do a front roll!"

used a lead sentence to introduce her topic and an exclamation mark in her last sentence to emphasize a job well done.

Yusef does so many things well! He capitalizes the important words in his title. He uses a lead sentence and concluding sentence. He has a good sense of logical order, at least for writing up this procedure. Yusef has a few typical issues at the kindergarten level. Although he uses space between words very well, he randomly capitalizes certain letters such as *y* and *p*. Yusef sometimes confuses the letters *b* and *d*.

Teaching Point: To help younger students form lowercase *b* instead of *d*, tell them to think about how they would write an uppercase "B" and take off the top loop. The *B* and *b* have loops that face in the same direction.

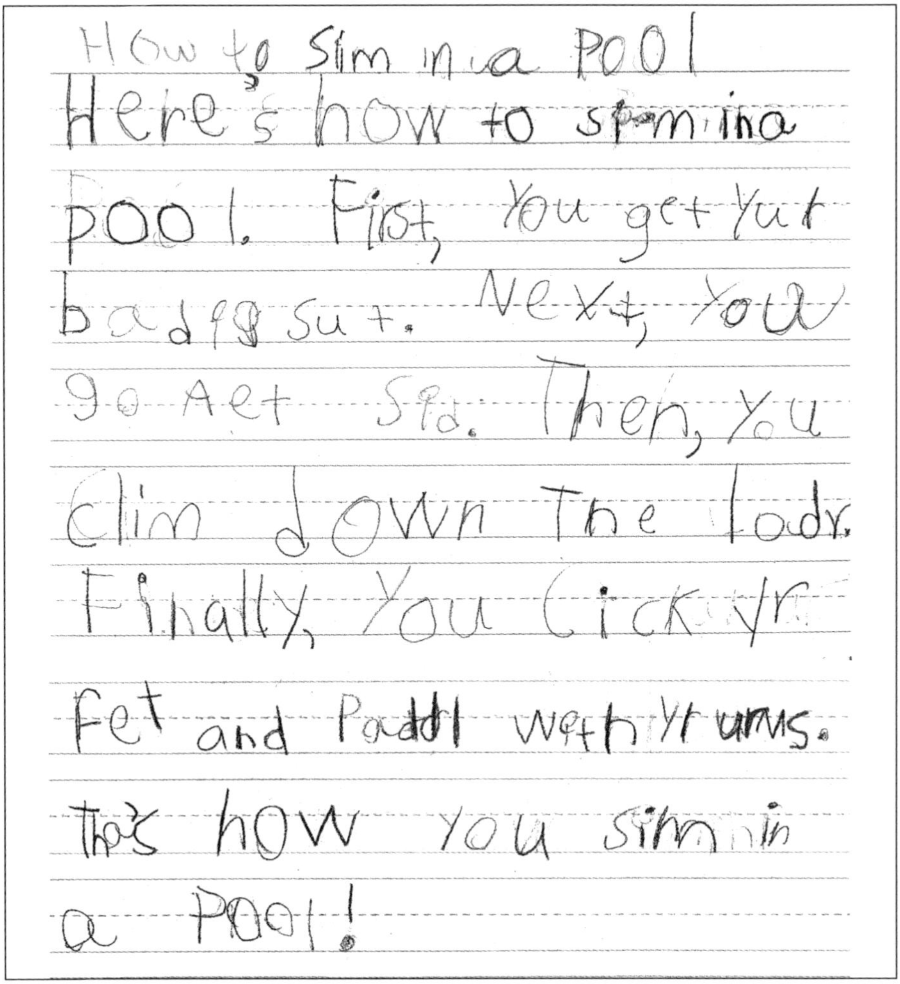
How to Sim in a Pool
Here's how to sim in a
pool. First, You get Yut
badgg sut. Next, You
go Aet Sid. Then, You
clim down The lodr.
Finally, You Cick yr
fet and Paddl weth yr arms.
Tha's how you sim in
a Pool!

Figure 8.3
Dilan instructs us in how to swim: "Here's how to swim in a pool. First, you get your bathing suit. Next, you go outside. Then, you climb down the ladder. Finally, you kick your feet and paddle with your arms. That's how you swim in a pool!"

As you can see, Dilan did quite a bit of writing. He had a topic sentence and used transition words to help organize his thinking. He wasn't afraid to try to spell words such as *bathing suit* and *paddle*. Dilan wrote in complete sentences and knew when to use end punctuation. His one sentence formed with a compound predicate shows he has a good sense of what ideas can logically be placed together—*kick with your feet and paddle with your arms*. Spacing between words is fairly consistent. He tries to use the apostrophe correctly in *here's* and *that's* and has some issues with uppercase and lowercase letters. In conferences, that's a grammar/language issue to work on, especially with students in grades K–2. Unfortunately, some upper elementary students continue to have issues with letter formation. The letters *j, k, p, s,* and *y* seem to be particularly troublesome for some children throughout elementary school. Nipping the problem early on is advisable. If students continue to form their letters incorrectly throughout the primary grades, it will be a difficult habit to break later on and one they should not have to spend time worrying about—there will be other issues!

As you can see, Mikel is doing many things well. It is her nature to be precise and always do her best. She begins with a lead sentence instead of beginning with the first instruction or step to follow. She uses a simple clos-

Figure 8.4
Mikel explains how to do a forward roll: "Here's how to do a forward roll. First, stand up. Next, bend down. Then put your head on the ground. Finally, tuck your head and roll. That's how to do a forward roll!"

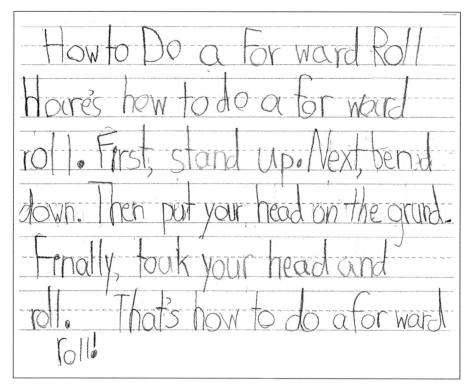

ing sentence. Mikel knows how to use some basic transition words to help organize her procedural piece. She knows how to write imperative sentences—a command that begins with an action rather than the subject noun. She begins her sentences with capital letters and ends with a punctuation mark, reserving the use of the exclamation point for her final sentence. She does a remarkable job placing the apostrophe in the correct place in *here's* and *that's* and could tell Shelly what two words stood for each contraction.

Gail Speers, a first-grade teacher in the Upper Moreland Primary School, also had students try out procedural writing. The students listened to Lois Ehlert's *Hands: Growing Up to Be an Artist.* After reading the mentor text aloud, Gail and Lynne shared a passage from the book on the whiteboard: "He [Father] builds things in his workshop. He measures with his ruler, marking the wood with a pencil. Then he measures again, just to be sure." They brainstormed a big list of all the ways they used their hands to do sports, help their parents, or make things and shared the idea they wanted to write about. Gail's knowledge of her students was helpful here. She knew their interests and areas of expertise and could offer them suggestions when they were stuck or provide gentle nudges if she felt they would really take an interest in writing about a particular skill or process. Lynne and Gail spent some time providing models for them. Lynne used "How to Plant Flowers" and wrote in front of the students orally while Gail recorded:

It is fun to plant flowers. First, you dig a small hole in the soil. Make sure it is not too deep or too shallow. Next, place the young plant in the hole. Then, fill in the hole with some potting soil and pat it down gently. Finally, give your new plant a little drink of water. Repeat this process for each new plant. Enjoy your flowers in the spring, summer, and fall!

Lynne and Gail asked the students to find the words that helped order the steps for planting a flower and wrote them on the chart. Gail used these words to create a template for her students as they wrote their procedural pieces. Johna's piece (Figure 8.5) offered a caution: *You have to be careful because you can get hurt!* Her drawing added another detail: *Look each way.* She clearly is emphasizing safety, and you can almost hear her parents talking to her and giving her instructions. She has a title, a lead sentence, and a closing sentence. Johna used the exclamation point in every section of her plan.

In a conference with Johna, Lynne asked her to choose one place where Johna felt the exclamation mark was really needed. As you can see from her piece, Lynne could not change this young writer's mind and the exclamation marks remained.

Figure 8.5
Johna explains how to ride a bike:
"Riding a bike is easy to ride. First, you have to get on your bike! You keep pedaling and you have to keep your balance. Next, you have to be careful because you can get hurt! Then, if you are turning, you have to stop and you look both ways! Finally, you have to wear your helmet. You have to be careful! That's how to ride a 2 wheeler bike!"

Figure 8.6
Nick explains how to catch a frog:
"Catching a frog is easy if you know how. First get a boat at a boat store. Next get a net at a store. Then if you see a frog try to catch it with your net. Finally you might catch a frog. Now you know how to catch a frog."

Nick's advice on how to catch a frog is quite expensive (Figure 8.6). He tells his reader, *First get a boat at a boat store.* Nick has a wonderful sense of sentence, uses end punctuation, and has spaces between his words. His spelling is remarkable.

Gwen wrote about fishing. She has a question lead sentence, a closing sentence, uses end punctuation, and has a sense of order. Her spacing is excellent, even though she tries to cram her final words on the last line because she has run out of room: *Do you no [know] how to catch a fish? First, get werms and Buy a fishing rode [rod]. Next, go to a Big rever [river] an sit on a rock. Then, put one of your wrems [worms] on your fishing rode. Finally, thow [throw] your fishing rode [rod] into the rever an [and] waet [wait] itill [until] a fish gets your werm. That's how to catch a fish.*

In Alison Navarrete's kindergarten class at Eagleville Elementary School in Methacton School District, students were eager to write in their journals after Lynne read *Hands: Growing Up to Be an Artist.* The students brainstormed on a chart a list of ways they use their hands. They added to this list after their field day where they engaged in activities like tug-of-war. Every student had at least one idea to write about. Lynne used the topic of planting flowers, revising her original piece slightly:

I use my hands to plant flowers. First, I dig a hole in the garden soil. Next, I place the flower in the middle of the hole. Then, I fill in the hole with the garden dirt. I pat the ground around the plant with my gloved hands. After that, I plant more flowers the same way until I am finished. Finally, I give my flowers a little drink of water with the hose. Now I am ready to enjoy my garden!

The students read and reread with Lynne. They noticed the transition words and how the writing started with a lead sentence to introduce the topic and ended with a closing sentence. The students drew a picture first and labeled it. Adiva wrote a piece that has voice and sophistication (Figure 8.7).

What an amazing piece! Adiva proves to us that we need to write about what we know and love. She writes with the voice of authority as she explains how to apply nail polish. When Lynne and Alison conferred with Adiva, they had her reread her sentence: *Next, I use my hand opin the top.* They asked her to read it several times. Each time, she said the word "to" after the word "hand," even though she had not written it. Only after pointing to each word and slowing down did Adiva realize she had omitted a little word that was important if she wanted to write a complete, logical sentence. Lynne explained how to use an upside down *v* (a caret) to show where something such as a letter or word should be inserted. She has so many conventions of writing in place: spacing between words, comma use after the transition words, end punctuation, and the correct use of upper- and lower-case letters. Alison praised her for her use of a good describing word such as *sparkly* and an effective closing sentence.

Figure 8.7
Adiva explains how she paints her nails: "I love to use my hands to paint my nails. First, I pick the sparkly color. Next, I use my hands to open the top. Then, I carefully put (on) the color! Finally, I put my hands under the fan to dry. My nails look great!"

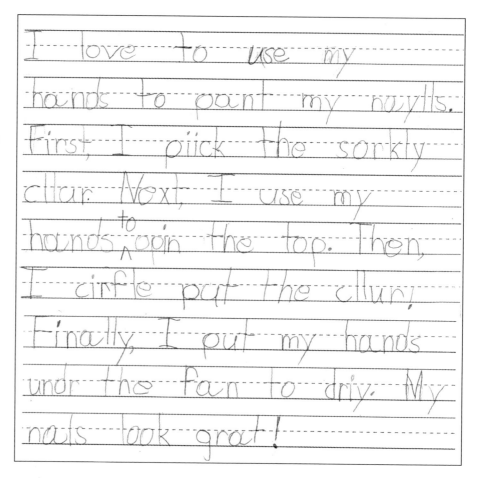

Kathleen wrote about tug-of-war (Figure 8.8). She understood where to place an exclamation mark and was able to use transition words, too. Alison and Lynne loved her engineered spelling for high-five—*hifif*.

Kathleen was able to spell "because" correctly by using the word wall. Alison placed words the students seemed to use often on the wall to help them become more independent.

Anthony's piece (Figure 8.9) was original and filled with details. He had trouble forming some lowercase letters, especially *g, b,* and *p*. Anthony has a sense of sentence, uses a lead sentence, begins his sentences with capital letters, and uses transition words to help him organize his piece. When Lynne conferred with Anthony, she suggested that he might use all capital letters to write *CRUNCH! CRUNCH!* since his exclamation marks told her that he wanted her to read these words in a louder voice.

Figure 8.8
Kathleen shows us how she uses her hands to play tug-of-war:
"I love to use my hands to play tug-o-war. First, I pick up the rope. Next, I pull the rope. Finally, I give my fans a high five because we won! I love tug-o-war."

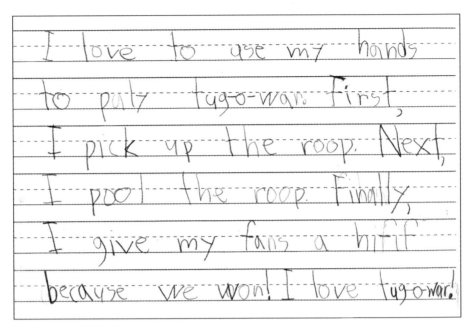

Figure 8.9
Anthony explains how he uses his hands to get breakfast:
"I love to use my hands to get out breakfast. I get out my bowl, and next I get out my spoon. Then, I get out my Fruit Loops. Finally, my dad helps me pour the milk. I spoon the Fruit Loops in my mouth. Crunch! Crunch! I love to eat Fruit Loops."

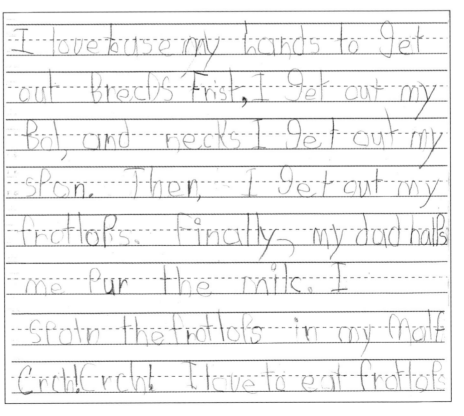

The procedural pieces in kindergarten gave the students a chance to create an expert list in their journal and write about a process or offer an explanation. Lynne talked about this kind of writing as informational writing—where sometimes writers teach their readers how to do something. Although writing about a process is not easy, these kindergartners eagerly embraced their writing and shared their pieces with partners, teachers, and the whole class. It is easy to make the mistake of choosing a topic that is too broad. If young writers make this mistake, then writing a procedural piece becomes almost impossible. In Shelly's and Alison's kindergarten classes and Gail's first-grade class, the teachers helped their students revise their thinking before they started drafting. Hence, writing to explain how to play baseball became either how to hit a ball or how to catch a ball, and how to play football became how to score a touchdown. The students learned some basic transition words and phrases and also learned that these words or phrases are usually set off from the rest of the sentence with a comma. Kindergartners need to continue to work on spacing between words and need to edit their papers for correct letter formation. At this level, many students randomly use uppercase letters in their sentences, not because they think those words should begin with capitals, but simply because some letters are troublesome to form as lowercase letters. A great addition to procedural writing at this level would be to add photos or to videotape the students as they demonstrate the skill or activity as a motivation for the writing piece.

Procedural Writing with Fifth Grade

Diane worked with Carolyn Dutton's fifth-grade class at James Buchanan Elementary School on procedural writing. She began by reading *How to Babysit a Grandpa* by Jean Reagan to the students. This delightful book is narrated by a preschooler who has tips for babysitting his grandfather. Diane read it through once and then, as she read it a second time, she asked students to notice that the narrator gives directions for many different procedures. For example, the narrator specifies how to stay quiet, what to do on a walk, how to entertain a grandpa, how to play with a grandpa, what to draw for a grandpa, and how to say goodbye to a grandpa. Each of these procedures is written as a bulleted list preceded by a colon as the mark of punctuation. Diane pointed out these features on the document imager. If your school does not have an imager, circulate around the room with the book so that every student can see at least one of the lists and the colon as you reread the book.

After the second reading, Diane asked the students to turn and talk about what procedural writing is and what it is not. She listed their responses:

It could be a list of ingredients or materials you need.
It could be a recipe.
It gives steps in order.
It tells why it's important to do.
It gives information.
It could tell you how to do something.
It does not tell a story.
It does not give an opinion.
It does not try to convince you of anything.

Diane accepted all answers and asked students to think of things they have read or heard about that could be thought of as procedural pieces of writing. Responses included recipes, instructions for playing a board game or a video game, directions or maps to a place, rules for behaving at recess or in the cafeteria, rules for Mrs. Dutton's class, and so on. Diane asked students to write a definition of procedural writing in their writer's notebooks and to add anything to the definition that they thought of that may not have already been mentioned.

Diane then explained how to brush your teeth on the whiteboard in front of the students.

If you want to have healthy teeth and gums, you should brush your teeth twice a day. In order to do this effectively, you will need a soft-bristled toothbrush, toothpaste, a sink with running water, a glass, and dental floss. You may want to add mouthwash to the list, but many dentists do not think that mouthwash is absolutely necessary.

First, wet the toothbrush with a little water from the faucet. Then, squeeze toothpaste onto the brush so that it covers the bristles. Then begin brushing. Place the brush at a 45-degree angle to your teeth and brush up and down paying close attention to each tooth surface. Be careful not to brush too hard because doing so can cause damage to the tooth enamel and may even cause your gums to bleed. Brush your tongue too in order to remove bacteria. Brushing your teeth should take around two minutes, but the important thing is that you reach every tooth surface. After you have brushed with the toothpaste, rinse the toothbrush, and rinse your mouth with water, spitting the rinse water into the sink. At least once a day, use dental floss to clean between your teeth, removing any food or plaque that has lodged there. Pull a length of floss from the roll and wrap one end of the floss around one index finger and the other end around the other index finger. Then, insert the floss between every tooth and the one next to it making sure to get all the way to the gum line. Finally, rinse with mouthwash if desired. Swish or gargle mouthwash for about thirty seconds. Then spit the gargled mouthwash into the sink.

Having clean teeth and healthy gums is important to your overall well-being. If you follow this procedure, you should have strong teeth and gums for your lifetime and you will never have to store your teeth in a glass by the bed!

Next Diane asked students to look at her "How to Brush Your Teeth" piece and also to check the list they had made naming what procedural writing is and is not, focusing on the characteristics of procedural writing. They turned and shared with a partner what they now believed necessary to write a procedural piece of writing. Here is their final list:

- Tells why the procedure is needed (why it's important)
- Gives a list of what is needed to complete the procedure
- Includes all the steps needed to do the procedure
- Lists the steps in the order in which they must be done
- Tells everything the reader needs to know to complete the procedure
- Leaves nothing out—assumes that the reader doesn't know unless the writer tells him

The final two items on the list may seem redundant, but Diane appreciated that the class noticed the importance of not making assumptions about the reader. As noted before, young writers often don't realize they are leaving out important information. This unfortunate lack of insight carries over to grammar issues as well. When students write fragments without meaning to, for instance, it is often because they make assumptions about the reader's knowing what the writer means to say. When the class suggested the final two items on the list, Diane mentioned that leaving nothing out that the reader needs to know applies at the sentence level too!

Students then paired up to write letters to next year's fifth-grade class telling them how to be successful in Mrs. Dutton's classroom. Emir and Summer began by noting why it is important to follow their suggestions.

We hope you succeed in Mrs. Dutton's class. It's not that difficult if you take care of your supplies and follow the rules. If you don't make an effort, you may be in fifth grade more than one year!

Jared and Mackenzie made a list of necessary supplies.

In order to succeed in fifth grade, you will need the following supplies: pencils, folders, notebooks, erasers, a flash drive, and plenty of books to read. You will also need to remember the rules: raise your hand to speak, be respectful, and do your best every day.

Jordan wrote the following steps to follow:

First, take notes and put the date on your papers. Doing this will help you when you study for a quiz. Second, always do your homework. Trust me, you will be rewarded. Third, keep track of all your papers so you don't lose anything important. That's what the folders are good for. Keep all of your papers in a folder marked for that subject. Finally, prepare to be challenged and face every challenge with confidence.

With the students' permission, Diane shared these excerpts with the class, asking them to decide what (if anything) the writers had left out that was important to know. Students liked the opening paragraph because it was attention-getting and had humor. However, Madelyn wondered if "take care of your supplies" was enough information for the reader. "What does that mean?" she wondered. The class decided that more explanation could be beneficial. Elle thought that taking care of your supplies might mean that you should be organized. Emir and Summer added the following:

It's not that hard if you keep your supplies organized so that you can find what you need easily. Have a place for everything in your desk and in your cubby. When you are running low on paper, for example, you will know it if you have an organized notebook and desk.

The lesson continued with suggestions about the supplies needed. The class decided that further explanation of the supplies—why they are necessary and how they will be used—was important. In a discussion about the order of the steps to follow, Austin wondered if it made any difference how the steps in this case were ordered. Since the topic is "How to Be Successful in Mrs. Dutton's Fifth-Grade Classroom," he wondered, should the writer start with what to do in the beginning of the year and then talk about how things change as everyone gets to know one another? Jordan thought that the steps should be listed in the order of importance. Diane agreed that order of importance seemed like the best way to organize this part of the procedure. Here is what the class wrote:

If you want to succeed, you will need to take these steps. First, and most important, remember to be respectful to everyone. That means that you will raise your hand to speak, and you will listen to the person who is talking whether that person is Mrs. Dutton or a classmate. Mrs. Dutton will be really annoyed if she can't hear what a student is saying because you are talking at the same time. The second most important thing is to follow directions. That means that you have to listen carefully to what Mrs. Dutton says to do, and then do it in the exact order she tells you. This is important because if you don't follow directions, you may not get credit for the work you do. Third, do your homework. Homework is important because you almost always use it in class the next day. If you don't do your homework, you may not be able to understand the next day's lesson. Fourth, no bullying! If Mrs. Dutton catches you picking on another person, look out. That's true in every class in school and even at recess. Finally, organize all your papers. It helps if you write the date on every paper and keep a folder for every subject. When it's time to study for quizzes and tests, you'll be glad you did this.

Diane pointed out that as the students revised the original pieces, they added important information that a reader would find necessary to following the suggestions. Since Diane was the scribe for the class writing, she added the necessary marks of punctuation. She decided to focus on use of the comma for introductory elements (like first, second, third or after introductory dependent clauses in complex sentences). She reminded them of how the colon was used to introduce a list in *How to Babysit a Grandpa* because she thought a colon would likely be used most often in writing their own procedural pieces.

Diane asked the students to brainstorm uses of the comma. They knew about commas in a series, commas in dates, commas to separate cities from states in addresses. One or two knew about commas in compound sentences. Then she asked them to look at the commas in the shared writing about the steps to take to succeed in Mrs. Dutton's class. Did they see a reason for all of the commas? Diane pointed out the commas following each of the introductory words (first, second, third, etc.) and also the commas after the introductory clauses. She asked students to notice the length of the sentences with the introductory clauses. "When you are reading aloud," she asked, "what does the comma tell you to do?" Commas tell us to pause in our reading. Commas are like road signs telling us to slow down. Commas help to clarify meaning.

The next day Diane brought in thirty sentence strips, enough for each student in the class to participate. One strip contained an independent clause and one strip contained a dependent clause. The strips were color-coded: six were on blue stock, six on orange, six on dark pink, six on yellow, and six on green. Diane did this to avoid confusion and also to give students the challenge of finding an appropriate match for their strips. Those with blue strips paired with others with blue strips, and so on. She used these sentences:

> As Ralph began climbing/the ladder slipped.
> When Leo lost his keys/he searched everywhere.
> When we finished eating/we cleared the table.
> The girls saw the movie/after they met for dinner.
> After the third inning/the game was tied.
> If I know Jim/he will be late.
> While the music played/the actors walked onstage.
> Because it was so cold/we couldn't stay outside for long.
> Although it was late/we still had time to see the show.
> Before we knew it/it was time to leave.
> Since it was raining/we did not have recess.
> When Mrs. Dutton read the book aloud/we were in suspense.
> As I listened to my iPod/I did my math homework.
> Whenever I go to the beach/I bring a book with me.
> If it rains on Sunday/we will not have a picnic.

Diane distributed the strips and asked students to find a partner with the same color strip and make a sentence. They took turns at the front of the class reading aloud the sentences they made. Diane asked the pairs to read the sentence two ways—with the adverbial clause first and with the adverbial clause after the main clause. Students decided that sometimes the sentences sounded "better" with the dependent clause first, and sometimes they liked the sentence better when the dependent clause came after the main clause. Diane asked several of the pairs to write their sentences on the board with the dependent clause first. She instructed them to put a comma after the last word in the dependent clause. Diane wrote on the board: *Use a comma after an introductory clause.* She reminded students that clauses have a subject and a predicate. Independent clauses are sentences and can stand alone. Dependent clauses are not sentences because they cannot stand alone.

Because students were going to write their own procedural pieces, Diane reminded them of the use of the colon to precede a list. Colons mean "note what follows." Do not use a colon immediately after a verb or a preposition. When Summer wrote *The supplies you need to be successful in Mrs. Dutton's class are:* the colon is unnecessary and should not be used. The instruction on the use of the colon is also an opportunity to remind students of the definitions of a verb and a preposition, parts of speech studied earlier in the year.

Students brainstormed lists of topics for procedural writing. In their writer's notebooks, they wrote as many topics as they could think of and shared them with the class. Some of these included How to Build a Snowman, How to Keep a Low Profile, How to Play Hockey, How to Play Solitaire, How to Play Black Ops, How to Wash Dishes, How to Make an Ice Cream Sundae, and How to Make a Peanut Butter and Jelly Sandwich. They then chose a topic and began writing. Diane asked them to remember to use commas after introductory dependent clauses and to use the colon before the list of the ingredients needed. As students wrote, Diane conferred with individual writers noting those whose pieces she wanted to share with the class. During these content conferences, Diane did not mention grammar or conventions. Only after the drafts were ready did Diane refer to the lesson on uses of the comma and the colon. Then, she asked her writers to edit for these two specific items.

 Teaching Point: Please remember that editing is only one part of the writing process. It does no good to point out editing errors to individual writers before they have their thoughts together. Sometimes errors get fixed by the writers themselves when they get their ideas organized. Sometimes errors are easier for writers to see when they read the piece to another person. Sometimes errors need to be addressed by the teacher, but only after the draft is complete and revised for content. Just because we are embedding grammar instruction into units of study in writing does not mean that grammar is the only thing we teach or the only thing we point out to students in their drafts during conferences.

When students had completed their procedural pieces, Diane, with student permission, reproduced examples of student writing that included correct use of the comma to introduce elements such as first, second, third, and so on and after an introductory clause and the correct use of the colon.

To make the perfect ice cream sundae you will need the following ingredients: your choice of ice cream, an ice-cream scoop, your choice of syrup, rainbow or chocolate jimmies, whipped cream, a cherry (optional), a bowl, and a spoon. (Alexis)

If you catch the ball, you are safe. (Javier)

If you are a shy person like me, you want to keep a low profile. (Jared)

When the shortstop runs for the ball, cover second base. (Jordan)

First, find a bowl big enough to hold three scoops of ice cream. (Madelyn)
Finally, cut the bread into two triangles and eat slowly to savor every morsel. (Garcia)

Together, Diane and the fifth graders developed an anchor chart on transition words and phrases that can be used as time signals. Diane suggested that they also place these words on a reference page in their writer's notebook. See the list that follows:

Transition Words to Tell "When" It Is Happening

when	immediately	now	then
lately	already	little by little	first
at the same time	simultaneously	during	first of all
later	once	subsequently	next
meanwhile	after	final	then
before	the first thing	afterward	in the beginning

Diane asked students to reflect about writing procedural pieces in their journals. Why is this an important skill? When will they use it? What did they learn from writing these pieces? These fifth graders noted that in order to write about a procedure they had to really know about that procedure. They also noted that leaving out information made it difficult to follow the instructions. Writing these pieces helped these writers understand that clarity of expression and clarity of thought are important factors in good writing no matter what the subject of that writing may be.

Comparative and Superlative Adjectives

Young writers, possibly for emphasis, often use both *more* or *most* and the *-er* ending or the *-est* ending, giving rise to such constructions as "more better" and "most greatest." These constructions not only are incorrect but also indicate that the student has not understood the concepts or how to construct the comparative and superlative. (Note: Adverbs also have comparative and superlative forms. Most classes will need a separate lesson on adverbs using the pattern discussed here.)

Hook: Read aloud to the class the book *If You Were an Adjective* by Michael Dahl. Pages 20 and 21 define comparative and superlative forms of adjectives and page 22 addresses irregular forms of comparative and superlative adjectives. Read the book for fun, but point out that the examples use only *-er* and *-est* and not "more *-er*" and "most *-est*."

Purpose: *Writers, I've been noticing that sometimes when I'm reading your work (or listening to you speak) I wonder why you use an adjective like "better" with the word "more." Today we're going to talk about comparative and superlative adjectives and how to form each kind.*

Brainstorm: Students brainstorm a list of adjectives or describing words in their writer's notebooks. Share lists in small groups. Together as a class make an anchor chart of adjectives that the class has brainstormed.

Model: Using a class-generated brainstormed list, model for students how to form the comparative and superlative forms for each.

Positive	Comparative	Superlative
fat	fatter	fattest
strong	stronger	strongest
loud	louder	loudest
neat	neater	neatest
warm	warmer	warmest
short	shorter	shortest
weak	weaker	weakest
eager	more eager	most eager
flat	flatter	flattest

expensive	more expensive	most expensive
long	longer	longest
curious	more curious	most curious
wide	wider	widest
thin	thinner	thinnest

Ask students what they notice about the words that use "more" and "most" in the comparative and superlative forms. (Generally speaking, words of one syllable form their comparative and superlative by adding *-er* and *-est*. Words of more than one syllable usually form their comparative and superlative by adding the words *more* and *most*. No words use both!)

Guided Practice: Send students on an adjective hunt in their independent reading books and their writer's notebooks. Working with a partner, students will make a chart of these adjectives in their positive, comparative, and superlative forms in the reference section of their writer's notebooks. Circulate around the room to be sure they are using "more" and "most" when necessary and never with the *-er* or *-est* ending.

Independent Practice: Ask students to go back to their drafts to find places where they have used the comparative and superlative forms and check to see if they have been used correctly. They should make any necessary corrections.

Reflection: Ask students to write in the reference section of their writer's notebooks about what they now know about making comparative and superlative forms of adjectives. Allow them time to share their discoveries with the class.

How do comparative and superlative forms of adjectives make a description more specific?

Your Turn Lesson

Contractions Using Pronouns

Many intermediate-grade writers (and even more experienced writers!) confuse possessive pronouns with contractions. These writers will mistakenly write *it's* in a sentence like: *The poor dog licked it's wounds and whimpered.* Using the apostrophe to show possession in pronouns is a common editing error.

Hook: The picture book *Punctuation Celebration* by Elsa Knight Bruno is a handy resource for the intermediate-grade classroom teacher. This book clearly explains punctuation marks and their uses, giving specific examples to illustrate each one. Read the pages on the topic of the apostrophe to the students. If possible, use a document imager to allow students to follow along. Point out that apostrophes have two uses: to show possession and to form contractions. This lesson will focus on apostrophe use in contractions.

Purpose: *Writers, I've noticed that when I'm reading your pieces, I'm sometimes confused by the apostrophes being used with pronouns. When an apostrophe is used in pronouns, it is a signal that a contraction is being used. The apostrophe takes the place of missing letters. For example, "we'll" is short for "we will," and the apostrophe replaces the letters* w *and* i *in* will.

Brainstorm: Ask students to make a list of common pronoun contractions (think of the pronouns: *I, he, she, it, we, you*, and *they*) in their notebooks. Remind them that the apostrophe in a contraction is used in place of the missing letters. Share lists in partners. Add examples to a class anchor chart.

Model: Reproduce sentences your students have written (or make up your own) using pronoun contractions. Read the sentences aloud, changing the contraction to the full words. For example, in the sentence: *They're the winners of the contest*, read: *They are the winners of the contest*. Training students to read out the contractions will avoid common apostrophe errors. When the sentence *The poor dog licked it's wounds* is read aloud as *The poor dog licked it is wounds*, the error becomes immediately apparent.

Guided Practice: Ask students to go back to their drafts to check for apostrophe use in contractions. Read each example aloud with a partner and make changes as necessary. Next, ask students to go back a second time and look for places where an apostrophe is necessary to form a contraction but is missing. For example, if a writer has written *were* in the sentence *"Were going to the zoo on* *a class field trip,"* reading that sentence aloud with a partner should pinpoint that error.

Independent Practice: Contractions should be used sparingly in writing. Ask students to look at their drafts to find examples of contractions. Ask them to notice how many times they are using contractions. Instruct them to try writing out these contractions as two words. They can then make decisions about whether using a contraction at that particular point in their piece is a good choice. Students should be able to articulate the reasons for using contractions when they do so. For example, if the piece is a narrative (or an anecdote), using a contraction has the effect of real speech and rings true. *Come on, Jack, let's get in line for the roller coaster* is certainly more effective than *Come on, Jack, let us get in line for the roller coaster.*

Reflection: Ask students to share the changes they made with contractions and to tell why they made those changes. Students should be able to explain the use of the apostrophe in a contraction, and to justify the use of contractions in their written pieces.

> *What types of writing would be most likely to use contractions? Why do you think so?*
>
> *How does reading contractions aloud as two words keep you from making errors using pronouns?*

Your Turn Lesson
●●●●●●●

Expanding a Sentence Using Compound Elements

Sometimes young writers get stuck in the practice of writing fairly simple sentences even though they may be presenting sophisticated ideas. Their sentences follow a noun-verb-direct object or noun-verb–indirect object–direct object pattern. Often they fear that longer sentences will be run-on sentences. While we do not want our students to fill their texts with unwieldy sentences, we do want them to vary the length and complexity of their sentences for stylistic purposes and interest for the reader.

Hook: Read *If You Were a Conjunction* by Nancy Loewen to the class. The book asks students to notice the big, colorful words on each page (so they can easily identify the conjunctions). Ask students to jot down the coordinating conjunctions in the reference pages of their writer's notebook: *and, but, or, nor, for, yet, so.*

Purpose: *Writers, today I'm going to show you how you can use coordinating conjunctions to create interesting sentences and vary your sentence length and structure.*

Brainstorm: Divide the class into pairs or triads, assigning one coordinating conjunction to each group. Generate as many sentences as possible using that conjunction in a limited time (say three to five minutes). In all probability generated sentences will include not only compound sentences but also sentences with compound subjects and/or predicates, as well as items in a series joined by conjunctions. What students are doing here is using conjunctions to join sentence elements. As the lesson progresses, the distinction of what constitutes a compound sentence as opposed to the other structures will be addressed.

Model: Choose several compound sentences from a mentor text such as the opening of *Sarah, Plain and Tall* by Patricia MacLachlan. For example, in Chapter 1:

> "It made a hollow scraping sound on the hearthstones, and the dogs stirred." Talk about how the author tied the scraping sound to the dogs' stirring. These elements are closely related.

> "Caleb thought the story was over, and I didn't tell him what I really thought." Talk about the fact that this is a compound sentence because each part can stand alone, independent of the other.

"He was homely and plain, and he had a terrible holler and a horrid smell." Talk again about the fact that the elements in these sentences are closely related. If students do not notice that the second sentence here contains three uses of the conjunction *and*, point that out to them and ask them what two things the first and third *and* connect.

"I wiped my hands on my apron and went to the window. Outside, the prairie reached out and touched the places where the sky came down." (Talk about how both of these sentences have compound predicates that expand the action but are *not* compound sentences.)

Guided Practice: Ask students to look at the sentences they have written in small group and to write two or three of those sentences in their writer's notebooks. Ask volunteers to come to the board to write their sentences. With class participation decide which of the sentences are compound (two independent clauses) and which have compound elements (subjects, predicates, items in a series) but are not compound sentences. Point out that a comma is inserted before the conjunction in a compound sentence but is not used when only the subject or predicate is compound. If students write sentences containing items in a series, be sure that they use commas to separate each of the items.

Independent Practice: Ask students to revisit the sentences they have written in their writer's notebooks and to make the necessary changes in punctuation (adding commas or deleting them). Circulate around the room to monitor student progress. Ask students to return to a piece of writing they are currently working on or to other entries in their writer's notebook to find a few places where they can combine sentences to create compound sentences or compound subjects/predicates.

Reflection: Ask students to share some of their revisions using compound elements. Ask them to reflect on these questions:

> *What do you now know about coordinating conjunctions?*
> *How did revising for compound elements change your writing?*
> *When revising for sentence fluency, how do you decide which sentences to combine?*

Improving Sentences with Pronouns

First graders through upper elementary grades have difficulty with pronoun usage. Young writers often overuse them, creating confusion for the reader. For the lesson, we are focusing on the practice of using pronouns as substitute nouns to eliminate redundancy and improve the flow of the words in the sentence or paragraph. (CCSS.ELA-LITERACY.L.3.1.A: "Explain the function of nouns, pronouns, verbs, adjectives, and adverbs in general and their functions in particular sentences.")

Hook: Read *I and You and Don't Forget Who: What Is a Pronoun?* by Brian P. Cleary. Listen for pronouns you hear and think about the ones you have not used in your writing.

Purpose: *Writers, today I'm going to show you how you can use pronouns as noun substitutes to avoid repetition that becomes boring to the reader and takes away from the sounds of your sentences.*

Brainstorm: Reread Cleary's book and ask students to listen for words they think are substitutes for nouns and what nouns these pronouns are a substitute for. Older students can use their "stop and jot" writer's notebooks to write down the pronoun-noun pairs they hear.

Model: Create a model that overuses the nouns and ask students what they think of your writing piece. Then rewrite using pronouns and ask them to compare/contrast the two models. Make sure you read both paragraphs aloud:

Once there was an old man. The old man lived in a house. The house was on a mountain. The old man had a dog. The dog lived with the old man. The dog's name was Skippy. Skippy barked too much. Skippy ate too much of the old man's food. The old man had to chase Skippy away from the old man's dinner table. That made Skippy sad.

Revision adding pronouns:

Once there was an old man who lived in a house. It was on a mountain. The old man had a dog. His name was Skippy. He barked too much. He ate too much of the old man's food. The old man had to chase him away from his dinner table. That made Skippy sad.

Note to students: In the fifth sentence in the revised version, "the old man's" was used instead of "his" because it would be impossible to know whose food you were talking about—the dog's or the old man's.

Guided Practice: With a partner, read the poem "Walking" by Grace Ellen Glaubitz aloud several times. Notice the placement of pronouns. Talk about what nouns they refer to and make a list of pronoun-noun pairs to share in whole group. As students share their pairs, chart them and discuss how the poem would sound if only nouns were used.

Independent Practice: Ask students to return to a piece of writing they are currently working on or to their writing folder/portfolio to find places where they can substitute a pronoun for a noun or places where they need a noun instead of the pronoun because the use of the pronoun confuses the reader.

Reflection: Ask students to share some of their revisions using pronouns. Ask them to reflect on these questions:

> *What do you now know about pronouns?*
> *How did your revisions using pronouns change your writing?*
> *Where did you have to use the noun form instead of the pronoun form? Why?*

"Walking"
by Grace Ellen Glaubitz

When Daddy
Walks
With Jean and me,
We have a
Lot of fun
'Cause we can't
Walk as fast
As he,
Unless we
Skip and
Run.
I stretch,
And stretch
My legs so far,
I nearly slip

And fall—
But how
Does Daddy
Take such steps?
He doesn't stretch
At all!

Prepositions and the Prepositional Phrase

Young writers can take advantage of the prepositional phrase to add sentence variety to their compositions. It is nearly impossible to write an essay without using prepositions and prepositional phrases. Students need to understand the prepositional phrase and its usefulness in writing.

Hook: Read *Rosie's Walk* by Pat Hutchins to the class. This delightful book is filled with prepositional phrases on each page as Rosie the hen goes for a walk around the barnyard not knowing that a fox is following her. Children will love the illustrations and the fact that the fox is foiled at every turn. Read it for enjoyment. Then, point out the prepositional phrases. Follow up with a reading of *If You Were a Preposition* by Nancy Loewen.

Purpose: *Writers, today I am going to show you how you can use prepositions and prepositional phrases to add variety to your sentences. We are going to practice moving prepositional phrases around in the sentences we write.*

Brainstorm: Ask students to brainstorm the job of a preposition using the information from the book *If You Were a Preposition*. Their list should include:

- Prepositions make sentences longer by adding more detail.
- Prepositions tell where things are.
- Prepositions tell when things happen.
- Prepositions never work alone. They are always part of a prepositional phrase.

In advance, prepare three-by-five-inch cards by writing one preposition on each card. Distribute them to the class so that each student has one card. Pair students with a partner. Together they can decide which of the prepositions to "act out" for the class. As the student pairs demonstrate the prepositions through role play, ask the class to state the preposition and the prepositional phrase, naming the object of the preposition each time. You may need to explain that the object of the preposition is the noun in the phrase. For example, Jordan and Gia walked around the desk. The preposition is *around* and the phrase is "around the desk." The object of the preposition is "desk." When Skye and Ashley acted out *down*, they sat down. That was the perfect opportunity to show that *down* in the sentence "they sat down" is not a preposition because prepositions never work alone. They are always part of a phrase and take an object.

Model: Use the prepositions on the three-by-five-inch cards to write sentences that include prepositional phrases. Show students how the phrases can be positioned in the sentence and how prepositional phrases can be linked together. For example,

By the side of the road I noticed an old bicycle with broken wheels.
I noticed an old bicycle with broken wheels by the side of the road.

Shared/Guided Writing: Ask students to use the prepositions on their three-by-five-inch cards to create sentences and to play with the placement of the phrases in the sentence. They may work in pairs or individually.

Independent Writing: Ask students to return to their writer's notebooks or to their current drafts to find places where they could add another prepositional phrase or change the position of the phrase in the sentence. Ask them to share what they changed.

Reflection: After students share their sentences ask them to think about what they did and how it worked for them.

> *Examine the lead sentences in some of your narratives or descriptions of setting in your writer's notebook. How could you revise the lead(s) to use one or several prepositional phrases to create a more detailed picture?*
> *Can you find sentences in one of your pieces where you could move the prepositional phrases to another position in the sentence? Explain which position fits your purpose better and why.*

ESL Learners: Prepositions, particularly *at, on*, and *in*, cause trouble for students who are not native speakers. These prepositions appear with regularity throughout writing pieces in all genres. For example, we say, "Jane lives at 1205 Durham Street in London, England, on the banks of the Thames." When we speak about specific addresses, we use *at*. When we talk about towns, cities, counties, states, countries, and continents, we use *in*. When we talk about street addresses, we use *on*. Idiomatic uses are difficult to address because there are so many of them. Teachers can help ESL students address these issues by copying examples in their writer's notebooks as they continue to study prepositional use. For example, when we use words such as *up, down, upstairs, downstairs, uptown*, and *downtown*, students should recognize that these are not prepositions and no prepositional phrase is needed. "Grandpa went downtown" (see Appendix F).

Part 3
Opinion Writing Units of Study

Chapter 9

Introduction to Opinion Writing

In *Write Like This: Teaching Real-World Writing Through Modeling and Mentor Texts*, Kelly Gallagher reminds us, "Writing well does not begin with teaching students how to write; it begins with teaching students why they should write" (2011, 7). Offering opinions is perhaps a natural consequence of growing up. School itself presents many opportunities for students of all ages to offer their points of view on various subjects, giving them myriad reasons to write: what should or shouldn't be included on the cafeteria menu, how much homework should be given, what books should make the required summer reading list, what options could be provided for students who complete their assignments and have some free time.

Today's technologically savvy youngsters possess other possible outlets for writing opinion pieces, including cell phones in the classroom and student response systems such as classroom clickers or audience polling technology. Parents know that their children often try to influence their decisions to buy certain products and brand names, be it cereal, backpacks, sneakers, pocketbooks, Wii games, movies, or jeans. Will our students understand the need to learn how to argue in ways that might convince their parents, teachers, and friends?

If writing instruction will help them win arguments and develop the power to sway others, will they be more motivated to experiment with craft, syntax, and mechanics? When students offer opinions and develop arguments, they learn to reason, evaluate information, and develop rational, meaningful support for their ideas. Why is teaching grammar and punctuation so important in this text type? In order to write with clarity and purpose, writers need grammar and conventions. As Barry Lane's *But How Do You Teach Writing? A Simple Guide for All Teachers* tells us: "It gives you flexibility and variety and helps expand your original voice as a writer. You also learn grammar so you don't look like a fool" (2008, 168). If students want their target audience to consider their opinions, they must have the "look of literacy" that includes proper spelling, capitalization, correct usage, and punctuation—and all that the word *editing* often implies. Persuasive writing (although not mentioned in the Common Core State Standards [CCSS]) connects directly with the real world and a real audience—not just the classroom teacher. Your students' voices will be much more likely to be heard if they are not monotone, limp, and fearful voices created by the use of the same sentence patterns, the same words, and a limited knowledge and use of parts of speech. Older and more sophisticated writers will be able to break the rules when it is appropriate for them to do so for emphasis, rhythm, and emotional appeal. Barry Lane recognizes the need to find ways to explore a "multiplicity of voices" and encourage students to create the kind of writing that "pushes its way out of the box and into the real world" (2001, iii).

It is important to note that one can write an opinion piece without trying to change anyone's mind, but one cannot write a persuasive piece without writing an opinion. Opinion pieces are opinions that are offered and then supported with facts, definitions, and details. Persuasive writing focuses more on the author's stance and his or her relationship with the audience. It often takes into account the author's credentials and trustworthiness. Argument writing, which begins in the sixth grade in the Common Core State Standards, is used to support claims through an analysis of the topic. In persuasive writing, the author appeals to the emotions and needs of the audience (pathos), but in opinion and argument writing, the author appeals to logical reasoning and evidence presented in his or her text (logos).

The Common Core State Standards states in its College and Career Readiness Anchor Standards for Writing that "To build a foundation for college and career readiness, students need to learn to use writing as a way of offering and supporting opinions, demonstrating understanding of the subjects they are studying, and conveying real and imagined experiences and events. They learn to appreciate that a key purpose of writing is to communicate clearly to an external, sometimes unfamiliar audience, and they begin to adapt the form and content of their writing to accomplish a particular task and purpose" (www.corestandards.org/ELA-LITERACY/CCRA/W). That's quite a philosophical statement! Take it apart and notice that opinion writing, informational writing, and narrative writing have equal importance. *All* writing that students accomplish needs to be a form of clear communication with an awareness of audience and task. The clarity of communication is the job of grammar and usage. Students need to realize that their study of grammatical principles, including punctuation, is intrinsic to the task of writing clearly for an audience. Nowhere is this more important than in producing an opinion piece.

In opinion writing, audience awareness is among the first things the writer should consider. For whom is this piece intended? What do I want this person / these people to understand about the topic? How do I convey my opinion to this audience in a forthright way? Is my piece intended to sway others to my way of thinking? If so, which arguments on the other side should I address and how do I counter those arguments? The answers to all these questions help young writers organize and clarify their thoughts.

As early as kindergarten, CCSS suggests that students "Use a combination of drawing, dictating, and writing to compose opinion pieces in which they tell a reader the topic or the name of the book they are writing about and state an opinion or preference about the topic or book" (CCSS.ELA-LITERACY.W.K.1). In this instance, a kindergarten writer likely would be forthrightly stating an opinion to an audience of other kindergarten students. As the writers progress through elementary school, their opinion pieces will develop from opinions about books to opinions about other topics and from an audience of classmates and teacher to possible audiences outside of school. In grade five, for example, students will: "Write opinion pieces on topics or texts, supporting a point of view with reasons and information"

(CCSS.ELA-LITERACY.W.5.1). These reasons and facts are to be "logically ordered" and supported by details. In the upper grades, students can choose to write about a topic of importance to them and to address an audience for whom that topic is of interest. By sixth grade, expectations include refuting counterarguments.

Young writers have strong opinions. Ask any parent of a three-year-old who wants a candy bar at the grocery checkout lane how many reasons the child can come up with for having that candy bar! The three-year-old wants what she wants and opinion supported by facts doesn't enter into the matter. However, student writers have to have more than just a strong opinion in order to write an opinion piece that resonates with its intended audience. Writers need to know how to distinguish between *facts* and *opinions*. They need to be able to formulate opinions that can be supported by factual evidence. They need to be able to use their knowledge of grammar and conventions to create a unique voice that clearly states their intentions. They need to understand how to write in a formal style and when it is appropriate to use personal pronouns and address their target audience in the first person or second person. Jeff Anderson tells us that "Students come to us aware of audience and purpose; we just have to apply their knowledge to their own writing" (2011, 50). In order to be able to write in different voices, students need myriad opportunities to try out opinion/argument writing. As writing teachers, we need to keep in mind these factors as we teach this unit of study.

Chapter 10

Opinion Writing
in the Primary Grades

In a unit of study on opinion writing, students will need to learn that their lives are full of reasons to talk and write about their opinions and argue to sway others to change their minds or actions. Think about all the synonyms we can use to talk about persuasion: persuade, convince, induce, coax, argue, inveigle, sway, woo, talk (someone) into, urge, advise, incite, prevail upon, entice, bring (someone) around, twist (someone's) arm, win over, influence, counsel, prompt. Examples of persuasive writing are everywhere—in television commercials, radio advertisements, flyers for extracurricular activities, supermarket product packaging, book and movie reviews, clothing sales, and toy store ads. They all offer claims, sometimes making use of propaganda techniques such as "testimonial" and "join the bandwagon," but these claims are not always substantiated. Students have opinions about everything in their world, but often try to convince others with whining, begging, or flattery. What they need to offer instead are the facts or evidence to support their opinions, but finding that support can often be challenging.

There are many topic areas to draw from when it comes to writing opinions. In primary grades, it seems logical to start with personal topics and, in upper elementary grades, to move to more substantive topics that revolve around school and the community. Middle and high school students can deal with larger, global topics such as climate change, world hunger, immigration laws, and the use of biological/chemical warfare. School shootings have sparked much discussion about gun control.

Lynne decided a good place to start might be to explore what Mrs. Keller's kindergarten class knew about fact and opinion. Mikel offered her thoughts to her partner. "A fact is something that is true like in the books we are reading about animals." Ava agreed and added, "Yes. You don't make up facts. Our storybooks are made up." Nick was confused. "But are the storybooks opinions?" Mikel thought for a minute. "No. I think you have opinions about real things." As Shelly and Lynne listened in on the various conversations, they heard the kindergartners talk about opinions as something you either agree with or disagree with. Hannah announced that it was okay to change your opinion. Shelly asked her if she could share an example. Hannah remembered the first time she changed her mind about eating broccoli. "My mom put melted cheese on top, and when I tried it, I thought it tasted okay. Before that I thought it was disgusting!"

Lynne and Shelly used some nonfiction books and pulled facts and opinions from them. They talked about the describing words that sometimes make a fact an opinion. Lynne wrote, "Spiders build webs." Then she rewrote the sentence: "Spiders build beautiful webs." The students talked about the difference and why the second sentence was an opinion and not a fact. Lynne and Shelly wanted to establish a very basic understanding, knowing that first- through third-grade teachers would also focus on this skill. Eventually, Lynne and Shelly created an anchor chart for fact and opinion from the students' ideas:

FACTS
1. true
2. in nonfiction

OPINIONS
1. what someone thinks
2. in nonfiction

3. sometimes in fiction
4. can prove it
5. can change¿¿¿

3. often in fiction
4. can give reasons
5. can change

The students were not convinced that facts could change. Lynne offered this thought. "Right now many of you are five years old. That is a fact. But very soon, most of you will be six. So a fact about you will change!" They ended the session with a read-aloud, *William's Doll* by Charlotte Zolotow, and created a two-column chart for students to respond to the question: Should William be allowed to have a doll? Every student placed a checkmark in either the AGREE column or the DISAGREE column. They talked about their thinking in whole group. "I liked what the grandma said in the story," Anthony said. "It will help William practice being a good daddy." Not everyone agreed, but the students understood a few big ideas:

- Everyone can have an opinion.
- You can change your opinion when you listen to others or read a book.
- It's better if you have one or two reasons to explain your thinking.

The students were asked to bring in their favorite book that Friday and be able to offer their opinion of the book to a partner. Shelly suggested that they spend some time over the weekend rereading the book with a parent or sibling or by themselves.

On Monday, Shelly held up *Charlotte's Web* by E. B. White and offered her opinion of the book. Then she told the students she was going to write a book review so that her opinion would be more permanent and others could read it, too. She wrote in front of her students gathered on a big carpet by the chart:

Charlotte's Web by E. B. White is a great book for children in elementary school. I love animals and I think it was sweet of Fern to want to keep Wilbur. The friendship between Wilbur and Charlotte is inspiring. It makes me think about my friends. Charlotte's Web helps readers think about how people should be treated. The author writes with lots of details to help me visualize the story events and characters. Charlotte's Web is my favorite book!

Lynne showed the students a few book reviews from the *New York Times* and from Amazon and asked the students why people write book reviews. Jalyn said that it is a good way to know whether you want to read a book. Hannah said that not everyone likes the same books. "You might like to read about snakes, but I wouldn't like to do that!" she added with gusto. Shelly and Lynne asked the students to share their books with a partner, offering their opinions. Since everyone brought a favorite book, Shelly suggested that the students give some reasons why they liked this book. She wrote some questions on the board:

- Why do I like this book?
- Who would like to read this book?
- Have I read this book many times? Why do I do this?

Lynne and Shelly listened in while the kindergartners talked about their books. Whenever possible, Lynne and Shelly nudged them to explain the thinking behind their opinions. Here are some snippets of conversation:

Mikel: I like when books help you learn new things. That's why I like to read nonfiction.
Jadyn: I like books with poems that rhyme. I like to say them with my mom.
Anthony: I like to read stories that take place in outer space.
Hannah: My book is very funny. It makes me laugh.
Dylan: I like any book by Mo Willems.
Jana: I like to read all the books about Fancy Nancy. I want to be just like her.
Ava: *Pete the Cat* has a song you can sing—"I love my white shoes . . ." (Ava sings some of the words.)
Nigel: I like to read about animals like turtles and snakes and animals that aren't pets like dogs and cats.
Jalyn: The pictures and words make me feel like I'm on a roller coaster. I like the sound words like WHOOSH!—all in uppercase to show how fun it is!

After the students had enough time to share their books with a partner and some with whole group, Shelly and Lynne tried to gather the group's thinking based on this question: What should I write in my book review? With little revision help from the teachers, the children's ideas were again recorded on chart paper. Shelly placed the poster paper on the front board where everyone could see it as he/she drafted a book review. Lynne shared one of her favorite books as she composed a book review for *One Tiny Turtle*. She talked as she wrote:

One Tiny Turtle by Nicola Davies is a good book for you if you like to read about turtles. I liked learning facts about sea turtles. I think readers will be amazed to learn that sea turtles come back to the beach where they were born to lay their eggs. If you choose to read this book, you will discover many interesting facts about these sea creatures. The two kinds of print make the book easy to read. Colorful pictures fill each page. Many of the pages have a blue-green color like the sea. This book is too good to miss!

After Lynne reread her piece several times, the students returned to their list of things to possibly include in their book review and added two additional items (see Figure 10.1; added items are starred). In order to motivate the class to do their best, Lynne and Shelly asked the principal, Susan Smith, if some of the students' book reviews could appear in her final newsletter. Shelly also decided that she would keyboard all their final pieces into her computer and print out all the book reviews to go home in the final report card envelope. In this way, the students, together with their parents, could find great summer reading material. The students were very excited about this real-world connection with home. Shelly explained how helpful this list would be. "You are doing the work of real authors because you ARE real authors!" she explained to them. The students returned to their desks to orally share their opinion one more time before writing their review.

Figure 10.1
What Should I Write in
My Book Review?

- how the author writes words to help us to get excited
- how the author helps us see the characters and places
- tell your favorite part
- how the author uses photographs to look at in books with facts
- how we can learn new things from our book
- the book has poems that rhyme
- the story takes place in outer space
- a favorite character is in all the authors' books (like Olivia in Ian Falconer's books or Fancy Nancy in Jane O'Connor's books)
- funny stories that make you laugh
- have riddles you have to figure out
- has a song you can sing
- can read about what you want to be when you grow up
- has amazing facts you can surprise your friends with
- makes you feel like you are doing what the character is doing like learning how to water ski
- tell who you think would like to read this book (the intended audience)*
- end with a closing sentence like, "Don't miss your chance to read this book!" or "This book is a must-read for your summer reading!"*

The next day Shelly reviewed their list of things to include in a book review. Lynne and Shelly demonstrated how to write book titles and author names on the board and chart paper. They talked about remembering to always capitalize the first word and last word in a title and all the important words in between.

Teaching Point: It is not always easy for students to write book titles correctly, especially if they are looking at the cover of a book. Sometimes all the words are written in lowercase, and sometimes all the words are written in upper-case. In Nicola Davies's book, the title is written like this: *One Tiny TURTLE*. Sometimes the title page will show the traditional way we capitalize book titles, but this is not always the case either. There doesn't seem to be a single set of rules for capitalizing words in a title. For most of us, it's a matter of selecting one convention and sticking to it.

Grammar Reference: Concerning book titles, the *Publication Manual of the American Psychological Association* instructs writers to capitalize only the first word of the title and any proper nouns when citing works in a reference list for print publications. It's now the standard form for titles and headlines in most countries; however, the United States has not yet adopted it. Headline style, or up style, instructs writers to capitalize the first and last words of the title and all nouns, pronouns, adjectives, verbs, adverbs, and subordinating conjunctions (*if, because, as, that*, and so on). Style guides often vary on instructions concerning little words such as articles, coordinating conjunctions, and prepositions, which usually are not capitalized unless they appear as the first or last word of a title. It is most important to decide on one format (style) and stick with it!

As Shelly and Lynne circulated to have roving conferences with the children and nudge them to keep thinking and keep writing, another lesson soon arose in the form of a brief mini-lesson. Lynne and Shelly both noticed that the students were using a generous helping of exclamation points. They reminded the students that exclamation points are not used like periods and should only appear at the end of a sentence that is brimming with emotion. Shelly cautioned that when exclamation points are overused, they cancel each other out. Later that week they addressed the issue of exclamation points by skimming through classroom library books and putting sticky notes on any page that contained one. If the page had more than one, they simply wrote the number on the sticky note. The students made a few important discoveries:

- The exclamation point IS a rare beast.
- Stories use them more, especially when characters are talking.
- Nonfiction books don't use them often and some nonfiction books don't have any exclamation points.
- They can be used after a single word such as "Stop!"
- You want to read these sentences in a louder voice.
- Sometimes, they end a sentence that sounds like an order such as, "Don't touch the stove!" or "Never swim alone!"

Teaching Point: As with everything we teach, students must feel safe enough to try things out and take responsible risks with their writing. The teaching of grammar and conventions can be overwhelming. It is important that students are not so focused on correctness that they will play it safe and not experiment with marks of punctuation they have not used yet or new sentence patterns. We want our primary students to try things out and gradually develop background knowledge and an ear for correctness.

As students continued to draft, revise, and edit their book reviews, Lynne and Shelly continued to confer. The students' enthusiasm ran high because they had a goal of real-world publication both in the principal's end-of-year newsletter and the book review publication that would be sent home with their final report cards. Lynne and Shelly reminded the students that their reviews would help parents, grandparents, and even parents of friends in other classes and schools choose books for summer reading. They created a three-star rating system that was posted on chart paper for all students to see. After some discussion of titles for their rating system, the students voted. This additional discussion provided yet another opportunity to practice capitalizing important words in titles as well as providing a chance to brainstorm appropriate titles for a piece of writing. Figure 10.2 shows the rating system (and title) they created:

Figure 10.2
Mrs. Keller's Kids Read and Rate Books

Too good to miss!	★ ★ ★
Worth the time to read!	★ ★
Okay. Read it if you have the time.	★

Several of the students' book reviews are included in their own handwriting. Alyssa (Figure 10.3) was attracted to the poetry that her book contained and mentioned four poems, doing a good job of capitalizing the titles in the first two she mentions. For a kindergartner, she has good control over spaces between words and uses end punctuation. Lynne loved how Alyssa decided who would like her book and addressed the target audience in the last sentence of her review.

When Lynne conferred with her on her final draft, she did not realize that Alyssa had not written the book's complete title, *Fancy Nancy: Poet Extraordinaire!*, but instead had shortened it to *Fancy Nancy*. They had a brief discussion about the meaning of "extraordinaire" and how that helped to describe the main character. Alyssa said that Nancy wrote really good poems that Alyssa liked reading aloud. They also talked about why the author chose to end her title with an exclamation point. Alyssa said, "Then you know that she [Nancy] is one of the best poets in her class—maybe in her whole school!" They also talked about the word *library* and why it would not be capitalized.

Figure 10.3
Alyssa reviews *Fancy Nancy: Poet Extraordinaire!* by Jane O'Connor: "*Fancy Nancy Poet Extraordinaire* is a great book because it has poetry like 'The Five Little Pumpkins,' 'Picking Berries,' and 'First Snow,' and 'As Soon as Fred Gets Out of Bed.' So get it at a library. You might like *Fancy Nancy*. It is great for you if you like being fancy!"

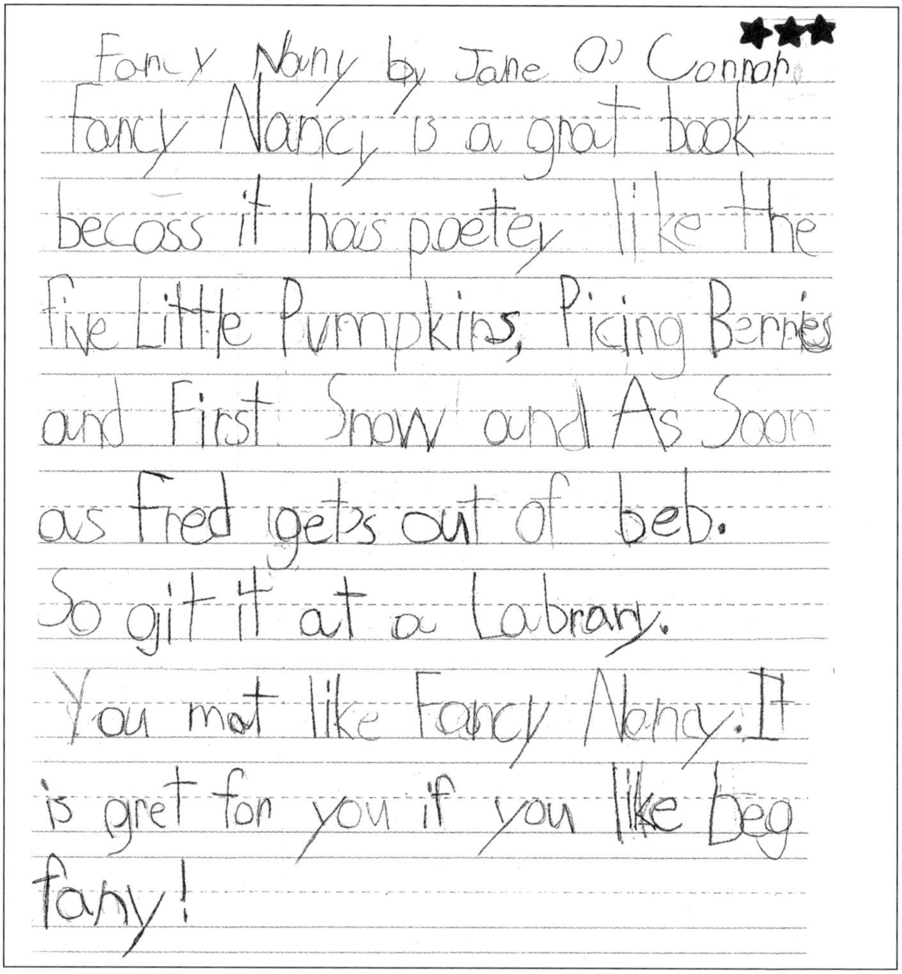
Fancy Nany by Jane O'Connor
Fancy Nancy is a grat book
becoss it has poetey like the
five Little Pumpkins, Picing Berries
and First Snow and As Soon
as Fred gets out of beb.
So git it at a Labrary.
You mat like Fancy Nancy. It
is gret for you if you like beg
fany!

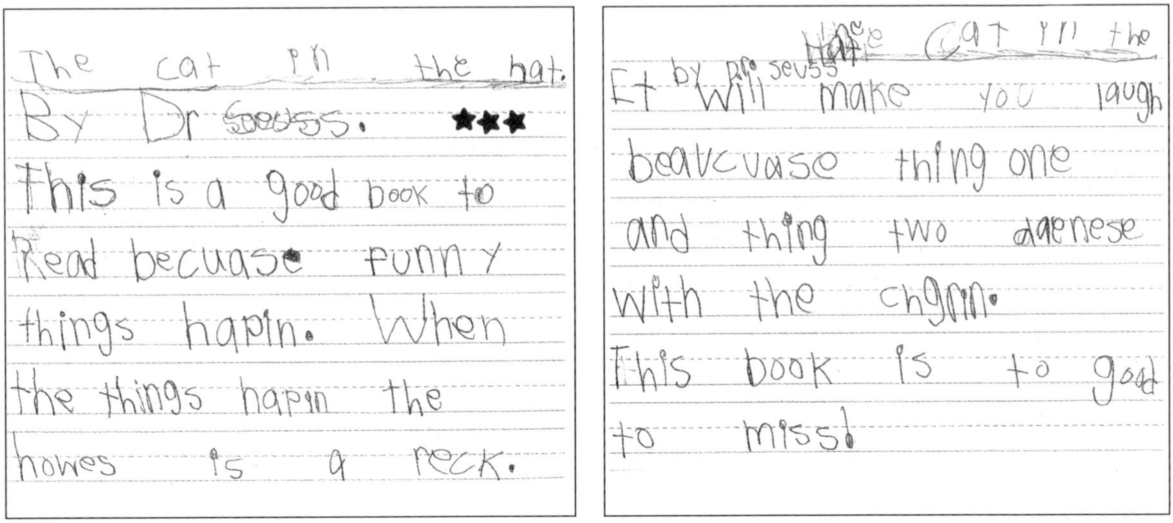

The cat in the hat.
By Dr Seuss. ★★★
This is a good book to
Read becuase funny
things hapin. When
the things hapin the
howes is a reck.

Hafe Cat in the
Et by Dr Seuss
Et will make you laugh
beavcuase thing one
and thing two daenese
with the chgrn.
This book is to god
to miss!

Figure 10.4
Hannah reviews *The Cat in the Hat* by Dr. Seuss:
"This is a good book to read because funny things happen. When the things happen the house is a wreck. It will make you laugh because Thing One and Thing Two dance with the children. This book is too good to miss!"

Hannah (Figure 10.4) wrote about *The Cat in the Hat,* also giving it a three-star rating. Hannah also had control over spacing and end punctuation. Although she did not capitalize *Thing One* and *Thing Two*, she did begin her sentences with a capital letter, and she is an amazing speller for a kindergartner, spelling words like "laugh," "funny," "when," and "things" correctly without any assistance. Her classmates often asked her for help with spelling when Shelly and Lynne were engaged in a one-on-one conference. Lynne did speak with Hannah about rules for capitalizing words in titles, something Hannah did not do, as well as her use of a period after the title and again after the author's name. They looked at a few books and Hannah realized that titles can end in a question mark or exclamation point but periods are not used.

Asher (Figure 10.5) spent a long time writing and rewriting his review. Lynne praised him for the specific content he placed in his review and his closing sentence. Additionally, Asher opened his piece with an invitation to a specific audience, and Lynne praised him for that. He had a good sense of sentence and used capitals to begin each sentence and end punctuation to close, although his periods were too big as well as his dots over the letter *i*. The revision was centered around the way he split compound words or any word, for that matter, on different lines. Lynne advised him to keep the entire word on the same line. At this point, he was not ready to make good decisions about where to split a word by using syllable knowledge. They also talked about spacing between the letters of a word such as *not* in the final sentence.

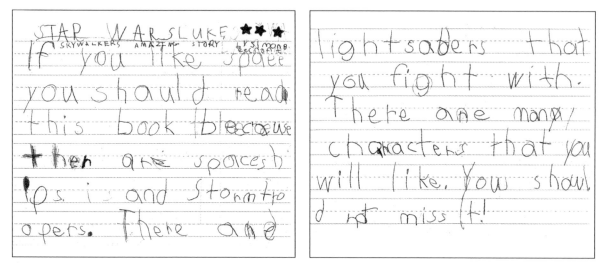

Figure 10.5
Asher reviews *Star Wars: Luke Skywalker's Amazing Story* by Simone Beecroft: "If you like space you should read this book because there are spaceships and storm troopers. There are light sabers that you fight with. There are many characters that you will like. You should not miss it!"

Mrs. Flaherty's first graders were excited to write book reviews to be included in Mrs. Smith's newsletter to the parents. Lynne modeled using *Thomas Jefferson's Feast* by Frank Murphy:

Do you like to eat? So did our third United States President, Thomas Jefferson! In Frank Murphy's historical fiction Thomas Jefferson's Feast, *we learn how Jefferson's trip to France was as much about eating as in cementing a friendship between the two countries. Did you know every time you enjoy some ice cream on a hot summer day, eat a French fry, or enjoy a "love apple," you have Jefferson to thank? Read this slice of life about Jefferson while learning a little French at the same time! If you love history, food, and writing that has a twist of humor, you won't want to miss* Thomas Jefferson's Feast *by Pennsylvania author and teacher Frank Murphy.*

The first graders used a four-star rating system that basically stood for a *must* read, a *good* read, an *okay* read, and a *probably-can-skip-this-one* read. The first graders decided that they had to include the title and author, spelled and capitalized correctly. Sam suggested that sentences should start with capitals and end with a period, question mark, or exclamation mark. Eowyn reminded everyone that they shouldn't use many exclamations, and Makenzie added that they had to remember to tell exactly why they liked the book. Mrs. Flaherty suggested that their details should help their readers know why they rated the book as a four-star or three-star read. The students had library that day, so they used the time to find a good book to review. In the next several days, the students talked about their book in small and whole group. Lynne returned to her review and asked the students if they would read this book based on her review. Patricia said she liked to read about real people, so she would read the book. Aidan added, "It's cool to know that Mr. Murphy teaches fifth grade in a school near our school." Ally said she wanted to read more about love apples. "What are they exactly?" she asked. At that point, Lynne gathered the class on the rug and read Frank's book to them. They talked about how the sprinkle of French words helped create a voice of authority for the author. As the students started drafting, they had Lynne's piece as a model and the shared experience they had created about *One Tiny Turtle*. Ally and Melanie shared their final drafts and participated in a whole-group praise-and-polish conference. The students had previous experience with this kind of conference. Typically, a conference begins with a specific praise like, "I like the way you helped me to form a picture in my mind of the main character." After one or two praises the responder(s) can ask a question for clarification purposes. For example, "Which part of this book was your favorite part?" A polish is a suggestion that the writer weighs and decides to use, partially use, or not use at all. Students are more likely to act upon the polishes given by their teacher, but this is not always the case. A polish could be, "I think it would be a good idea to tell us the name of the illustrator, too." A polish could ask the writer to add another detail or a closing sentence. Figures 10.6 and 10.7 show their final drafts.

If you love friendship, you'll want to read Chrysanthemum by Kevin Henkes. You will be surprised by the amazing pictures in the book! Did you know Chrysanthemum loved her name first and then did'nt love it? You'll love this book because it teaches you that feeling can change every day when you're in school or at home or even at dance or at a game! She is a girl that is named after a flower but she's a very great girl.

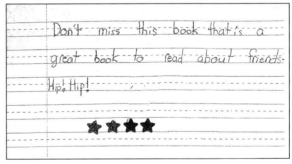

Don't miss this book that is a great book to read about friendship! Hip! Hip!

Figure 10.6
Ally's review of *Chrysanthemum* by Kevin Henkes

If you love books about learning a lesson you should read Silverlicious by Victoria Kann. My favorite part was when Silverlicious apologizes to Cupid the Easter Bunny and Elf #351. It teaches you that you need to be nice to each other If you lose your sweet tooth you should always be

sweet like your sweet tooth. Don't miss this great book.

Figure 10.7
Melanie's review of *Silverlicious* by Victoria Kann

In Maribeth Batcho's second-grade class, students voted for a four-star rating system. The students created the descriptors shown in Figure 10.8:

Figure 10.8
Batcho's Book Reviews

Award-winning, exceptional, don't miss it.	★ ★ ★ ★
Worth the time. Enjoyable.	★ ★ ★
Average. Okay. Read it if you have the time.	★ ★
Dull. Not worth your time.	★

Maribeth and Lynne decided to collaborate to draft a review for *The Mysteries of Harris Burdick* by Chris Van Allsburg. The students were already familiar with this author since Maribeth had read *The Widow's Broom* around Halloween and returned to this author before the winter holiday to share *The Polar Express*. Lynne and Maribeth thought the second graders might return to this book to write a story that would accompany one of the striking illustrations, so they took the opportunity to introduce the book by writing an opinion piece. As they composed orally, Lynne recorded their thinking on chart paper:

If you love to draw or if you choose a mystery when you visit the library, you will enjoy The Mysteries of Harris Burdick. *At first glance, the picture book may appear to be simple. However, you will find that the black-and-white pictures challenge you to use your imagination! What would happen if you tried to skip stones across the lake, and the third time it came back to you? A story idea such as this can be found in Van Allsburg's strange and wonderful book.*

A title for each piece of artwork is followed by a sentence that could be used to write an original story. Do you like to write? The pictures and story starters will keep you busy all summer long. You'll never be bored and will entertain family and friends with your fantastical narratives. Even published authors you know and love have tried their hand at writing a story for one of the pictures!

The students reread the book review aloud with their teachers in different pieces. Kaylee suggested that we should include information about the award Van Allsburg won for *The Polar Express*. Lynne and Maribeth stopped to talk about the Caldecott Medal and also to note that this author won it twice (also for *Jumanji*). The class agreed, and Max pointed out that the author's full name should follow the title in the first sentence. Logan agreed. "If you say the title and the author more than one time, it will stick and kids will remember it." Jake thought the book would appeal to kids who like to draw. Lynne and Maribeth encouraged the students to notice things that made the review easy to read. John commented, "You know how to read it because there are periods and questions and exclamations. Will thought it needed a closing sentence. He suggested, "Check it out in your school library!" Aidan noticed that the review had two paragraphs. "It makes it easier to write a book review—first for content and again for a grammar read." Together, they made a list of things to remember when developing a story line and grammar and conventions to watch out for:

Book Review: Developing Content
- Talk about who would like to read this book.
- Include the title and author at the beginning and again somewhere else.
- Give a specific example of what you liked.
- Tell the readers if the book is fiction or nonfiction.
- Include any important features like photos and captions.
- Include a star rating using the rating system and the reviewer's name.

Book Review: Paying Attention to Grammar and Conventions
- Use capitals to begin sentences.
- Correct capitals in words that don't need them.
- Indent to begin a new paragraph about a new idea.
- Capitalize the first word, the last word, and all important words in between to write the title.
- Capitalize the author's first and last name.

- Use variation in print (ex. BIG) to say a word with emphasis.
- Do not use apostrophes when you only mean "more than one."

Maribeth and Lynne added this last rule because the students had spent some time studying contractions as well as the possessive use of the apostrophe since they were using these various forms in their everyday writing. Shortly after several lessons involving modeling, guided practice, and independent practice, the second graders began using apostrophes everywhere, especially in sentences with plural nouns or even words using the singular form of the verb (My brother *plays* guitar). Maribeth copied the lists so the students could paste them into their writer's notebooks for easy reference.

The students spent a week choosing a favorite book from their home library, school library, or classroom library. They sat with several different partners and orally shared their thoughts about the book they chose to review. The second graders were very honest and did not always rate a book with four stars or even three stars. The reviews included in this chapter are the final drafts.

In Aidan's review (Figure 10.9), you will notice the specificity of content, the neat handwriting with proper spacing between letters and words, the capitalization of proper nouns, and use of transition phrases such as "For example, . . ." Lynne praised the correct use of the apostrophe for *it is*, the caret to include an omitted word (*big*) in that same sentence, and loved his vocabulary—words like *challenge, family members, choices, especially,* and *characters*. His last sentence offered a satisfying close. They talked about including the name of the title or author in a different spot, finding variations of *I liked* to begin sentences, and possibly omitting *I think* to strengthen the opening sentence.

Ryan's piece (Figure 10.10) was interesting because he chose to review a nonfiction book. Ryan readily admitted that he was drawn to any book about sharks and loved reading books about animals in general. He included that thought at the end of his review because he felt it would be important information for him if he

Figure 10.9
Aidan's review of *Those Shoes* by Maribeth Boelts

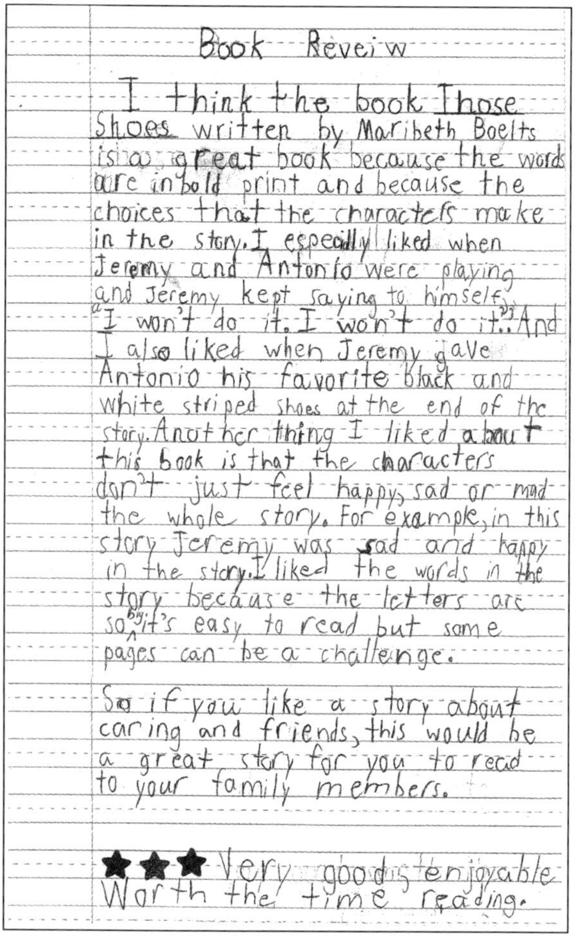

Figure 10.10
Ryan's review of *Sharks* by Seymour Simon

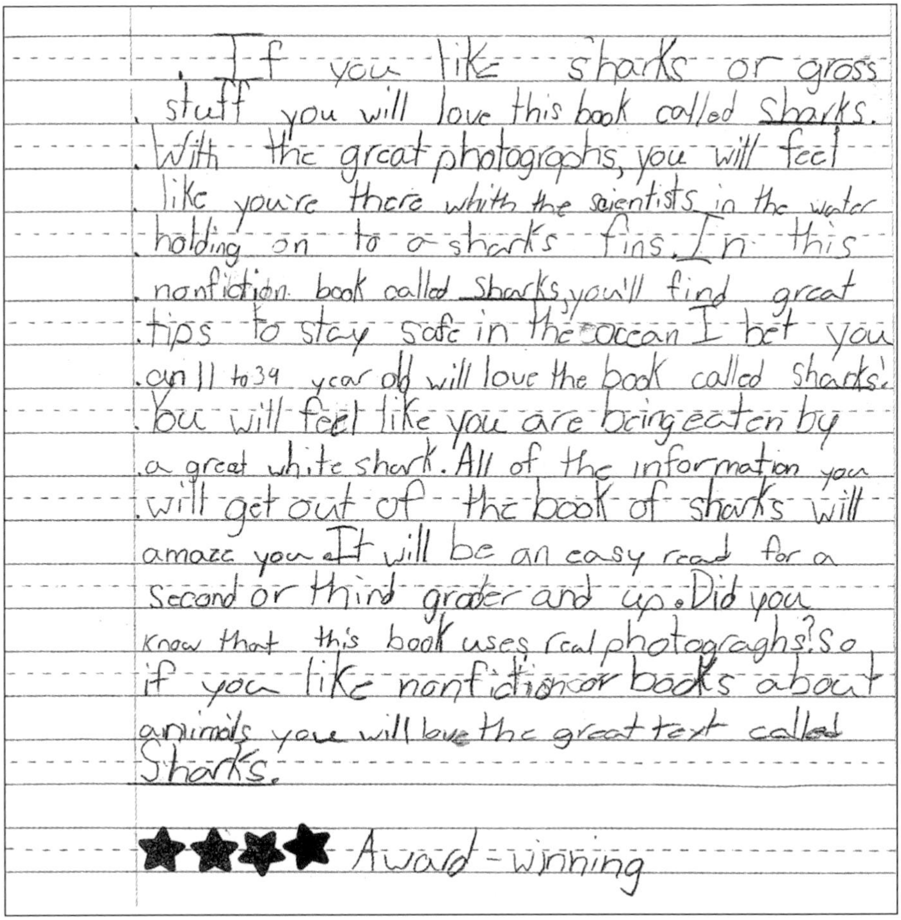

> If you like sharks or gross stuff you will love this book called Sharks. With the great photographs, you will feel like you're there whith the scientists in the water holding on to a sharks fins. In this nonfiction book called Sharks, you'll find great tips to stay safe in the ocean I bet you all 11 to 34 year old will love the book called Sharks. You will feel like you are being eaten by a great white shark. All of the information you will get out of the book of sharks will amaze you. It will be an easy read for a second or third grader and up. Did you know that this book uses real photograaghs? So if you like nonfiction or books about animals you will love the great text called Sharks.
>
> ★★★★ Award-winning

decided to read a book based on a review. Ryan mentioned the title twice, called attention to the incredible photographs, and talked about the target audience in other ways—age level (*11 to 34*) and level of difficulty (*It will be an easy read for a second or third grader and up.*). His praise: Lynne and Maribeth loved his enthusiasm. His polish: he forgot to include the author's name!

Will's piece (Figure 10.11) is short and sweet. He calls attention to the humor and the illustrations. Will shows us he has read the "About the Author" section and includes information about Kinney as a game developer. Even though he really enjoyed this book he offered this thought to the class after he shared his review: "I think a lot of kids would like it, but the book is not as good as some other books my teacher has read aloud to us." He rated this book accordingly with three stars. Lynne and Will talked about the meaning of "the dog days of summer" and why Kinney probably chose *Dog Days* as his title. Lynne praised his question lead, his attention to a target

Figure 10.11
Will's review of *Dog Days* by Jeff Kinney

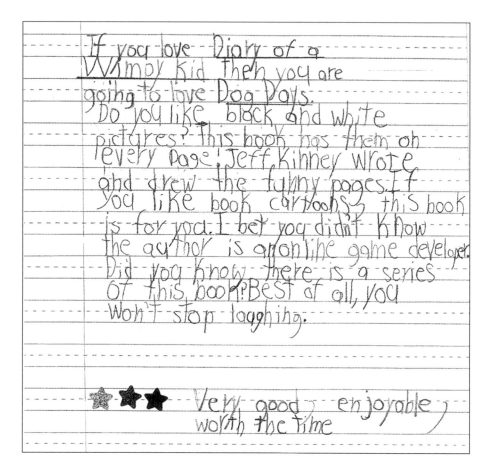

audience (*If you like book cartoons*), and his transitional phrase to close (*Best of all*). She noticed that Will knew how to use apostrophes correctly in contractions such as "won't" and "didn't." They looked at the spacing between sentences and agreed more space was needed. Additionally, Lynne called attention to letter formation for lowercase *k* and sometimes *n, y,* and *p*.

Clearly, these kindergarten, first-grade, and second-grade students addressed the Common Core State Standards by stating their opinion and providing a reason(s) to support their opinion and a concluding sentence. The second graders used transitional words and phrases such as *for example, best of all, I also liked, so if you liked,* and *did you know* to connect their opinion with reasons. As teachers, we must remember that children and adults learn to write by writing. The opportunities we provide for our students grow out of many different purposes with specific target audiences. Standards should not confine us or narrow the possibilities we offer our children. They are a measure that we can use to help us interpret the ongoing needs and progress of the students in our classrooms.

Chapter 11

Opinion Writing
in the Upper Grades

Writing an opinion is different from writing a persuasive piece. In persuasion (as in advertisement) the writer seeks to appeal to the reader through connecting to the reader's interests or emotions. In opinion or argument, though, the writer seeks to convince an audience based on evidence and facts. Aristotle divided the means of persuasion into three categories: ethos, pathos, and logos. *Ethos* (ethical appeal) means persuasion by means of trust. We tend to believe people for whom we have respect. *Pathos* means persuading by means of appeal to emotions. *Logos* means persuasion by the use of reason. Argument/opinion relies mainly on logos. Because Diane wanted to help students distinguish between persuasion and opinion in order for them to write clear opinion pieces, she began by introducing Aristotle's terms to the class. Then she read Karen Kaufman Orloff's *I Wanna Iguana*, an example of persuasion, in which Alex and his mother exchange letters about the possibility of Alex's keeping his friend's baby iguana when his friend moves. Diane read the book to the class and asked them to consider the reasons Alex gives for getting the iguana as a pet. They listed:

> "If I don't take it, he goes to Stinky and Stinky's dog, Lurch, will eat it. You don't want that to happen, do you?" (pathos)
> "Iguanas are really quiet and they're cute too. I think they are much cuter than hamsters." ("quiet" = logos; "cute" = pathos)
> "I'll keep his cage in my room. You'll never even know he's there." (logos)
> "It takes 15 years for an iguana to get that big." (six feet) (logos)
> "I need a new friend now. Your lonely child, Alex" (pathos)
> "I could teach it tricks and things." (it would be fun) (pathos)
> "Your son who has learned his lesson." (ethos)
> "I'll pay for the lettuce with my allowance." (logos)

After the class had explored how authors of persuasion use these techniques, Diane shared multiple pieces of opinion writing with the class, including picture books, op-ed writing from the local newspaper, articles from *Time for Kids*, and book reviews. She asked students to consider how the authors of these pieces used logos to advance their arguments.

Teaching Point: Immersion in many pieces of writing in a particular genre gives students the opportunity to intuit the features of that genre. We suggest keeping a place to organize samples of writing in each genre. Diane keeps three crates handy: one for narrative samples, one for informational samples, and one for opinion samples. As she's reading she will cut out suitable pieces or note picture book titles on index cards and drop them in the appropriate crate. When it's time to begin that unit of study, a quick perusal of the samples in the crate will yield multiple examples for student use.

Students read and discussed the articles and listed the logical reasons given. Afterward, Diane asked students to list the characteristics of argumentative (opinion) writing. Here is their list:

States specific facts as reasons
Gives evidence for opinions
Does not ask the reader to change his or her mind
Researches facts and tells where they came from
Does not always give a "counterargument"
States the opinion clearly (just puts it out there)
Clarifies which statements are fact and which are opinion

Diane accepted this list as a beginning for this fifth-grade class. Since these students had been accustomed to writing persuasive pieces, she wanted to be sure they understood what they would be writing, while having persuasive elements, differed in some ways. For one thing, the goal of persuasive writing is to get the reader to agree with the writer's point of view. The goal of opinion writing is to get the reader to acknowledge that the writer's side is valid. Also, persuasive writing relies on both facts and emotion, while opinion writing relies mainly on the presentation of relevant facts and evidence. In addition, the audience for persuasive writing tends to be specific—a particular person or group of people—while the audience for opinion writing may be more general. When students consider ideas for writing persuasive pieces, they consider hot-button issues, while in opinion writing they may choose to write about issues of interest to them that may or may not lend themselves to persuasion. It wouldn't take much convincing nowadays, for instance, to persuade most people that wearing seat belts as a passenger in a car is an important safety issue. However, one may choose to write an opinion paper about the benefits of safety belts in school buses. The goal of the piece may not be to change the reader's mind but to provide information that proves the validity of the point of view that providing seat belts in school buses is a worthy goal.

The class brainstormed ideas for topics about which they and others their age might have strong opinions. These included such things as favorite time of year/best holiday, favorite sports to play, best video game, why I need a (new) pet, going to a new (different) vacation spot, best book I ever read, best subject in school (why I like…), why recess is important, why the (beach, mountains, city) is a perfect vacation spot, why it's important for kids to have chores, why kids should get an allowance, and why it's important to know a language other than English. The class seemed most interested in the issue of recess, since their recess time in fifth grade is shortened on a regular basis. Diane suggested that the class write an opinion piece about why recess is important. First, they listed reasons why recess is important:

Recess gives us a chance to let off steam.
Recess is a chance to be with our friends outside of class.
Recess is good exercise.
Recess gets us out in the fresh air.
Recess is freedom from the classroom.
Recess gets us moving.
Recess monitors need their jobs.
Recess is a good chance to make new friends.
Recess lets us see kids who are not in our class.
Recess is the only time in school when we decide what we want to do
for ourselves.

With this list on the board, Diane asked students to limit their reasons to the three most important. They decided on the following: Recess is a break from the classroom, it's good exercise, and it provides jobs for monitors.

Teaching Point: Diane limited the reasons to three, since that number lends itself to the standard five-paragraph piece. While not all pieces of writing have to be five paragraphs, the structure is useful in teaching expository writing and, in particular, opinion pieces. Students not only need to express reasons in their pieces, they also need to prioritize those reasons and to introduce their opinions with a "hook" that will draw the reader. They also need to provide a conclusion that will stick with readers, giving them something to think about. Each of these structural components becomes a paragraph: an introduction to list the reasons, first reason, second reason, third reason, and conclusion. Children can follow this pattern to write successful opinion pieces. Later, as they become more experienced writers, they can experiment with different numbers of paragraphs.

Diane reminded students about leads. What hook could they use to draw the reader in to reading their opinion piece? Emir thought that it would be a good idea to quote an expert who was on their side. Diane asked the class to think of an authority or an expert who might agree with them that recess is important. They mentioned their teachers, especially their physical education teacher, because teachers know that students need to be active; their parents, because parents want their children to be healthy and exercise more; and Michelle Obama, because of the posters they've seen in their cafeteria promoting her *Let's Move!* initiative and healthy eating. The class decided to use Mrs. Obama as the authority to begin their piece. This is what students, Diane, and their teacher, Mrs. Dutton, wrote together:

First Lady Michelle Obama speaks out for healthy living for all children. Her Let's Move! initiative calls for exercise and nutritious food in schools. Yet, some elementary schools are considering eliminating recess. We, Mrs. Dutton's fifth-grade class at James Buchanan School, believe that this is a terrible idea.

    The most important reason to keep recess is that exercise is good for the brain as well as the body. Getting outside to play wakes us up and prepares us for more school work. Besides sunshine us a source of vitamin D, essential for strong bones.

    Another reason for keeping recess is that recess gives students a "jump start." After working hard all morning, getting out for recess energizes us and prepares us for a long afternoon. Without recess we would be sleepy or fidgety. Neither would be good for learning.

    Also eliminating recess will eliminate jobs for monitors. In this economy we don't want anyone to lose their jobs.

    For all of these reasons we believe that recess is important for the kids, the teachers, and the monitors. We believe that recess should not be eliminated.

Diane asked the students to look at what they wrote and to turn and talk with each other about what they thought was the strongest reason and why it was the strongest reason. Responses were all over the place, as Diane suspected they would be since there was little support for any of the reasons listed. Mrs. Dutton suggested that what was missing from their opinion were authoritative voices. The piece the class wrote is what they think, but what would make readers believe that theirs was a valid opinion? The class took another look at the opinion/argument samples they read earlier in the week. They saw that all these pieces used examples, reasons, facts, anecdotes, proof, and/or specific information. The class agreed that their five paragraphs needed more supporting details. With help from their teachers, the students also agreed to change their final reason from the need for monitors to keep their jobs to the needs of students to socialize with their friends, since the latter reason is more likely to apply to students in any school district.

    Since students did not have access to the Internet, Diane brought in a sample of informational articles from various sources, including the Council on Physical Education for Children, the *New York Times*, and the National Association of Early Childhood Specialists in State Departments of Education as well as specific web resources like educationworld.com and pediatrics.aapublications.org. Students were grouped into three sections and instructed to read the articles, highlighting support for any of the following three reasons: recess as good exercise and to promote overall health, recess to promote increased concentration in class, or recess as a way for children to learn to problem-solve with their friends. Each group highlighted specific details that supported their reason for keeping recess. Diane placed these on the document imager and provided a reminder lesson on summarizing. As an example, students read a blog entry by Ali Kelley from February 28, 2013, titled "New Program Will Help Bring Physical Activity Back to Schools" and posted in the U.S. government's Let's Move! blog. They highlighted the following portion:

> According to the Physical Activity Guidelines for Americans, children and adolescents need at least 60 minutes of moderate to vigorous physical activity each day to stay healthy. Physical activity enhances important skills, like concentration and problem solving, which have been shown to improve academic performance. However, kids today are the most sedentary generation in America's history. Only 1 in 3 children is active on a daily basis and only 4 percent of elementary schools, 8 percent of middle schools and 2 percent of high schools currently offer daily P.E. Meanwhile, only 9 states require recess in elementary schools.

Diane posted the highlighted portion on the imager and with the class paraphrased the information that could be uses as support for their opinion that recess helps maintain good physical health.

On February 28, 2013, Ali Kelley posted on the Let's Move blog that Physical Activity Guidelines for Americans state that children need at least sixty minutes of physical activity every day to stay healthy. Unfortunately in that same posting, we see that only one in three children today is active every day. Surprisingly, just nine states require recess and only 4% of elementary schools have daily PE classes.

Practicing as a class with a shared writing experience is an efficient way to teach summarizing. It is important for students to learn to paraphrase and to learn to use direct quotations sparingly. It may take multiple lessons to get students comfortable enough to use their own words to summarize what they are reading. Remember, too, that summarizing is a good study skill as well as an important writing skill. Teaching summarizing is a true two-for-one learning experience.

Teaching Point: Many student writers of all ages simply copy what they are reading word for word if it supports their opinion or argument. Sometimes students will use quotation marks to indicate that these are not their own words, and sometimes they won't. As teachers we need to instruct students about when and how to summarize and when and how to use direct citations. Even though the unit Diane taught had as its primary focus writing opinion pieces, it was necessary to include writing summaries as well. Summary writing follows these steps: (1) Read the material to get the gist. (2) Reread to highlight main idea(s). (3) Write one sentence explaining each main idea in paraphrase. (4) Use examples from the article that reinforce the main idea(s). (5) Write a draft of the summary using your own words.

Since this fifth-grade class had already written summaries in previous units of study, Diane's task was to remind them of what they had already practiced. After several shared summary-writing practices, each group of students presented their supporting details to the class, writing those details on the whiteboard. With these added pieces of information, the class revised their previous shared writing as follows:

Recess . . . It's Important

First Lady Michelle Obama speaks out for healthy living for all children. Her Let's Move! initiative calls for exercise and nutritious food in schools. Yet, some elementary schools are considering eliminating recess. We, Mrs. Dutton's fifth-grade class at James Buchanan School, believe that this is a terrible idea. Children need recess for exercise, to "jump start" their brains, and to interact with friends. All of these benefits of recess not only help students, they help their teachers too.

The most important reason to keep recess is that exercise is good for the body. On February 28, 2013, Ali Kelley posted on the Let's Move! blog that <u>Physical Activity Guidelines for Americans</u> state that children need at least sixty minutes of physical activity every day to stay healthy. Unfortunately in that same posting, we see that only one in three children today is active every day. Surprisingly, just nine states require recess and only 4% of elementary schools have daily P.E. classes. In a May 2006 position paper, The Council on Physical Education for Children writes that lack of exercise may lead to health problems like diabetes, obesity, and other serious conditions. Daily recess can be an important source of exercise and may prevent such problems.

Recess and exercise is also good for the brain. Getting outside to play wakes kids up and prepares them for more school work. Time magazine reported on December 31, 2012 that when children sit for hours at their desks, they become fidgety and jumpy and get off task. Recess gives children's brains a "jump start." Students of all ages need a break from school work, and they return to the classroom better prepared for their school subjects.

One more reason for keeping recess is that it gives students the chance to get together with their friends. Children need to learn to solve their own problems without parents' or teachers' involvement. This can happen only at recess, not in the classroom. In fact, recess is a chance for children to make friends. Friendship is important for everyone. Without recess, spending time with friends in school can happen only at lunch time, which is a very short period.

For these reasons we believe that recess should not be eliminated. Children need exercise, they need time to "jump start" their brains, and they need a chance to build friendships. As Arne Duncan, Secretary of Education, said, "We need more of our schools creating environments that promote physical activity and play and encourage our students to get moving." We agree with Mr. Duncan.

This shared writing provided the opportunity to embed several lessons on conventions. First and foremost, it is a lesson on transitional words. As the students suggested content, Diane pointed out the need for transitions within and between paragraphs. For example, use of phrases such as *in fact, for instance, for example,* and *to illustrate* help readers recognize when the writer is clarifying a previously stated fact or idea. Transitions like *yet, however, nevertheless, on the other hand,* and *still* show contrast. As students composed the shared writing, Diane steered them toward using effective transitions. She also pointed out the use of the apostrophe in paragraph four—*parents'* and *teachers'*—asking why the apostrophe comes after the -*s* instead of before the -*s* (see the Your Turn Lesson "The Apostrophe to Show Possession" following Part 1).

Students were now ready to begin to write their own opinion pieces. They brainstormed topics that they were enthusiastic about. Diane and Mrs. Dutton conferred with students, helping them to limit their topics. For instance, video games was on many lists, but neither "video games" nor "why I like video games" is a viable topic for an opinion piece! Students love their video games. When they write about them, they get more wrapped up in the minutiae of how to play the game than the reasons that support why children should be allowed to play video games. However, "Why Madden NFL 25 is more fun to play than Madden NFL 11" narrows the topic nicely. Help students generate lists of possible topics and then share those lists in whole group. Sharing lists allows students who "can't think of anything" to borrow a topic from someone else's list. If each student takes a turn sharing one item at a time, every student has an opportunity to participate and borrow.

Teaching Point: For instruction in grammar and conventions to be effective, students have to be given many chances to produce their own written work. Helping them select and narrow a topic they are passionate about may take some writing workshop time. However, it is time well spent. Allow students to explore their selected topics and give them the option to abandon a piece that is not working for them. While conferring with students, keep a record of the errors in grammar and conventions they are making while drafting, not for the purpose of correcting errors during the drafting stage, but to help plan grammar and convention lessons. Often the errors students make while drafting transfer to their revisions as well.

After students had selected and narrowed a topic, they partnered with another student to tell what they knew about their topic, to discuss where they thought they would find supporting information, and to rehearse what they thought they would write. Their partners were to listen actively, suggesting possible resources and restating their partner's opinion. Each student received feedback from at least one other student. Once students had an opportunity to talk to one another about their intended opinion pieces, they began to draft. As Diane circulated among the writers, she listed their topics to facilitate finding authoritative sources. Once the drafts were completed and students found support for their opinions, they revised, including supporting details.

In conferring with students in the editing stages of their pieces, Diane noticed that the following lessons were necessary for the class: rules for citing evidence, including direct quotations; when to begin a new paragraph, including transitions; and subject-verb agreement.

Diane presented students with a scaffold for taking notes and summarizing their findings. The scaffold proved helpful for students as they took notes and for Diane when she presented the lesson on citations that follows. Students found support for their opinion/arguments and summarized those findings. Inserting that support proved to be a problem for the class. Even though the class had practiced a shared writing about the importance of recess, which remained on display in the classroom, one practice did not suffice, of course. Here is a paragraph from Jordan's first draft of a piece about why baseball is a great sport for kids.

My team is like family. We work together to defeat opponents. In Livestrong.com it says that teamwork is important in baseball. You are always moving on the diamond, if the ball is hit to right field and you play second base, you want to move toward right field to be the cut-off man. You want to try to keep the ball from getting to 2nd base.

Here's a paragraph from Mackenzie, whose topic is that summer is the best season of the year.

Another reason I believe summer is the best season is because I love to go camping. It doesn't matter if I am in a tent or an RV. Either way I get to be outdoors. That's good for health and fitness because I can hike or swim. USA Today says that's great for getting strong muscles and bones.

Many students in the class presented their citations by simply stating the source as Jordan and Mackenzie did. A lesson was needed to demonstrate how to insert citations with full information. Fortunately, students could refer to their scaffolds to find what they needed. Jordan was able to go back to his notes and include the date of the Livestrong post. He revised his paragraph by beginning with the Livestrong citation:

In July 29, 2011 article Livestrong.com said that teamwork is important to building a good baseball team. That is true for me because my team is like family. We work together to defeat opponents. For example, if the ball is hit to right field and you play second base, you want to move toward right field to be the cut-off man. You want to try to keep the ball from getting to second base. If the runner gets to third base, there's a 50/50 chance that they score on the next hit. You don't want to let your team down.

Mackenzie, too, was able to add the June 2009 date to her citation.

Another reason I believe summer is the best season is because I love to go camping. It doesn't matter if I am in a tent or an RV. Either way I get to be outdoors. That's good for health and fitness because I can hike or swim. A June 2009 article in *USA Today* states that summer exercise, like hiking and swimming, builds strong muscles and bones. At least it's better than sitting in front of television all day.

Diane explained that it's important to include these dates (as well as title and author if one is mentioned) not only for veracity, but so that readers can find these sources for themselves if they want more information. (Note: Neither citation example is complete. Subsequent lessons with this fifth-grade class were needed. Often, collaboration with the school librarian helps to reinforce correct citation skills with elementary and middle school students.) As students progress through the grades, they will be required to write longer and more detailed research reports. Giving them experience in summarizing, note-taking, and showing citations accurately in the early grades will serve them well as they begin to tackle these tasks.

Because opinion writing relies on presenting reasons and support for those reasons, teaching paragraphing is an easier task than it might be for other types of writing (see the Your Turn Lesson "When to Make a New Paragraph in a Narrative" following Part 1). Diane asked students to limit their reasons to three. After the introduction or hook, each of the body paragraphs explained one reason. The conclusion paragraph ended the piece. What Diane focused on in these lessons was the need for transitions between and within paragraphs. She referred to the shared writing and, with students' help, circled transition words as they pointed them out. Together the class defined the uses of these transitions: to repeat, to clarify, to show contrast, and so on (see the Teaching Point that follows). As students revised their pieces, Diane asked them to circle their transitions. If transitions were absent or rare, students were instructed to add them where needed.

Teaching Point: Encourage students to notice transitions in their reading. Keep an anchor chart of transitions and their uses. You can set up the categories: transitions that repeat an idea; transitions that illustrate or clarify; transitions that show contrast or change; transitions that show time order; transitions that restate an idea; transitions that add to what has already been stated; transitions that show cause and effect; and transitions that are good for endings. Ask students to add to the anchor chart when they meet these transitions in their reading and to use the words on the anchor chart in their own written pieces.

Because opinion writing frequently includes more than one reason or more than one point of view, students often make mistakes with subject-verb agreement. One of the reasons for this difficulty is the consequence of students' writing longer sentences. Often in these sentences, the subject and verb may be interrupted by an intervening phrase, leading to errors in subject-verb agreement. Students may write *Eating fatty or junk food when I'm playing games make me gain weight.* The subject of the sentence is not *games* but *eating.* Therefore, the verb should be *makes,* not *make.* With student permission, Diane duplicated sentences her student writers had constructed. She led the class in deconstructing the sentences for subject-verb agreement. Then, students went back to their pieces to edit for correctness of subject-verb agreement. (See the Your Turn Lesson "Subject-Verb Agreement" following Part 3.)

Students changed the following sentences:

The smell of freshly cut grass, the bright white chalk lines, and the morning sun rising over the horizon warming my legs welcome me to my softball heaven. (Alexis changed *welcomes* to *welcome*)

There are no school related responsibilities. (Mackenzie changed *is* to *are*)

Playing softball because of all the complicated plays makes you feel healthy. (Elle changed *make* to *makes*)

Hot stuffy classrooms even with the best teacher in charge are not the best places to learn. (Jordon changed *is* to *are*)

Dedicated coaches who know baseball and love the game make going to practice fun. (Jared changed *makes* to *make*)

Other topics for opinion writing can come from book and/or movie reviews, travel brochures, restaurant reviews, favorite school subjects, and even favorite video games. Students have strong opinions and usually are eager to express them! Our job is to help them express themselves clearly and concisely. Grammar and conventions lessons for this unit, in addition to the ones already discussed in this section, can include capitalization rules for titles, the formation and spelling of regular and irregular plural nouns, proper forms of helping verbs and linking verbs (*to be*), as well as pronoun-antecedent agreement (in grades three and up).

Adding Appositives to Paint Pictures and Combine Ideas

There are many ways authors add details to describe characters, objects, settings, and events. An appositive is a noun or noun phrase that renames another noun right beside it. The appositive can be a short or long combination of words.

Hook: Choose some of the mentor texts you have been using in the classroom and examine sentences containing appositives closely with the students. Look for books that your grade-level students would be familiar with and use as mentor texts.

- "Igor Stravinsky had a hat, a tattered, battered green beret." From *Do You Have a Hat?* by Eileen Spinelli
- "I was sitting on the front porch and I saw a strange car, a big white one, come down the road and turn left at the T, head down to the building site, and park." From *Ida B and Her Plans to Maximize Fun, Avoid Disaster, and (Possibly) Save the World* by Katherine Hannigan
- "I took the pearls out of my pocket, the three milky spheres the Nereid had given me in Santa Monica." From *The Lightning Thief* by Rick Riordan
- "But behind him, on a much higher seat in the middle of the sledge sat a very different person—a great lady, taller than any woman that Edmund had ever seen." From *The Lion, the Witch, and the Wardrobe* by C. S. Lewis

Purpose: *As we have been discussing, there are many ways to build content in any type of writing. The appositive is one effective way to do this. Appositives not only give you a chance to include some details to help your readers get a clear mind picture from your words but also create some sentence variety in your writing as well. The appositive or appositive phrase always sits next to another noun to rename it or to describe it in another way. The word itself comes from the Latin for "to put near."*

Brainstorm: In this case, brainstorming is closely tied to the use of literature in the hook. As students examine books and discover different ways appositives can be added to a sentence (at the beginning, as an interrupter, and at the end), they are actually engaging in a type of brainstorming using an inquiry approach. Students can work with partners to find more examples and copy them into their notebooks or post them on a class anchor chart.

Model: Either read a previous notebook entry of your own or compose a new entry in front of the students. Perhaps begin with a literature model such as this one from J. K. Rowling's *Harry Potter and the Sorcerer's Stone*: "Filch owned a cat called Mrs. Norris, a scrawny, dust-colored creature with bulging, lamp-like eyes just like Filch's."

As you write in front of your students, let them know that although the appositive most often appears as an interruption in the middle of a sentence, an appositive phrase can also be found at the beginning or at the end of a sentence as well.

From Lynne's notebook:

Dorothy's shoes, ruby-red and glittering like fiery stars, would take her home.
Ruby-red and glittering like fiery stars, Dorothy's shoes would take her home.

Important to tell your students: Appositives can be omitted from the sentence and the sentence can stand alone without the appositive phrase. Appositive phrases can help students combine thoughts into one sentence to avoid writing too many short, choppy sentences in one passage or piece of writing.

Guided Writing: Ask students to return to a previous notebook entry or piece of writing. Ask them to consider how they could add appositives to paint pictures with words or to combine two or three short sentences into a longer one. Invite some students to offer their pieces for group revision, or hold a guided conversation in front of the group. Maggie, a second grader, had written a short description of her stuffed animals. With a little more questioning and some help from the class, her sentences were revised to include appositives as follows:

The first one I got was Zebow, a zebra with thin stripes and soft fur. I named my second stuffed animal, a brown bear with big feet, Cinnamon.

Lynne guided the students to realize that appositives are easy to add to a piece of writing. The students noted the use of the comma (or commas) when the phrase interrupted the sentence midstream. She circulated around the room with the classroom teacher as students tried to add an appositive to a notebook entry or to the piece of writing they were currently drafting.

Independent Writing: Ask students to continue revisions of previous pieces by adding an appositive or appositive phrase. Students may also wish to start new pieces and concentrate on using appositive phrases possibly to start or end a sentence.

Reflection: After students have the opportunity to revise or write, ask them to share in whole group or small group. The following questions can help guide their thinking.

How did your use of appositives change your piece?

How is it satisfying for your reader?

Does the appositive you wrote improve the story (opinion piece, report, etc.)?

Would a different appositive or appositive phrase be better?

What kinds of things should you think about as you write appositives to add to your piece?

Your Turn Lesson

The Movable Adverb

Many upper elementary and middle school writers often place adverbs (when they use them) at the end of their sentences. These writers are still tied to basic sentence patterns. For third and fourth graders, the *-ly* adverb presents an opportunity to teach students how to vary their sentence patterns by recognizing three different positions for adverbs within a sentence.

Hook: Read *Suddenly Alligator: An Adverbial Tale* by Rick Walton. Ask students to listen for words that end in *-ly*.

Purpose: *Writers, today I'm going to show you how you can use adverbs to create sentence variety. Remember that many adverbs answer the question "how" and end in -ly. Today we are going to concentrate on these kinds of adverbs because they can be moved to different locations in your sentences and still the sentences will make sense.*

Brainstorm: Individually generate a list of verbs that show action in the past tense: *climbed, hopped, swam, flew, gobbled, closed, opened, danced, rode, drove, jumped, strolled, jogged, trotted, sauntered, baked, sang,* and *wrote* are a few. Have students turn and talk in small group and add to their lists. Ask for examples of strong verbs and create a two-column anchor chart labeled: Verbs/Adverbs.

Model: Reread *Suddenly Alligator: An Adverbial Tale* by Rick Walton and ask students to use their notebooks to stop and jot the adverbs they hear as you read. Make a list of these adverbs and ask students what they noticed about where they were placed in the sentence. Choose several sentences from the mentor text and model for students how you can move the adverb to different locations. For example:

> "I picked them up and slipped them into my left pocket easily." (From the original text)
> Easily I picked them up and slipped them into my left pocket.
> I picked them up and easily slipped them into my left pocket.

> "The alligator smiled at me hungrily." (From the original text)
> Hungrily the alligator smiled at me.
> The alligator smiled hungrily at me.

Guided Practice: Continue to use the mentor text to find other sentences. Have students work in pairs to move the adverb to two different locations and share their sentences. Ask students to return to their writer's notebooks to find where they used an *-ly* adverb or could add an *-ly* adverb. Experiment with the sentence by moving the adverb to different locations. Each time read the sentence before and after the adverb sentence and evaluate the placement of the adverb. Discuss which version works best and why. Share your thoughts in whole-group discussion.

Independent Practice: Ask students to return to a piece of writing they are currently working on and find a few places where an *-ly* adverb could be used. Try to use the adverbs in three different locations to change your sentence patterns slightly.

Reflection: Ask students to share some of their revisions using the *-ly* adverbs. Ask them to reflect on these questions:

> *What do you now know about -ly adverbs?*
> *How did changing the placement of the adverb affect the flow of your paragraph?*
> *When can you envision using movable adverbs again?*

Expanding a Sentence Using Complex Elements

Many sixth-grade writers get stuck in the practice of writing fairly simple sentences even though they may be presenting sophisticated ideas. Their sentences follow a noun-verb–direct object– or noun-verb–indirect object direct object pattern. Often, they fear a longer sentence because it could be a run-on. While we do not want our students to fill their texts with unwieldy sentences, we do want them to vary the length and complexity of their sentences for stylistic purposes and interest for the reader.

Hook: Read *If You Were a Conjunction* by Nancy Loewen to the class. This book asks students to notice the big, colorful words on each page (so they can easily identify them). Although they may easily recognize the coordinating conjunctions, they may not be aware of the subordinating conjunctions (or at least, not be using them in their writing).

Purpose: *Writers, today I'm going to show you how you can use subordinating conjunctions to create interesting sentences and vary your sentence length and structure.*

Brainstorm: Individually generate a list of conjunctions you regularly use. You may want to search through your writer's notebooks or writing folder/portfolio to help jog your memory. Copy a few sentences that use a subordinating conjunction to share later.

Model: Choose several sentences from a mentor text such as *Shoeshine Girl* by Clyde Robert Bulla. Discuss how the use of compound, compound-complex, and complex sentences creates a rhythm and interest in the subject. For example, *Shoeshine Girl* by Clyde Robert Bulla uses three sentence patterns in the opening paragraph:

> "The train stopped at Palmville, and Sarah Ida had a sudden thought." (Talk about how the author created a faster pace by combining these thoughts.)
> "Maybe she could find a place where everything was new and she could start all over again." (This sentence uses a coordinating conjunction "and" and a subordinating conjunction "where." This allows the author to give necessary information with the fewest number of words. Economy of expression is important for quality writing.)

"While Aunt Claudia paid the driver, Sarah Ida looked at the house."
(This complex sentence allows the writer to communicate two different things occurring simultaneously.)

Guided Practice: With a partner, use picture books such as *The Girl on the High-Diving Horse* by Linda Oatman High and their independent reading books to find other sentences with complex and/or compound-complex elements. Have students work in pairs to discuss these sentences and how they work to tell the story. Share in whole group and record the most interesting sentences on an anchor chart with the students' explanations.

Independent Practice: Ask students to return to a piece of writing they are currently working on or to their writing folder/portfolio to find a few places where they can combine sentences or parts of sentences to create complex or compound-complex elements.

Reflection: Ask students to share some of their revisions using complex or compound-complex elements. Ask them to reflect on these questions:

What do you now know about conjunctions?
How did your revisions for complex or compound-complex elements change your writing?
Where could you do this kind of work again?

Subject-Verb Agreement

Subjects and verbs must have matching forms; that is, they must show *agreement*. If a subject is singular ("one student"), the verb must also be singular ("studies"). If a subject is plural ("all students"), the verb must be plural ("study"). Forms that match in this way are said to be in agreement. Common Core State Standards expects that students in the third grade will master this skill (CCSS.ELA-LITERACY.L.3.1.F).

Hook: Revisit the picture book *The Relatives Came* by Cynthia Rylant as a read-aloud to the class. Children enjoy this book for the narrative and should remember the story with pleasure. This book is a good one to use for the purpose of this lesson because it's obvious that "the relatives" are plentiful. This is a large family.

Purpose: *Writers, I'm noticing that sometimes when I'm reading a draft (or writing one myself) I have to think about whether the verb I'm reading or writing "goes with" the subject of the sentence it's in. If the subject of the sentence is one person or thing, it is called a singular subject; if it is more than one person or thing, it is called a plural subject. If the subject of the sentence is singular, the verb must be singular too. If the subject is plural, the verb must be plural. This is called subject-verb agreement. When we write sentences in which subjects and verbs agree, our readers can pay attention to what we are writing instead of being distracted by thinking that something doesn't "sound right."*

Brainstorm: Conduct a group brainstorming with the class. Ask them to list as many nouns as they can in one minute. Write these on the board or anchor chart as students share them aloud. Then, ask students to list as many pronouns as they can in one minute. Write these on the board as well. Ask students to decide which are singular (one) and which are plural (more than one). Separate the nouns and pronouns into two columns labeled *singular* and *plural*.

Model: Using the anchor chart of singular and plural nouns and pronouns compose several sentences, adding a verb and modifiers to the original noun or pronoun on the list. For example, use the singular noun *brother* to compose a sentence: *My brother is excited about being in the playoffs.* Compose about five sentences for the students in which the subject and verb agree in number. For older grades (fifth and sixth) compose sentences where the subject is followed by modifiers before the verb. These sentences make the choice of verb more difficult to decide. For example, *My brother with his excellent hockey* *skills is excited about being in the playoffs.* The prepositional phrase *with his excellent hockey skills* does not affect the choice of verb. The subject is still *brother*, which is a singular noun. Remind students that collective nouns like team, family, band, jury, for example, are usually considered singular.

Guided Practice: Ask students to work with a partner to compose sentences using singular and plural nouns. Challenge them to use interrupters between the subject and verb. Have students share their creations on sentence strips posted in the classroom.

Independent Practice: Instruct students to return to their writer's notebooks or current drafts to check their sentences for subject-verb agreement. Ask them to revise some of their sentences to add interrupters between the subject and predicate. Not only will this give them additional practice, it will add sentence variety to their written pieces.

Reflection: Ask students to reflect on the following questions:

What does it mean when subjects and verbs agree?
Look at some of your writing in your notebook or the piece you are currently drafting. How does subject-verb agreement help to make the meaning of a sentence clear?

Verb Tense Consistency

Though Common Core State Language Standards do not specify consistency in use of verb tense until grade five, as early as grade one students are expected to "use verbs to convey a sense of past, present and future," and in second grade, students should "form and use the past tense of frequently occurring irregular verbs," while subject-verb agreement is expected in grade three. Clearly, we teachers need to teach verbs and their functions in sentences. Even in first grade we can begin to point out that if a writer is using present tense, she should use present tense throughout the entire piece.

Hook: Read *How to Babysit a Grandpa* by Jean Reagan. This book not only is filled with active verbs but also serves as a hook for writing procedural expository text. Children love the idea that the babysitter in this story is the grandchild.

Purpose: *Writers, today we're going to talk about verb tense. Tense is another word for time. Things that happen right now are in the present tense; things that happened before now are in the past tense; and things that will happen later on are in the future tense. Remember, too, that sentences are groups of words with a subject and a predicate verb that make complete sense by themselves.*

Brainstorm: Tell students, "As I read a few of the pages of *How to Babysit a Grandpa*, list the verbs (the action words) that you recognize." If you have a document imager, show the students the pages as you read them. Read the pages with the lists "How to Stay Quiet" and "What to Do on a Walk," for example. List the verbs students recognize on an anchor chart.

> *wiggle*
> *giggle*
> *yell*
> *pretend*
> *act*
> *says*
> *pop*
> *shout*
> *grab*
> *cross*
> *remind*

       step
       look
       show

Mention that the lists are sentences in which the subject is "you under-stood," and tell them these are called imperative sentences.

Model: After listing the verbs on the anchor chart, ask students what tense (time) the verbs represent. These are all present tense verbs. Together with the class change the present tense verbs to past tense. All the verbs except *say* are regular verbs and form the past by adding *-ed* to the present form of the verb. If the word ends in a silent *-e*, drop it before adding *-ed*.

       wiggled
       giggled
       yelled
       pretended
       acted
       popped
       shouted
       grabbed
       reminded
       stepped
       looked
       showed
       "say" becomes "said"

Guided Practice: With the class, write several sentences explaining the procedure of saluting the flag, something that happens daily in school. It will look something like this:

Stand at attention by your desk. Face the flag. Place your hand over your heart. Recite the Pledge of Allegiance. Put your hands at your side. Sit at your desk. Listen to the morning announcements.

    Working in pairs or individually students will identify the verbs and the tense of the verbs.

Independent Practice: Ask students to return to their writer's notebooks or their current drafts to find the verbs in their sentences. Ask them to identify the tense of the verbs.

Ask them to change any verbs in their pieces that are not the same tense as the other verbs in that same piece. Students can share their verbs and why they changed or did not change them. This lesson may be repeated many times as needed. Once is rarely enough.

Reflection: Ask students to reflect on why verbs are important in any sentence. Ask them to explain why they changed verbs for tense in their writer's notebooks or draft.

> *Find an entry in your writer's notebook that describes a person, place, or event. First, check for verb tense consistency and then rewrite a paragraph or two in a different tense (for example, past to present or present to past). Read both entries aloud and talk with a partner about which tense is more powerful for this piece of writing. Explain why you think so.*

Part 4

Conversations About Grammar and Conventions

Chapter 12

Introduction to Grammar and Conventions Conversations

Teaching grammar isn't a discrete part of the day. It's something that often happens in reading and writing workshop in elementary classrooms and the English/language arts classrooms in middle schools. However, conversations about grammar and conventions can naturally occur across the day and across the curriculum.

Take reading nonfiction, for example. Often lists are introduced with a colon, which is an excellent opportunity to point that out. Appositives are used in nonfiction to add detail. Commas get messy for students, so it is a good idea to talk about their appropriate use in many places, including how they are used in science and social studies texts. Proper nouns abound, and rules for capitalization are important within a text and within a reference list. In order for any of the grammar and conventions rules to stick, they have to make sense to students. The best way for that to happen is to show them how "following the rules" makes meaning clear to the intended audience.

In reading fiction, the obvious conversations may involve the use of dialogue, consistent verb tense, sentence types, and the use of end punctuation such as the exclamation point and the question mark. Issues of style are important here and can include elements such as movable adverbs, adjective interrupters, and prepositional phrases.

Important to note is that these conversations about grammar and conventions do not supersede the conversations about the science or the history or the literature we are studying. Throughout the day, you can point out the grammar and conventions connections as they occur in the daily classroom activity or when they directly connect to what your students have been learning about in reading and writing workshop. In writing workshop, as you introduce and review the traits of writing—ideas, organization, word choice, voice, sentence fluency—issues of grammar, usage, and conventions are always there in the background. For example, as you're teaching sentence fluency, you will talk about compound and complex sentences and the marks of punctuation that accompany them. When you talk about word choice, that's the time to talk about strong verbs, specific nouns, or appropriate transition words and phrases.

We can certainly schedule conversations about grammar and conventions as a regular part of our reading/writing workshop as well. Instead of spending time with isolated workbook pages or daily edits correcting some imaginary writer's errors, we can look at what real authors are doing and what our own students are doing, shifting the focus to correctness whenever we can. Our job is to show our writers how the smaller focus lessons and the larger Your Turn Lessons connect with the things that professional writers do every day on the job as journalists, historians, scientists, speech writers, and authors of the picture books and novels our students are reading. We want to be sure that our students, through study, imitation, and reflection, understand that professional writers use grammar and conventions etiquette to make their meaning clear to their readers.

Chapter 13

Whole-Group Conversations About Grammar and Conventions

Ongoing conversations about grammar will help students grow in knowledge, in application, and in their writing process. During the day, as students contribute to class discussions, collaborative group work, and literature circles, and as they talk to other students at lunch, during recess breaks, and on the playground, we can "listen in," noticing their speech patterns (including errors), which frequently transfer to their writing.

Looking over their shoulders as students are drafting (clipboard cruising), we may find evidence of the tracks of our teaching. For example, are students using the apostrophe correctly in contractions and to show possession? Is their writing a solid block, or are they breaking it up into paragraphs? Noticing students at work and at play can inform our instruction.

It is important for students to understand that success in school and in the real world depends on having the look of literacy. We should have this conversation with students at every grade level; it's that important. Too often great ideas remain unexplored because their written explanation is muddied by errors. Readers discount ideas when there are grammar and conventions errors because the readers focus on the errors instead of the message. The writer appears to have no authority. How many times have we as teachers made an error while drafting something quickly on the board? Isn't the error the first thing students will point out to us? Students notice errors; teachers notice errors; readers notice errors. Your listening audience in formal and in informal conversations notices errors. Students need to realize that errors get in the way of communication. Using standard grammar, usage, and conventions gives our speech and writing that look of literacy. As teachers, we need to find the time to have conversations about grammar and conventions during the day.

Not everything is a teachable moment; it is important to link this information to our ongoing focus lessons, Common Core State Standards, and school district curricula. We need to note where we already have presented focus lessons that obviously did not stick. We may notice that common homophone errors are still occurring or that students are placing commas or apostrophes everywhere in their writing. They may be in love with the exclamation point. The grammar and conventions lessons we choose to present are based on perceived student needs and should be developmentally appropriate.

Remind students of the kinds of conversations we have throughout the day—with our friends, with family members, with other writers in writing workshop. In writing workshop, for example, we talk about strong verbs, using dialogue to advance the action in a story, and adding adjectives or adverbs for description. As writers we are wordsmiths. We want to make our meaning clear to the reader. Sometimes our conversations can lead us to make new discoveries or to seek clarification—in a thesaurus, an online dictionary, or a grammar reference book such as *Mechanically Inclined* by Jeff Anderson. As teachers, our job is to initiate these kinds of conversations with our students. The rest of this chapter discusses possible grammar and conventions conversations you can facilitate with your writers.

Early in the year a conversation about sentences might be a good place to start. As students talk about what makes a sentence, the teacher listens in on the conversation as a kind of formative assessment. What do students know about how a sentence is constructed? This is a good conversation at any grade level. It could start out as a think-ink-pair-share followed by a whole-group share. Before students share with a partner, they need some thinking time and a few minutes to jot down their thinking. This method allows students to listen carefully to their partner's thinking, since their own thinking will not be forgotten (because it has been written down on paper). The responses can be charted, and the group, with teacher guidance, can agree on whether to revise or eliminate the charted responses. In Ms. Batcho's class, for example, William shared that a sentence must be longer than one word. Later in the discussion Aidan questioned William's contribution, giving the examples "Help!" and "Quiet!" as sentences that could be used in a story. During conversations such as this, the teacher learns what students know and what they remain confused about. After the discussion, the anchor chart can be left on display to add information or to revisit for review or clarification at another point in the year.

Another ongoing conversation about grammar and conventions can involve students in talking about what rules they may have found difficult to carry over into their writing. To give students ownership in the process, chart the common responses and ask them to vote on the top one or two so the students have an input in the topic of the classroom conversation. This, too, can inform instruction for future focus lessons. In Cathy McParland's ESL kindergarten class, for instance, Jana and Kishan found it very difficult to limit the use of the exclamation point in their writing, especially when they were writing about summer activities. The rest of the students agreed that they liked to use exclamation points in all their writing. Lynne and Cathy felt that a conversation about the use of exclamation marks would result in a rich discussion and perhaps change the students' thinking. In the following shared experience, Lynne suggested that two or three of the sentences might end with a period instead of an exclamation point.

Our Playground

Our playground is a happy place! I sit and rock on the jumpy, bumpy ride! Today I'm playing on the swings! I slide down the slide and go up again! I like to play at recess with my friend!

The students talked with each other and did not want to make that change because they said that each sentence showed they were very happy and excited. Also, Alan said, "We are happy when we are at recess on the playground." They read the sentences they had volunteered for the shared writing out loud. Each student read in a louder-than-usual voice and emphasized certain words such as "happy" and "swings" again and again and again. While a rich discussion took place, the students' thinking remained the same. The best Lynne could do was to suggest that the students think of one more sentence that would have a different mark of punctuation at the end. She suggested a question. Nathaniel offered, "Do you want to play with me?" The class agreed that this question would be perfect to add to their shared writing. Later in the year after many more shared and guided writing experiences, the issue of the exclamation point can be revisited in another classroom conversation.

Conversations about errors that students notice in everyday talk as well as in movies, on television, and in the books that they read are appropriate for upper grades. Give students several days or a week to listen for these errors or to find them in their reading. They should jot these down in their writer's notebooks to share in the whole-group discussion. They might notice such things as double negatives, pronoun and verb misuse, slang (like *outta* and *lemme*, for example). Have students share the errors they have discovered in small groups and find those that they have in common. Choose one or two common errors from the list they have created and lead a discussion about when these errors are purposeful and, if so, in what types of writing they are appropriate. For instance, in *Mick Harte Was Here* by Barbara Park, the following exchange is noted: "Hiya, Wocket. How ya doin', girl?" he'd say. "You doin' okay today?" Students may also find examples of dialect. *The Sign of the Beaver* by Elizabeth Speare has this passage in the beginning of the book when Matt's father gives him a watch that belonged to Matt's grandfather: "Aye, it's yourn. Be kind of company hearing it tick." . . . "Aye. I knowed you would. Mind you don't wind it up too tight." The conversation with students can focus on when and where it would be appropriate to use this kind of writing. Lead them to discover that, while using these structures in narrative may work, they distract the reader from the point we are making when used in informational or opinion writing.

Another conversation for students in third grade and up may be about breaking the rules, a hot topic for students and teachers alike. Students will often discover that writers do not always follow rules of grammar and conventions. For example, they may use fragments or run-ons; they may write paragraphs containing one sentence for dramatic effect. Gary Paulsen, in *Hatchet* (1996), uses one-sentence and even one-word paragraphs in several places. In the second chapter, he writes: *"The thinking started./Always it started with a single word./Divorce./Secrets."* Authors also might end a sentence with a preposition; they may even make up words that can become part of the language, like *motel* and *smog*. These are called portmanteau words, formed by blending two or more other words—in this instance, *motor* and *hotel* to make *motel* or *smoke* and *fog* to make *smog*. Students may be familiar with other examples like *humongous* (huge and monstrous), *Internet* (international and network), and *fantabulous* (fantastic and fabulous). What students need to realize is that writers who break the rules do so with a purpose. As teachers, we can help students to recognize the reasons behind the rule breaking. Some rules should never be broken: for instance, spelling (outside of slang or dialect), subject-verb agreement, correct use of the apostrophe, and shifting verb tense. When having a conversation with students about rule breaking, genre and audience need to be part of the discussion. If the piece of writing is intended for the newspaper or if it is a letter to an official, for example, standard conventions need to be followed. Students need to consider whether their writing requires a more formal tone. Certainly, what they write as a text message, Facebook entry, or e-mail may not be acceptable in writing intended for public view. If students are unsure about whether to "go formal," advise them to err on the side of formality.

Reading drafts aloud may train the ear to listen for mistakes in writing. This can be a conversation the class may find helpful. Sometimes all one needs to do is to hear the sentence read aloud to recognize the mistake. For example, "Mary and Jim has gone to school" just doesn't sound right. Not everyone has a perfect ear for grammar, but a conversation about close listening and practice may help students develop an ear for grammatical correctness. Of course, focus lessons in certain areas will improve a student's ear for grammar. Some things to train students to listen for are errors in pronoun case, verb tense shift, and double negatives. More sophisticated students may recognize errors in parallel structure and dangling modifiers, in addition to those listed here. Individual students can share with the class the kinds of problems they have been able to identify when they read their writing aloud to another person or to themselves. They may know, for example, that when they stumble over a sentence they are reading aloud, something is wrong in the sentence. The reader/writer may simply run out of air because the sentence is too long.

Danny, a fourth grader, recognized this problem when he tried to read the following sentence: "I told him [Danny's Doberman] to come about, well, I don't know 8,000,000 times, but he didn't come so after me saying 'come' so many times, I tugged at the leash." Reading that sentence alerted Danny to the fact that it was too long. In conferring with Danny, Diane suggested that he find a spot where he needed to take a breath and try to break that one long sentence into two or more sentences. This is how Danny revised his sentence: "I told him to come about 8,000,000 times, but he didn't come. So after me saying 'come' so many times, I tugged at the leash." Is the revision perfect? No, but the sentences are more readable. Sharing examples like this one will help all your students train their ears and get into the practice of rereading their work aloud as well as silently.

Sometimes it is the word order that needs to be changed, as in Victor's sentence from a narrative he wrote in a fourth-grade classroom. Victor volunteered to share his narrative to receive whole-group praise and polish. Here is one sentence he read aloud from his narrative. "Maggie lost her kitten Mitchell on a warm summer day with people all over the place when playing in the park." When Victor read the sentence to the class, Diane asked, "Who is playing in the park?" Ellie thought Maggie was playing in the park and Cotton thought that the "people all over the place" were playing in the park. Zandy thought everyone was playing in the park. Diane asked Victor to clarify his intended meaning. He wanted Maggie to be playing in the park. Diane asked Victor and the class to revise the sentence to make the meaning clear. Victor decided to revise the sentence by starting with the subject noun and read, "Maggie lost her kitten on a warm summer day while playing in the park filled with people all over the place." Again, is the revision perfect? No, but Victor's intended meaning is clear.

In both cases reading aloud pointed the writers to make changes that helped the writing. The subsequent conversations allowed the entire class to participate in training their ears for errors. We cannot say enough about the power of the read-aloud to help train students' ears for correctness. They need to hear a fluent reader (the teacher) reading quality texts by different authors and in different genres. Language is an oral imprint first and foremost.

Another conversation can involve sentence patterns. Sentence variety is an element of style that has a profound effect on any piece of writing. Students can go back to their drafts to find examples of various sentence patterns to share with the class. This discussion could be a good review.

Students can also talk about the issues that are ongoing struggles for them. What do they need to return to for deeper study? What is still confusing them or tripping them up? Let their confusions help to inform your instructional planning through classroom conversations.

What is grammar all about? What is it for? What are the benefits of understanding grammar? What does it allow us to do? How do correct grammar, usage, and conventions help us communicate effectively? Any of these questions can become the basis of a classroom conversation. Grammar is a common language for us all.

Chapter 14

One-on-One Conferring with Grammar and Conventions in Mind

When you confer with a student writer, you hope to teach the student one writing strategy he can use in a current piece of writing and apply to future writing. Teachers of writers teach the writer and move the writer forward rather than the individual piece of writing. Calkins talks about four effective ways you can teach writing in conferences and focus lessons: modeling, guided practice, explicit instruction that makes use of an example from a

229

mentor text, and sometimes inquiry (2005, 11). In Diane's and Lynne's conferences, you will see these methods embedded as teaching points unfold.

Although conferences can be held before a piece is drafted to determine the topic choice, Lynne held conferences with students after they had completed a first draft and had at least tried to give a second look for revision purposes. In these one-on-one conferences with first and second graders, Lynne first looked at what each student was already doing well as a writer and offered some specific praise. Students sometimes naturally do incredible things as writers but are unaware of what they are doing until the teacher or a peer points it out.

Then Lynne focused each student on a writing strategy or craft technique to help that student grow as a writer, particularly looking at needs such as focus, developing their ideas, and choosing exact words to carry those ideas. She tried to name the strategy and relate it to a familiar mentor text that the students had recently used if possible and/or show how she used the strategy in her own writing. Lynne had two of her writer's notebooks on hand for this purpose. Another way to help students is to use the shared writing that is produced on an anchor chart or interactive whiteboard. Most important, be sure to explain how the student can use the strategy or technique in his own writing.

All her conferences modeled the instructional language or nomenclature of writing. Lynne's purpose was also to move students forward in editing skills, so she looked at issues of punctuation, capitalization, and spelling. In some instances, Lynne focused on parts of speech such as the use of specific adjectives when students wrote descriptions. Before Lynne brought her conference to a close, she asked the students to try it out or gently nudged the students to talk out how they could use the strategy in their writing. It is a good idea to remember that, if your students could fix everything, they probably wouldn't need you. Too many negative comments overwhelm student writers and discourage them from revising their writing. Focus on what your students really need and can (at present) handle as writers to move forward.

In October, Lucy, a first grader, wrote about her Halloween costume (Figure 14.1). Lynne praised her for her use of adjectives such as *fantastic* and *pink*. In her original draft, Lucy knew to capitalize *Halloween* and admitted to Lynne that she had used the anchor chart to spell the word correctly, as well as the word *costume*. Again, Lynne praised Lucy's use of environmental print. All the first graders were encouraged to scan the room for spelling help. Lynne also praised Lucy for her use of two question sentences that helped draw in her readers to make a connection and establish interest by asking them to guess.

Figure 14.1
Lucy's Polished Draft

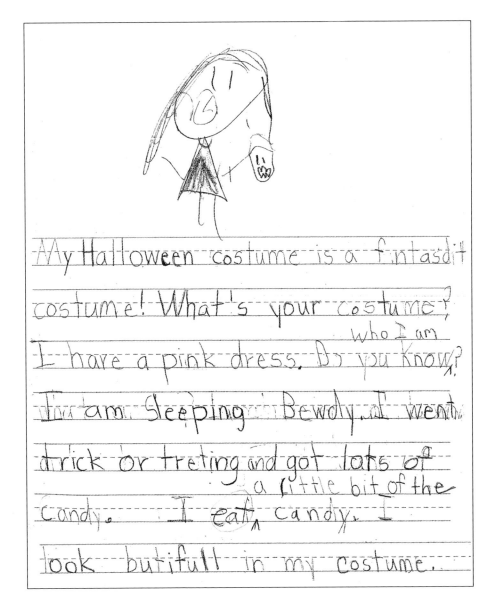

My Halloween costume is a fintasdit costume! What's your costume? I have a pink dress. Do you know who I am? I am Sleeping Bewdy. I went trick or treting and got lots of candy. I eat a little bit of the candy. I look butifull in my costume.

She asked Lucy to look at the words *sleeping bewdy* and asked her if she thought something should be changed here. At first Lucy was puzzled, but then Lynne shared her notebook entry about her Ms. Frizzle costume:

I'm ready for my Halloween party in my out-of-this-world costume! My wide-brimmed felt hat is as black as outer space. Sparkly, gold stars dangle from it on tiny threads. My black-as-midnight dress is covered in paper cutouts painted to look like the planets. My patent leather shoes shine with large gold stars glued onto a ribbon.

In my hand, I am carrying a long telescope. I am Ms. Frizzle, a teacher who plans the most incredible field trips ever!

Lynne also had her look at a page from *The Night Before Halloween* by Natasha Wing: "Count Dracula grinned and slicked back his hair." Lynne pointed to the word *Frankenstein* and then to another part of the text: "which set every monster and goblin in motion." Lynne asked Lucy to compare the proper nouns to the common nouns by simply pointing to the words. "They are all naming words, Lucy. Can you notice something different about them?" Lucy noticed the capitals. When Lynne asked her why *Frankenstein* was capitalized but not *monster*, Lucy explained, "There is only one Frankenstein but there are lots of monsters!" Lynne then asked her to revisit *sleeping bewdy* and Lucy decided to capitalize the *s* and *b* to show that it named only one specific fairy-tale character. Lynne also talked with Lucy about the use of an apostrophe in her sentence, *Whats your costume?* Lynne showed Lucy her notebook entry describing Ms. Frizzle and her use of the apostrophe in this sentence: *I'm ready for my Halloween party in my out-of-this-world costume!* Lucy was able to tell Lynne that *I'm* stood for two words, *I* and *am*. On a blank paper, Lynne wrote a few more contractions: *it's, let's,* and *can't.* Lynne explained that sometimes two words are shortened into a contraction—to make smaller—with the use of an apostrophe. (See the Your Turn Lesson "Contractions Using Pronouns" following Part 2.) Together, they talked about the two words each contraction was made of before returning to Lucy's writing. Lucy was then able to tell Lynne that *what's* replaced *what is* and was able to place an apostrophe before the *-s*.

Teaching Point: Lucy made a new reference page in her journal for contractions. All lists and reference pages can be placed in the back of the journal/writer's notebook with a colored sticky note protruding from a title page (lists and reference pages) that started this section. Reference pages are marked with a capital *R* in the top corner of the page inside a square that is filled in with a yellow highlighter.

The conference took seven minutes, about two minutes longer than Lynne wanted to spend with each child. It is easy to lose track of time when conferring. In order to get to every student within three to five days, conferences must be highly focused and brief. Lynne did not try to overwhelm Lucy by correcting every mistake in spelling. If pieces are going to be published in a newsletter or displayed in the hallway, post an explanation of "engineered" spelling or a "Work in Progress" sign.

Annalise, also a first grader, wrote about her soccer games (Figure 14.2). Lynne noticed her spacing and letter control to form a lowercase *s* and *y* as well as the capitalization of the pronoun *I* every time Annalise used it. Lynne immediately praised Annalise for her topic choice and told her it is important to write about things we know and love. She told Annalise that she helped her readers know that soccer was so enjoyable for her because her parents came to watch her play the game. Her most interesting sentence conveyed emotion in a show-not-tell fashion: *When my Dad was waching, he smild.* Lynne saw that Annalise needed help with end punctuation. She had none. Lynne asked Annalise to count sentences while Lynne held her paper and read Annalise's piece back to her. Annalise counted seven sentences.

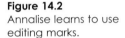

Figure 14.2
Annalise learns to use editing marks.

Lynne wrote the number down, and then asked Annalise to read aloud and Lynne counted. Lynne told Annalise that she thought there were seven sentences, too, but couldn't tell because sentences begin with capital letters and end with periods, question marks, or exclamation points. This time, when Lynne read over Annalise's shoulder, Annalise held the pencil to place end punctuation where it belonged. Then she went back to the piece to add three editing lines under the letter that began each sentence so she would capitalize that letter in her final draft. Lynne asked Annalise if any of the sentences should show excitement or another strong feeling. Annalise chose two sentences to use an exclamation point instead of a period. Lynne did not address spelling issues since Annalise's piece was easy to read and understand. It is interesting to note that Annalise made several mistakes in capitalization when she rewrote her piece for publication but used the editing marks (three underlines for capitals and a slash for lowercase) to correct some mistakes. Another time, she wrote through a letter to make it a capital. There are a few issues Lynne would have addressed if it had been March or April instead of November. If Annalise continued to write soccer stories (and she probably did), then *soccer* is a word that Annalise needs to learn how to spell. Also, a word like *had* needs to be become a sight word spelled correctly. By midyear, Annalise should be using an *-ed* ending to show the past tense of verbs such as *smiled* and *scored*.

Teaching Point: At this grade level, some things are just not important enough to address. For example, it is difficult to learn the rule about capitalizing words such as *dad, grandma, mom,* and *grandpa*. When used in a sentence and preceded by a possessive pronoun (*my, his, her, our, their, your*), these nouns are not capitalized. Only when they stand alone as you would use your own name in a sentence should they be capitalized.

Colin, a second grader, wrote about his dad in a "My Something Beautiful" piece (Figure 14.3). Colin had no trouble with content and had many reasons why he chose his father as his "something beautiful." Lynne and Colin talked about the wonderful picture he painted with words describing the scene in the ocean where Colin sat on his dad's shoulders when the big waves rolled in. He had a solid sense of sentence and knew where to place end punctuation. Colin was able to write sentences using dependent clauses naturally: *When I want to practice sports with him, he will!* At this point in time, instruction in complex sentences is not appropriate, so Lynne only pointed out that she liked the way Colin began his sentence with the word *when*. It was easy to praise Colin's use of the word *truly* as a

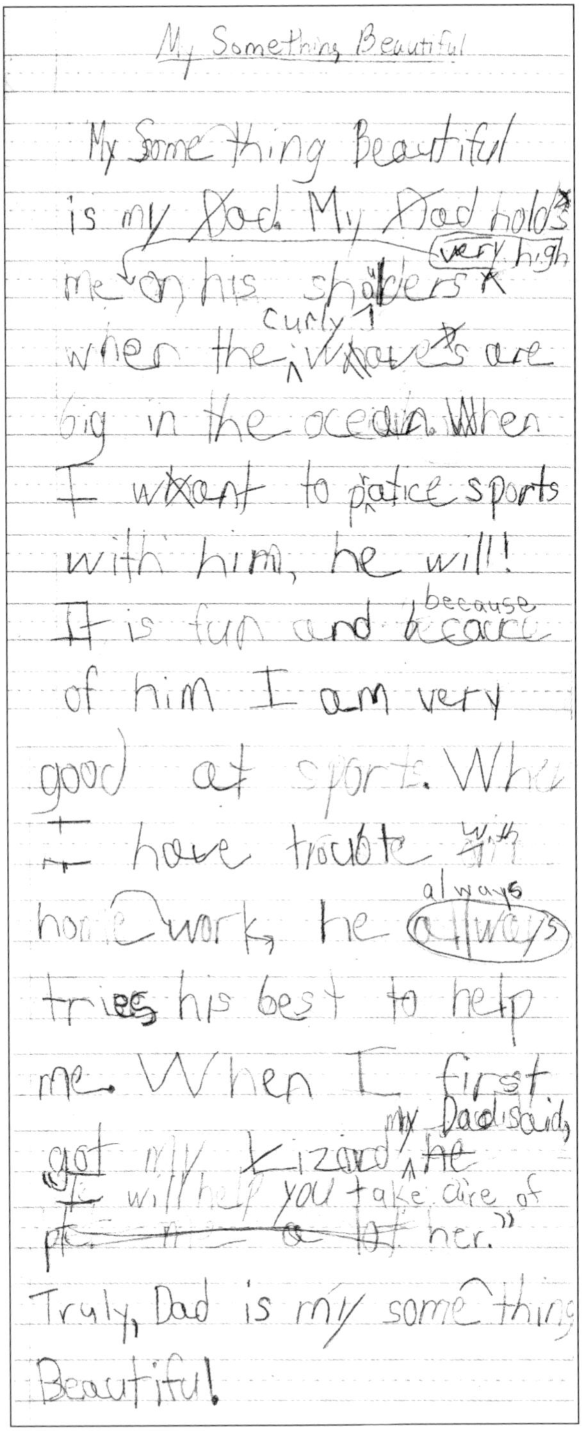
My Something Beautiful

My Some thing Beautiful is my Dad. My Dad holds me on his sholders very high when the curly waves are big in the ocean. When I want to patice sports with him, he will! It is fun and because of him I am very good at sports. When I have trouble with home work, he always tries his best to help me. When I first got my lizard, my Dad said, "I will help you take care of her." Truly, Dad is my some thing Beautiful!

Figure 14.3
Colin's draft with revisions and edits

transition word to indicate (sometimes) that a piece is drawing to a close. The class had spoken about transition words and phrases before they wrote their "Something Beautiful" pieces, and Colin used his new learning to try out a word not commonly used by elementary school students. Furthermore, Lynne was thrilled that Colin tried out dialogue and placed the quotation marks in the correct location. He had used his reference pages in his writer's notebook from the focus lessons on using direct quotations in dialogue for story writing and the November activity on turkey talk (see Chapter 16 for an explanation of this term). The only thing he needed to add was a comma to separate the explanatory words from the rest of the sentence. Lynne gave Colin three words to add to his list of "Must Spell Correctly" words: *want, always,* and *because*. Words that are repeated often across writing types should be learned so that correctness is reinforced. It is important to have the look of literacy, and high-frequency words need to be correctly spelled.

Lynne also talked with Colin about compound words such as *something* and *homework*. Together, they brainstormed a list of other common compounds such as *sidewalk, airplane, classroom, bedroom,* and *sunshine*. Colin and Lynne reread the sentence about the ocean waves. Lynne asked Colin if he could describe the waves in another way by placing an adjective in front of the word waves. Colin first said "enormous," but Lynne asked him to read the whole sentence aloud again to see if he had already described the size of the waves. Colin read the sentence two times before responding, "Oh, I said, 'big' but I could change it to 'enormous.'" Lynne agreed but directed him to the place in the sentence before the word *waves*. Then she wrote in her notebook: the wave. Lynne asked

Colin what adjectives could fit in this frame. Colin thought for a moment and suggested *blue, green, strong,* and *curly.* Lynne told Colin to choose one or two words to revise his sentence, and Colin chose *curly.* Here was the perfect chance to review the use of the caret to add words to a draft. Lynne reviewed her notes and noticed that quite a few second graders were adding an apostrophe to form the plural of nouns and the -s form of verbs. Although she addressed this point briefly with Colin, she made a note in her conference log to do a focus lesson on apostrophe use and misuse the next day with shared and guided practice. (See the Your Turn Lesson "The Apostrophe to Show Possession" following Part 1.)

Teaching Point: When conferring with students, create a simple system for keeping notes on each child. The name of the child, the title of the piece or topic, and the date are pieces of information that will help you keep track of progress and goals. For younger students, write a few revision suggestions on index cards or sticky notes so they can take them back to their seats. Otherwise, they will be back to see you because they have forgotten what they might try out. In upper elementary grades and middle school, have your students jot a few ideas on a sticky note or card as you confer. Every week, review the conference notes to find common problems for areas of instruction either in focused, flexible groups or as whole-class instruction.

Conferences with student writers are a great way to assess individual knowledge about grammar and conventions. This is not to suggest that teachers use conferences to edit student papers or to "correct" every grammatical, spelling, and conventions error. That is not the purpose of a writing conference. Typically, a writing conference addresses content. However, as we are conducting our conferences, we can note the areas where individual students and the class as a whole appear to be having difficulties. For example, if, during conferences, it becomes apparent that many of your students are inconsistent in using verb tenses, you will know that it is time to address that issue with the entire class (see the Your Turn Lesson "Verb Tense Consistency" following Part 3). Often, though, you may discover that only one or two students need a particular lesson. This is the time when you can have conversations about grammar addressing that issue with a small group or even only one student during conference time.

In one fourth-grade classroom in early October, Diane encountered the following entry in Lily's draft folder:

Maggie was so sad. She was starring out at the falling red and brown leaves she lost her kitten. Bing was walking through the park and meowing loudly but to the giant rotweiler it looked like dinner then the dog charged and barked! All through the street. Up the street. She went.

Lily's draft has many praiseworthy elements. Notice how she shows the season without naming it. Lily also catches attention with the phrase *to the giant rotweiler* [sic] *it looked like dinner.* In a content conference, Diane would point out these successes and let Lily tell her what she wants to say in this piece and where she wants it to go. However, Diane needed to know whether Lily has a sense of sentence. Is this draft typical or an aberration? A scan of entries in Lily's writer's notebook as well as written work from other content areas quickly demonstrated that Lily did need a lesson on what makes a sentence. Diane did not use Lily's draft to make corrections though. Instead, she said, "Lily, I wonder if we can talk about what makes a sentence. Remember the book *In November* by Cynthia Rylant that we read last week when we were talking about showing, not telling, in our writing? Let's look at it now. How do you know when one sentence ends and another begins?" Lily replied that there was a capital letter at the beginning of each sentence and a period (or some other mark of punctuation) at the end. Then, Diane asked Lily to read one of the sentences aloud. Covering up the second part of the sentence, Diane asked Lily to read only the subject part of the sentence. "Does that make sense all by itself?" she asked Lily. Diane covered up the subject part of the sentence and asked Lily to read only the predicate part of the sentence. "Does that make sense all by itself?" she asked. Lily decided that neither reading made sense.

What does a sentence need? It needs a "who" or "what" and it needs that who or what to do something or to be something. Diane asked Lily to look around the room and to pick out an object to describe. Lily chose the flag. Diane wrote *flag* in her notebook. Then, she asked Lily to tell her something about the flag. Lily said, "The flag is red, white, and blue." Diane wrote that sentence in her notebook. She said, "A sentence has two parts, a subject (the who or what) and a predicate (what the who or what does or is). Together Lily and Diane decided that "flag" is the subject. Lily identified the predicate as "is red, white, and blue." Diane accepted that answer. Diane asked Lily to choose a student in the class and tell her what that student was doing. She responded, "Danny is talking to Jayden." Again, Lily was asked to identify the "who" (Danny) and the "what Danny is doing" (is talking to Jayden). After eliciting several more examples, Diane suggested that Lily look back at her writer's notebook and/or drafts to revise groups of words to make complete sentences. Over the next several days, Diane made an effort to check in with Lily to review the changes she was making in her notebook.

In a third-grade classroom, Diane conferred with Nicholas on his narrative draft, the touchstone fiction piece "Maggie's Kitten" (see Chapter 4).

Once there was a girl named Maggie. She always wanted a kitten. On her 6th birthday her parents finally gave her a kitten. It was a super small orange tabby cat. Maggie loved her cat so much, but she couldn't think of a name. Maggie wanted some fresh air. She thought about going to the park. When Maggie stepped outside, the idea hit her. The name should be Fluffy. Then she took Fluffy to the park. When they got there, the saw a giant evergreen tree that towered over everything, even the tall, tall trees that have been there for decades. Fluffy was so scared she ran so fast she pulled the leash handle out of Maggie's hand. When Fluffy went running, she almost got hit by a ice cream truck. Maggie started running but not after Fluffy, she wanted ice cream. She wanted some mint chocolate chip ice cream so bad she forgot about Fluffy. Fluffy was chased by a big dog. She was stuck and frightened and hid in a UPS box. Maggie couldn't remember when she last saw Fluffy. She was in a mint chocolate chip wonderland. She wished she had her Sesame Street phone to call 911, but she didn't.

Nicholas's narrative draft shows a problem with focus; it is difficult to determine the conflict in the narrative: Is it that Maggie can't decide on a name for the kitten, or is it that Maggie is careless about taking care of the kitten or is it that the kitten gets lost and Maggie doesn't have a phone? The lack of focus is not a grammatical error, but before we as teachers can engage in any kind of conversation about conventions, the student writer must have something on the page that matters to both the writer and the reader. Sometimes simply asking what the student has in mind—What is your story about? What is the most important part of your story? What have you written that tells about that most important part?—can steer the student toward a focus for his or her piece. Diane asked Nicholas which of Maggie's three conflicts was the most interesting to him? Which did he think would be most interesting to a reader? Nicholas thought they were equally interesting, but agreed to focus on Maggie's absent-mindedness, which resulted in the loss of the kitten.

In addition to the conversation about focus, Diane praised Nicholas's use of punctuation: the comma in compound sentences, the comma after introductory elements, and the comma to separate coordinating adjectives (see Appendix G). She made a note that Nicholas could be a resource for peer editing. One-on-one conferring is also a great way for teachers to know what their students can do well!

In a fifth-grade classroom, Cotton's narrative draft began with a focus problem as well (Figure 14.4). The title, "My First Roller Coaster," leads the

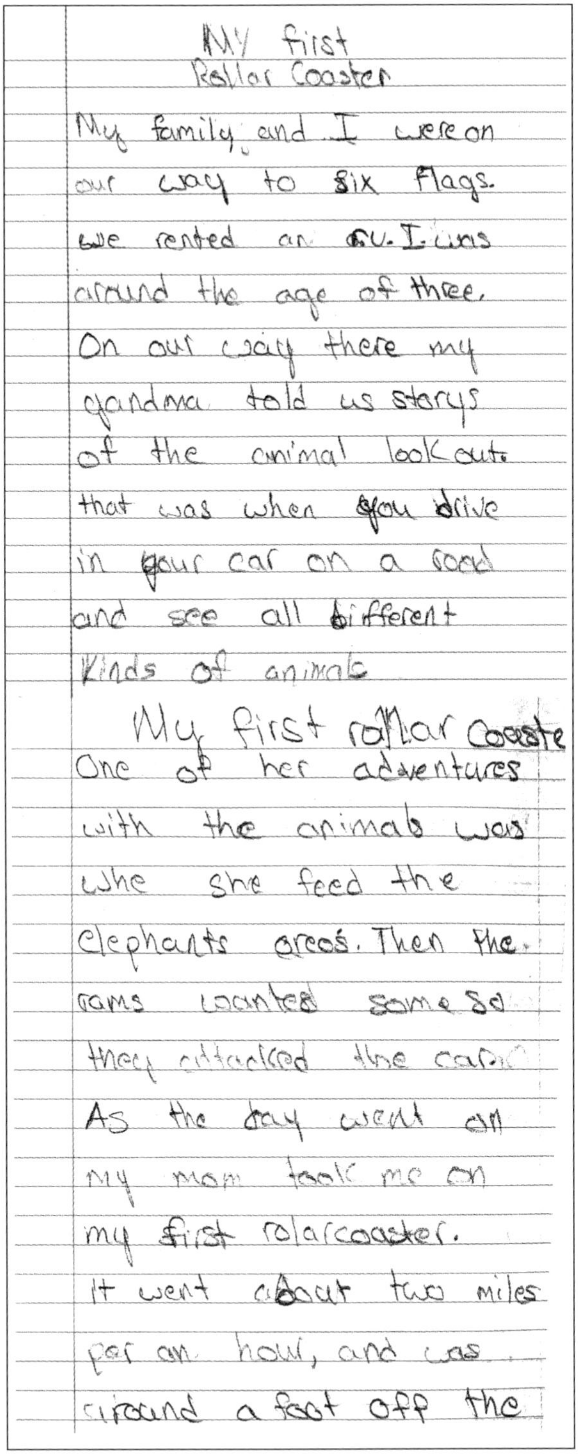

My First
Roller Coaster

My family, and I were on
our way to six Flags.
We rented an R.V. I was
around the age of three.
On our way there my
grandma told us storys
of the animal lookout.
that was when you drive
in your car on a road
and see all different
Kinds of animals

My first rollar coaste
One of her adventures
with the animals was
when she feed the
elephants oreos. Then the
rams wanted some so
they attacked the car.
As the day went on
my mom took me on
my first rolarcoaster.
It went about two miles
per an hour, and was
around a foot off the

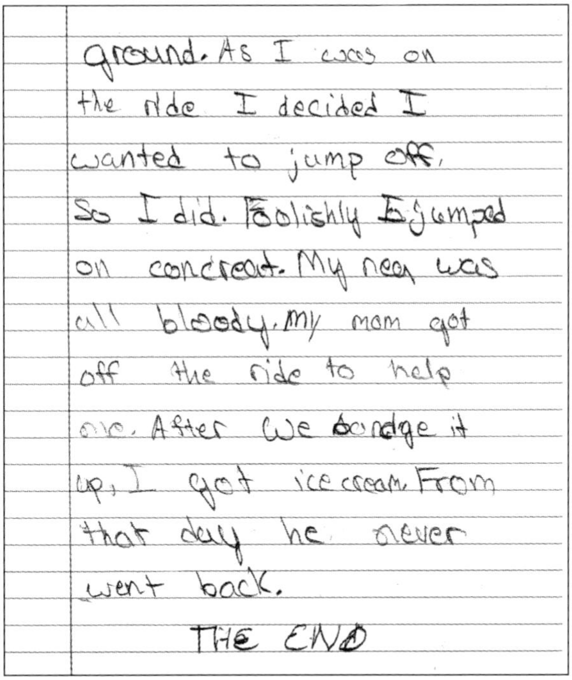

ground. As I was on
the ride I decided I
wanted to jump off.
So I did. Foolishly I jumped
on concreat. My neck was
all bloody. My mom got
off the ride to help
me. After we bandge it
up, I got ice cream. From
that day he never
went back.
THE END

Figure 14.4
Cotton's draft used in a conference with Diane

reader to believe that the narrative will be about a roller coaster ride; however, the writer adds details about renting an RV and about his grandma telling stories of the animal lookout. Diane noted the most interesting detail about the ride is Cotton's unusual exit! She praised Cotton's use of specific nouns and verbs: *adventures, Oreos* (not just *food* or *cookies*), *concrete, attacked,* and the use of the adverb *foolishly*. Cotton admitted that he didn't really have any memory of the events in question since he was only three years old when it happened. He knew only the stories that had been told by the family about the day. Diane suggested that he might want to change his topic to write something about which he did have a vivid recollection. In the meantime, Diane noted Cotton's need for a lesson on when to begin a new paragraph. Since his draft was not the only one in the class that demonstrated the need for this lesson, Diane decided that she would address this issue as a whole-class conversation. Often our one-on-one conferences inform our grammar and conventions instruction.

Diane conferred with fourth grader Skye on her narrative draft about her trip to Disneyworld.

When you go to Disneyworld theres fun every where you go. The best ride there is the Hauted Mantion. When you walk in theres 5 stuped heads that won't shut up.

When your standing in line you hear them sing badly.

When you actually git on the ride you have to git on quick. There is this room and the wall stretches and litting and thunder appear.

In the beginning of the rid theres a coffin. And a person comes out and back in. That ride is fun. Then theres a glass round spheer and a head appears and tells scarry furtions. That is the best ride ever!

Diane praised Skye for focusing on only one ride since Disneyworld is such a big topic. Diane asked Skye to tell her more about the ride and why she liked it. As Skye talked, Diane took notes for her to use in revising her draft. Diane also took this opportunity to talk to Skye about contractions. Diane read Skye's draft aloud and used two words everyplace there was a contraction without an apostrophe: *there is fun everywhere, there is five stupid heads, you are standing in line, there is a coffin, there is a glass round spheer*. Skye noticed that *there is five stupid heads*, "didn't sound right." Though subject-verb agreement was not the focus of this lesson, Diane was pleased that Skye noticed the error by hearing it. She explained that the sentence didn't sound right because *five heads* needs the verb *are*, not *is*. Diane wrote the pronouns *I, you, he, she*, and *it* in a column in Skye's writer's notebook reference pages. Together Skye and Diane made a list of common pronoun contractions: *I'm, I'll, I'd, you're, you've, you'd, he's, he'll, he'd*, etc. Diane instructed Skye to use an apostrophe to show that there are missing letters when two words are shortened to one word. Additionally, Skye's draft has multiple spelling errors. Diane corrected the word *furtions* (fortunes) because a reader would not necessarily know that Skye meant *fortunes*. The word *get* is so commonly used that Diane needed to know whether Skye really didn't know how to spell the word or if she was merely being careless.

Teaching Point: It is important that students, even in their drafting, spell words correctly if they know how because that's what writers do. Sometimes, student writers spell words the way they hear themselves say them. For example, they often write *are* for *our* because that's the way they pronounce the word.

You can determine if mispronunciation is the root of the problem by having your student read the sentence or passage aloud to you during conference.

．．

Other spelling errors would have to wait for correction until Skye had revised for content. Clearly, Skye's draft needs more description of the ride and why this ride is so memorable to her.

Once Skye had revised her draft and had described the Haunted Mansion ride to her satisfaction, Diane conducted an editing conference. In this conference Diane corrected spelling errors (*git* and *haunted mantion*, for example), but she was pleased that Skye remembered to use the apostrophe appropriately in contractions. Below is Skye's revised and edited description of the Haunted Mansion ride.

Disneyworld's Best Ride

Everywhere you go at Disneyworld there are fun attractions. The best ride there is the Haunted Mansion. When you walk in, there are five stupid heads that won't shut up. When you're walking by the heads, you hear them sing badly. They sing so bad I have to bring ear plugs just to block out the sound!

When you actually get on the ride, you have to get on quickly. There is this room and the wall stretches out and lightning flashes and thunder rumbles. Then the ride begins. Right off the bat, there's a coffin and a person rises up out of the coffin and then goes right back inside. That part of the ride is fun.

Finally, there's a glass round sphere. A head appears in the sphere and tells scary fortunes. The head doesn't tell everyone's fortune, but it is fun to listen to what will happen in the future. All of these things make Haunted Mansion the best ride ever.

．．

Teaching Point: A word about spelling needs to be said here. Nancie Atwell in *Lessons That Change Writers* gives specific instructions for students to keep personal spelling lists. Spelling lists devised by the teacher or by a book company rarely find their way into students' everyday writing experiences. They study the words for the test and mainly forget about them because there is nothing for them to attach the individual words to in their memory banks. We can teach them spelling rules: the *ei-ie* rule, the rule for forming plurals, or the rules for prefixes and suffixes, for instance. For spelling to stick, students need to have a stake in their learning. Nancie Atwell's strategy for personal spelling lists might just work for your students too.

．．

Chapter 15

Conversations with Educators: Assessing Growth in Grammar and Conventions

When writers write, they use the standard conventions of writing. They write in complete sentences with appropriate punctuation and correct spelling *if they know how*. We should encourage students to do the same things as they draft. At the beginning of the year when we circulate around the room during writing workshop, we become aware of our students' writing knowledge. Do they begin each sentence with a capital letter? Do they end sentences with an end mark of punctuation? Do they write in paragraphs? Do they attempt to use correct spelling? The answers to these questions become the baseline for instruction. If, for example, most of the students are not paragraphing, we know that paragraphing is a needed focus lesson or set of lessons. (See the Your Turn Lesson "When to Make a New Paragraph in a Narrative" following Part 1.) It is not fair to hold students accountable for things they do not know or have not been taught. In this chapter, we will discuss ways to assess growth in grammar and conventions and suggest ways to have conversations with our colleagues about this assessment.

Writer's notebooks can be an effective means of assessing grammar and conventions knowledge. Although we often do not evaluate notebooks for correctness, they can be a tool for assessment. We can ask our students to bring their notebooks with them to a writer's conference or to use them during reflection time at the end of writing workshop. Using a writer's notebook as a tool for assessment, we can look at student experimentation with their new understandings about grammar and conventions. Through examination of their multiple drafts, including revision and editing attempts, we can look for evidence of students' application of grammar rules. Have they found examples in mentor texts? Can they imitate them? Do they copy grammar and conventions rules and attempt to make sense of them using their own words? Ask students to reflect on how focus lessons have helped them write better sentences. They can either highlight errors that they find in their notebooks and revise them or highlight places where they have used the focus lesson correctly. They can share these examples with the class.

How we keep track of the information we have gleaned from our study of student notebooks can be shared with our colleagues at our grade level and/or school. For some of us, a checklist is an easy way to keep track of the kinds of things our students do with their notebooks to help them deepen their emerging understandings of the English language. A system using anecdotal record-keeping could be created by using sticky notes to notice what individual students are capable of doing or not ready to do at this point in the year. These sticky notes can be transferred to a manila folder for each child. Adding a date will help teachers to track growth throughout the year.

A separate section of the writer's notebook for reference purposes can start at the back of the notebook, or students can simply use tabs to indicate reference pages. The students will use this section for note taking during focus lessons on grammar and conventions. Instruct them to include examples from their reading and to imitate those examples themselves to illustrate the subject of the focus lesson. A simple checklist can be kept to note what students have imitated correctly and seem to understand as evidenced by their notes in their reference sections. In a narrative unit of study for one

Name _____		Genre _____	
Month _____		Title _____	

Focus Lesson	Definition	Example	Imitation
Sentence unit			
Simple sentence			
Compound sentence			
Commas in a compound sentence			
Commas in a series			
Quotation marks			
Specific nouns			
Strong verbs			
Maintaining verb tense			
Apostrophe with contractions			
Apostrophe to show possession			

Figure 15.1
What Have I Imitated
in This (type of writing)
Unit of Study?

fifth-grade class, the checklist in Figure 15.1 was useful for both teacher and students.

Copies of the checklist were made—one for the teacher and one for each of the students—so the students could also easily track their progress and their independent attempts.

As we teach our younger students to be their own editors, we can offer them a bulleted list of suggestions to help them as they read their first and revised drafts for grammar and conventions. Use this list in conferences with your students. Share lists with your grade-level colleagues and ask them for their input. Should something be added? Is something not appropriate at this point in the school year? Here is a bulleted list from Ms. Batcho's second-grade class:

1. Frame the first sentence with your fingers.
   - Check for a capital letter at the beginning.
   - Check for a period, a question mark, or an exclamation at the end.
2. Read the whole sentence to see if it sounds right.
   - Does it seem too long? You might need two shorter sentences.
   - Are there any words that are missing?
   - Are there any words that don't belong?

3. Read it again and tap each word lightly with your eraser end of your pencil as you read it aloud. Tap for a space between sentences.
    *   Circle any words that don't look right to you. Check with a spelling buddy.
    *   Look at your spacing. Are your letters too close together or too far apart?
    *   Are there spaces between sentences?

Other checklists look at spelling, punctuation, and grammar issues. It is important to limit the list for students to make it more doable. In elementary school grades, it is a good idea to reread for spelling mistakes only. The next read can be a punctuation check with a particular emphasis on one or two areas or skills like commas in a series or end punctuation. Students can work through an editing conference with a peer by actually exchanging papers and noting errors on sticky notes. After students offer suggestions to the writer, the writer then has to try out the suggestion(s) to see if it makes sense. He may want to consult with a grammar reference book or another peer or wait for a teacher-student conference. Here is an example of a third-grade classroom's spelling checklist (also see Appendix E):

Spelling Checklist
*   No excuse—spell these words correctly all the time! Provided by the teacher and may come from the Dolch Sight Word List (such as *about, myself, today, only, try, laugh, full, warm, when,* and *said*)
*   Homophone pairs (and triplets) that are often misused, even by adults! *too/to/two, your/you're, their/they're/there, hear/here, plain/plane, meat/meet, it's/its, know/no* (see Appendix C)
*   Irregular past tense verbs: *bring-brought, keep-kept, come-came, go-went, swim-swam, take-took, break-broke*
*   Environmental print—any words in the room on posters or chart.

Other checklists, for fifth grade and higher, include some common concerns about convention and grammar issues such as the following:

*   Apostrophes—Look for all nouns ending in the letter *-s*—plural nouns do not need an apostrophe. Look to see if they show ownership, then follow the rules for singular possessive and plural possessive.
*   View contractions for apostrophe usage.
*   Commas—Review for comma of address, comma splices (a comma joining two independent clauses without the presence of a coordinating

conjunction), and commas used in a series or a comma for appositives or adjective interrupters.

- Colons—Check colons for introducing long quotes, announcements, and introducing a series without expressions such as *namely* and *that is*.
- Semicolons—Fix comma splices by joining independent clauses with a semicolon when stylistically correct.
- Dashes and Hyphens—Make sure dashes are not excessively used and they maintain a space on either side. Check whether your adjectives are using hyphens correctly (no space on either side but not attached to the noun with a hyphen; i.e., *bare-branch tree*).
- Other Punctuation—Review for excessive exclamation points and ellipses.
- Conversation—Check placement of quotation marks for words directly spoken and punctuation that should be placed inside the end quote: period, comma, question mark, exclamation point. (See the Your Turn Lesson "Adding Conversation to a Narrative" following Part 1.)
- Run-on Sentences—Find every occurrence of coordinating conjunctions—e.g., *and, but, or*, and *yet*—and revise any run-on sentences.
- Sentence Structure—Check for unclear syntax and passive voice (avoid whenever possible).

At the beginning of the year, start to make a list of editing skills you think your students need. Talk with your grade-level partners. They may have some of the same needs and some different ones. Decide what is necessary to move the writer forward—not the individual piece of writing. And please remember—writing cannot be taught in a year!

With our grade-level colleagues we can also have conversations about what constitutes mastery of grammatical concepts. For example, if kindergarten, grade one, and grade two students all study nouns, how do our expectations differ at each grade level? A practical conversation can include what we observe our students accomplishing. What does mastery look like? Are kindergarten students differentiating between singular and plural nouns? Do first-grade students match singular nouns with their singular verb form? Can second graders form sentences that contain collective nouns and irregular plural nouns? Can our students demonstrate correct use of these conventions consistently? As teachers, we have a responsibility to assess student knowledge, of course, but we also must acknowledge the means by which we perform this assessment. Conversations with our colleagues help us all clarify our thinking about instruction and assessment.

Chapter 16

Using Mentor Texts for Whole- or Small-Group Instruction

Mentor texts are a friendly way to gather writers in small or whole groups for instruction. In this fashion, writers can study one or several skills they will need to become more adept and sophisticated in grammar and conventions concepts and applications. As a teacher, when you come to a part of a text where you believe your students could notice, for example, how the author helps us understand an action, a character, or an event through the specific use of nouns, verbs, and/or adjectives or where punctuation is used to show that someone is actually speaking, simply mark the text and jot a few notes on a sticky note to show how the passage or page of text can be used.

Then get ready for a rich conversation with your students about the "noticings"! In *Notice and Note: Strategies for Close Reading*, Beers and Probst talk about getting students to read like they are inside of the text, ". . . noticing everything, questioning everything, weighing everything they are reading against their lives, the lives of others, and the world around them" (2013, 3). We want our writers to notice everything, too, weighing what they are reading and writing against other works of mentor authors, the work they are producing in their writer's notebooks, and the pieces of writing they are currently drafting or are about to draft.

These passages from mentor texts can help the teacher transfer some of the responsibility to their students. What your students are doing could be called a "close read" as a writer. The student is highly focused and totally engaged with the text. He is thinking about how he can transfer the author's craft to his own writing. Ideally, it would be a good idea to make time for this type of instruction around grammar and conventions at least once each week. In upper elementary grades and middle school, these conversations can occur across content areas such as science, social studies, and foreign languages. During these lessons, students should have their notebooks open. As they read the passages and jot their noticings, they are "reading with a pencil," as Doug Fisher (2013) advises readers to do when they are giving a text a close read. Your writers are asking themselves to think about how the text works—looking at the author's choice of words, punctuation, sentence lengths, sentence types, and sentence structures.

In Maribeth Batcho's second-grade class, the students were getting ready to write a notebook entry about their "something beautiful." Maribeth had read *Something Beautiful* by Sharon Dennis Wyeth, brainstormed a list of her "something beautifuls" on the board, and then chose to write about her red boots. Maribeth wrote and revised in front of her students. The students looked at her final draft as their first mentor text to use for instructional purposes.

My Something Beautiful
by Maribeth Batcho
My cowgirl boots are my something beautiful. My husband, Frank, gave me these boots for Christmas one year, and I really love them. Not only are they cute, they are the most comfortable shoes I own. When I wear these boots, I feel sassy and fiery, like I can do anything I set my mind to do. In addition, I love the way they clickety-clack

when I walk down the hall as if they are saying, "Look out! Here she comes!" Red cowgirl boots. Sassy. Strong. SOMETHING BEAUTIFUL!

Maribeth read the piece aloud two times and asked the students to chorally read with her for the third reading. Then she asked them to take out their notebooks and think about what they noticed about the words she used, the punctuation, or anything else that jumped out at them.

After a few minutes, she asked the children to gather on the rug in front of the chart stand to turn and talk about their discoveries. As she called on them to talk about her text, she underlined the major points they discussed. Kadden said that he liked the sound words *clickety-clack* because he remembered hearing Ms. Batcho walking down the hallway to the recess door in these boots. Ms. Batcho underlined those words and asked the students to notice how the words were written. Kadden again responded and said the words were connected with a little line. Ms. Batcho wrote *hyphen* on the board and reminded the class about some nouns and adjectives they know and have used in their writing that use a hyphen, such as *X-ray, jack-in-the-box, star-shaped,* and *well-liked*.

Maggie noticed the dialogue. She said that the boots are talking when they click down the hall. Maribeth asked Maggie to read only the words the boots seem to be saying and underlined them. With a strong voice, Maggie belted out, "Look out! Here she comes!" Then Maribeth asked a volunteer to highlight the punctuation that lets the reader know there is conversation or a thoughtshot. After Jayla pointed out the quotation marks and the final end mark—an exclamation point—Maribeth simply told the students that a comma had to be used to separate the actual words that the boots are "speaking" from the rest of the sentence.

Then she moved on. "What else did you notice? What kinds of words help you to form a picture in your mind of my boot?" Mikey came to the chart and underlined *red* and *cowgirl*. Maribeth asked the students if they knew what job these words did in the first sentence. Dennis told the class they described the boots. Maribeth drew arrows from the adjectives to the noun they described. "Are there any other words that do this same job?" JuneSeo underlined *comfortable* and drew an arrow to the word *shoes*. Michael said he liked the words *sassy* and *fiery* because they told about Ms. Batcho. Maribeth listed all of these words in one column on the board and the words they described in the second column. The students talked about a name for each column. Then they labeled the columns "Adjectives" and "Nouns" to use the nomenclature of grammar. When we teach our students to notice things about an author's writing, the writing of their teacher or peer, or even their own writing, it is important to develop the nomenclature of writers. Having that common language enables us to talk about the same things and apply that learning to other texts as well. Esther talked about the use of all capital letters and the exclamation point in the final sentence. She said, "They are clues that tell us to read those words louder because you are excited."

Shawn noticed that the word *Christmas* started with a capital letter because it named a specific holiday. Aliece said *Frank* was also capitalized. The students talked about other possibilities for proper nouns. Maggie said that if the name of the shoe was used it would also be capitalized, like *Nike* or *Skechers* for sneakers.

Maribeth asked the students to look at the final four sentences. "What do you notice?" Emily said that some of the describing words like *red, cowgirl,* and *sassy* were already used. The writers turned and talked about the repetition—was it a good thing or a bad thing? Maribeth asked for a thumbs-up or thumbs-down. The class liked the repeated words because they reminded the reader at the very end of the piece what the boots looked like and how Ms. Batcho felt about the boots. Kadden was confused. "I am not sure that *sassy* and *strong* are describing the boots or Ms. Batcho when she wears her favorite boots." Maribeth asked them if the words could be describing both the boots and Ms. Batcho wearing the boots. The class decided it could be both. "These sentences are much shorter than the others," Esther commented. Chris asked if a sentence could only be one word. Ms. Batcho surveyed the class. Maura, Eric, Kathleen, and Ismael didn't think so. Then Mikey gave an example: "Help!" Ms. Batcho said that the sentences in her piece of writing were really fragments—a part of a sentence. She asked them to think about what kinds of words were used in the last four sentences. Maggie pointed out that most of them were adjectives, and Jayla found a noun—*boots*. Again, Ms. Batcho explained that most sentences have a noun and verb, but sometimes writers use fragments for a special effect. Readers notice the drama that fragments often create. She asked the class to read the last four sentences with her aloud after she modeled how she would read them. The students looked over their noticings and were told to return to them when they revised their "something beautiful" pieces.

The following day Lynne opened writing workshop with a read-aloud, *White Owl, Barn Owl* by Nicola Davies. After the reading, she showed one page of text on the document imager.

And then, one spring night, just as the sky went pink, a pale face looked out of our box . . .

An owl!
A white owl!
A barn owl!

Before they wrote about their noticings, they also reread Ms. Batcho's piece about her red boots. A few of the students immediately noticed a similarity as muffled "Oooohs!" arose from the group. When the students talked in small groups, they talked about the following points:

- the use of adjectives such as *spring, pink,* and *pale* to paint a vivid picture
- the use of three dots (ellipsis points) to get the reader to pause and get ready for a surprise
- the use of larger print to show excitement
- the use of exclamation points to show excitement
- the idea that some words can do more than one job, depending on how they are used in a sentence, such as the word *spring,* which usually is a noun but acts like an adjective here and sometimes can even be a verb!

Almost all the groups had these points covered. Mikey thought that the word *one* could also be a describing word. Lynne explained that all number words can act as adjectives in sentences if they are not just naming a number but describing something. Two groups noticed the short sentences that were really fragments because they used only adjectives and nouns. Kadden noticed how this text was just like Ms. Batcho's and made the words in these sentences very important even though there weren't many of them. Emily added, "It's because that's how you would think inside your head if you finally saw the owl in the nesting box. Those are the words you would think." The rest of the class agreed.

Then they looked at another page of text.

The owl flew back and forth over the field. Then another owl came to join it. "That's its mate," Grandpa whispered.
One owl dropped to the ground and came up again. "Look! Look, Grandpa!" It's caught something!" I said.

After spending time with their notebooks and partnering for discussion, the students again shared their noticings. "People are talking," Sam shared. "You can tell by the funny marks that look like commas." Lynne asked Sam to highlight the quotation marks on the chart paper that contained the text

Lynne had shared on the document imager. Sara explained who was talking. Michael read the words spoken by grandpa, and Maura read the words spoken by the granddaughter. Several other pairs of students read the words—grandpas whispering the words and granddaughters saying the words with excitement and much louder. Colin talked about the action word *flew* and Maggie found *dropped* and *caught*. Lynne agreed that the verbs were important to these passages. She asked the students to look at any other unusual punctuation. Jayla noticed the contractions *that's* and *it's* in the passage. The students talked about the job of the apostrophe and why contractions are used in story. Kadden found the one-word sentence and questioned if it was really a sentence. After much debate, the students decided that "Look!" can stand alone because it is a verb that gives a command or order just like "Help!" Since it was just before Thanksgiving, Ms. Batcho told the students they would use conversation with quotation marks for a *turkey talk* writing activity the next day, a technique used to motivate the students to write some dialogue and pay attention to the conventions of written conversation.

Students reviewed their noticings and the page from *White Owl, Barn Owl* that used conversation in order to write dialogue in the voice of a turkey to comment on the upcoming Thanksgiving Day. Students were urged to use the third-person voice and use their own name to call themselves Turkey Kadden or Turkey Sara. Lynne and Maribeth first modeled with a book the students were all familiar with: E. B. White's *Charlotte's Web*. She used part of the opening conversation, placing the page under the document imager:

> "Where's Papa going with that ax?" said Fern to her mother as they were setting the table for breakfast.
>
> "Out to the hoghouse," replied Mrs. Arable. "Some pigs were born last night."
>
> "I don't see why he needs an ax," continued Fern, who was only eight.

The students noticed the quotation marks, the use of a comma or question mark after words that were directly spoken, and the use of explanatory words that help the reader know who is speaking. Mikey added, "There's more. The author also tells us that Fern is eight years old." Kadden pointed out that every time a different speaker was talking, the writing began on a brand-new line. Maribeth told them that indenting and beginning on a new line is still another way the writer helps his readers understand who is speaking.

Next, Lynne and Maribeth gave the students several examples of "turkey talk" using different kinds of sentences but always placed the explanatory words after the spoken words, in the same way E. B. White wrote his opening conversation in *Charlotte's Web*. Maribeth and Lynne wanted the second-grade students to be able to imitate this structure and did not want to confuse them by writing some sentences that started with the explanatory words. They also wanted the students to have fun with language, so they tried to add humor to some of their examples:

> *"I am feeling a cold November breeze," Turkey Dorfman told Turkey Batcho.*
> *"Could the b-b-b-big feast day be near¿" gobbled Turkey Dorfman nervously.*
> *"Run for your life!" bellowed Turkey Batcho.*
> *"Is it getting hot in here¿" Turkey Batcho complained loudly as the heavy oven door closed.*

After myriad shared experiences on the whiteboard to practice punctuation, the students wrote several sentences on paper and practiced placing dried elbow macaroni noodles around the words that would be directly spoken. They then drew and colored turkeys on a piece of paper and cut them out. On a second piece of paper, they wrote and revised their sentences, then cut around these to make a speech bubble. The turkey and the bubble were glued to a piece of construction paper to look like the turkey was talking. They then pasted the noodles around their words to act as quotation marks (see Esther's turkey in Figure 16.1). Esther imitated the lead sentence used in E. B. White's *Charlotte's Web* and added another sentence with subtle humor. She also effectively used the ellipsis for dramatic pause!

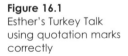

Figure 16.1
Esther's Turkey Talk using quotation marks correctly

Figure 16.2
Mikey uses direct quo-
tations for "Turkey
Talk."

Students read their final pieces in small groups before they were posted in the hall for other second graders to view. Mikey tried his hand at humor and used quotation marks correctly (Figure 16.2). During a conference with Lynne, they briefly discussed the homophone pair *weight* and *wait*. Lynne praised Mikey for remembering to capitalize the *t* in *turkey* since it was being used as part of a specific naming word, a proper noun.

Chris used two sentences that ended with exclamation marks (Figure 16.3). In conference, Maribeth noted his correct use of the apostrophe in the

Figure 16.3
Chris's "Turkey Talk"
using direct quotations

contraction *don't* and the capital letters to begin the words *Hunter* and *Turkey* since they were being used as part of a proper noun like *Aunt Sally* or *Uncle Chris.*

 Teaching Point: When teaching the use of quotation marks for the first time, try to use examples with explanatory words used only at the end of the sentences or find examples that use explanatory words only at the beginning of the sentence. Don't introduce both sentence constructions at the same time. It is too confusing! With primary students in grades K–3, cut out or draw speech bubbles and use hands-on manipulatives like dried macaroni noodles to emphasize the placement of quotation marks. Ask a lot of questions as you study the model. The answers to these questions will help you and your students create an anchor chart about writing conversation correctly and will guide them in subsequent drafts:

- Why are quotation marks used?
- Where is the comma in each sentence? What is its job?
- Notice the capital letter in the quotation. Why is it used?
- Are the question mark and the exclamation mark inside or outside the quotation marks?
- Why do you think there is never a period used at the end of the exact words a speaker says (for sentences that begin with the direct quote and end with the explanatory words)?

In upper grades, your class's shared writing experiences can also be a valuable resource for ongoing conversations about grammar and conventions. In Mr. Chindemi's fifth-grade class, Diane used the story the class wrote to accompany the wordless book *a boy, a dog, a frog and a friend* by Mercer and Marianna Mayer to elicit conversations about conventions and grammatical concepts. Here is the text the class produced:

a boy, a dog, a frog and a friend
Mercer and Marianna Mayer, words by Mr. Chindemi's fifth-grade class

Early one spring morning, Carl went fishing with his dog Sparky and his frog Croaky. He casts his homemade fishing pole into the pond. Immediately he gets a bite! He caught something big . . . so big that it pulled him into the water. Sparky and Croaky jump in after him. Carl stands up and shouts as he notices a turtle taking his fishing rod up on the shore. The turtle bites Sparky's paw and Croaky is frightened and hops away! Carl attempts to pull Sparky away from the vicious turtle. But the snapping turtle doesn't let go. When they are half way across the pond he releases his grasp. On the shore Sparky licks his paw while his tail is in the water. The turtle bites his tail and pulls him into the water. Carl is frightened! Before Carl jumps in he notices Sparky is afloat.

Croaky takes up his space on the lily pad where they all notice the turtle floating on his back appears to be dead. Although Carl is relieved his dog is safe, he is sad. Unfortunately the turtle is dead. He uses his fishing pole to pull the turtle to shore. Croaky is sad, but he is mad at the dog. Carl is unhappy with his dog. He thinks Sparky drowned the turtle. Carl begins to dig a grave for the turtle. He digs it deep. In the meantime, the turtle wakes up. Sparky and Croaky noticed that the turtle is awake but Carl does not. When he does notice he is happy! The turtle brings the fishing pole over to Carl and they all celebrate. Carl says to the turtle, "I name you, Mr. Snappers." Carl, Sparky, Croaky, and Mr. Snappers all go home friends together.

After reading the piece aloud with the class, Diane asked them to look at the page. "Where is the white space? It is one paragraph; it appears that everything in the paragraph is of equal importance and of equal interest. The page looks cluttered." Diane helped students to come to these conclusions by asking them questions: "Is more than one thing happening? Are all of these events happening at the exact same time? Do all these events happen in the exact same place? Do you find it easy to read the page? What is missing that would make the page more readable?" Once students decided that paragraphing was necessary, Diane reviewed three markers for when to begin a new paragraph:

- New event
- New time
- New place

Diane mentioned that there are other markers for changing paragraphs as well (see the Your Turn Lesson "When to Make a New Paragraph in a Narrative" following Part 1); however, for this lesson and for this piece the class looked at just these three. Diane then asked students to work in pairs to decide where the paragraph breaks should be in the mentor text they had written as a class. As students worked on the task, Diane conferred with them. She asked students to tell her why they started a new paragraph when they did, and she kept a list of those who got it right. She asked those students to share their new paragraphing with the class, allowing them to explain their reasoning each time.

The class decided to organize the text into six paragraphs. The first ended with the sentence *Carl stands up and shouts as he notices a turtle taking his fishing rod up on shore.* The second ended with the sentence *When they are half way across the pond, he releases his grasp.* The third . . . *the turtle, floating on his back, appears to be dead.* The fourth ended with *Carl is frightened!* The fifth *He digs it deep.* The final paragraph ends with the friends going home together.

Note that the paragraphing decisions depended on a change of location and/or event.

Teaching Point: Teachers can expand on the paragraphing lesson with other mentor texts across the curriculum—science and social studies as informational writing, for example, where paragraph breaks depend on change of topic rather than change of setting. Also, students may notice one-sentence paragraphs, particularly in their novel reading, where the author changes paragraphs for dramatic effect. Point out, too, that paragraphs change when the speaker changes. These are ongoing conversations. Try not to do too much in any one lesson. What is most important is that students begin to have conversations about why they make the choices they make in their writing and that they are able to explain their choices.

Once the class agreed on the paragraphing, Diane underlined all the predicate verbs in the sentences on the interactive whiteboard and asked students to identify the time in which these actions are taking place. It didn't take long for students to realize that some of the verbs are past tense and some are present. Diane asked the class to decide if the story would be better told in past or present tense, explaining that writers use the same tense throughout a piece of writing. Although Diane encouraged the students to try out present tense for the entire story, the students wanted to use past tense for all the predicate verbs. As often as possible, a teacher must let the student writers make decisions so they can own the process.

With these two major revisions done Diane felt that students were ready to revise the piece for other issues of clarity. Diane pointed out two sentences: *Carl attempted to pull Sparky away from the vicious turtle, but the snapping turtle didn't let go. When they are half way across the pond, he releases his grasp.* Who is *he* in the second sentence? Couldn't *he* be *Carl?* For clarity, *he* needs to be changed to *the turtle.*

Diane pointed out a sentence that she had trouble reading aloud: *Croaky took up his space on the lily pad where they all noticed the turtle floating on his back appeared to be dead.* She noted that what made this sentence a problem to read is the phrase *floating on his back.* They notice the turtle floating on his back and they also notice that the turtle appeared to be dead. What could we as writers do to make that sentence easier to read and to make the meaning clear? Diane suggested that the phrase *floating on his back* is an interrupter. She punctuated the sentence as follows: *Croaky took up his space on the lily pad. They all noticed that the turtle, floating on his back, appeared to be dead.* She explained that she made it two sentences because only Croaky was on the lily pad.

Finally, the class revised their shared writing for paragraphing, for clarity of expression, and for detail. Below is their revision and edit:

Early one spring morning, Carl took his dog Sparky and his frog Croaky to the pond to go fishing. He cast his homemade fishing pole into the pond and immediately felt a tug on the line. He caught something big. In fact, it was so big that it pulled him into the water! Sparky and Croaky jumped in after him.

Carl saw a turtle carrying the fishing pole onto the shore. "You come back here!" Carl shouted. Barking and snarling, Sparky ran after the turtle. The turtle dropped the pole and snapped at Sparky's paw, biting him. Carl tried to pull Sparky away from the vicious turtle, but the snapping turtle would not let go.

When they were half way across the pond, the turtle finally released his grasp. Poor Sparky whined and licked his paw. He did not notice his tail hanging below the water, but the turtle did notice! He bit Sparky's tail and pulled him into the water. Carl was frightened. He thought Sparky was drowning. He stripped down to his underwear to jump into the water to save his pet.

Before Carl jumped in, Sparky came to the surface. The turtle, however, floated on his back and appeared to be dead. Croaky, perched on a lily pad, watched the scene. Although Carl was relieved about Sparky's safety, he was sad about the dead turtle.

Using his fishing pole to pull the turtle to the shore, Carl prepared to bury him. He dug a deep grave. He even picked a few flowers to leave on the grave. "Bad dog," Carl scolded. Sparky was responsible for the turtle's death.

Suddenly, the turtle woke up! Sparky and Croaky were surprised, but Carl did not notice. When he found the turtle alive, Carl smiled. The turtle carried the fishing pole over to Carl and everyone celebrated. Carl shouted, "I christen you, Mr. Snappers." Carl, Sparky, Croaky, and Mr. Snappers all went home friends together.

Notice that the class made some changes beyond those Diane pointed out in the previous discussion. Again, it is important to allow students to make decisions about the writing they are producing so that they own the process and product. Teachers can encourage students to use specific verbs and nouns, for example, and sometimes might even make suggestions. In the final analysis the choice should always be the class choice and not the teacher choice.

Shared-writing mentor texts provide multiple opportunities for conversations about grammar, conventions, and clarity. Keep in mind that "rightness" per se is not the goal of these conversations. Instead, the goal is to help your students to investigate language, to become aware of the choices they are making in their editing, and to be able to communicate their reasons for making those choices.

Afterword

Grammar to a writer is to a mountaineer a good pair of hiking boots or, more precisely, to a deep-sea diver an oxygen tank.

—A. A. Patawaran

Teaching grammar and conventions is a daunting task because of the breadth and depth of the subject compounded by the wide range of understanding about grammar and conventions in almost every grade, from kindergarten through high school and beyond. Still, our students need to have the look of literacy and the sound of literacy in their writing and speaking. Otherwise, what they say and what they write will have little impact on their target audience. Our job as educators is to improve the lives of our students in and out of school. Be it in relationships with family or friends, in the workforce, or in the community at large, having a knowledge of language and the ability to express language will benefit and empower our students throughout their lives.

The Common Core language standards set explicit grammatical and conventional expectations for each grade level. Our fear is that packaged programs with multiple worksheets and isolated exercises might be seen by some as the answer to grammar and mechanics instruction in the classroom. We wrote this book to help teachers embed that work into meaningful practice within the writing workshop structure. As we wrote over the course of one-and-one-half years, we revisited traditional grammar rules and learned some new ones.

Getting students to put words on the page by creating their own drafts is our first priority. Then they must learn, as the first reader of their own drafts, to criticize and begin the revision process. Finally, they learn to take a closer read and edit further. It is true that sometimes errors jump off the page at us, even as we draft, and it is okay to correct them then. During the writing process, we can revise and edit as early as our planning stage and until we have to turn something in because we have a deadline to meet. Even after publication, writers sometimes lament one last chance to add a detail or move a sentence or change a mark of punctuation.

But we must never make writing a matter of grammar and conventions *only*. Students need to develop ways to sharpen their focus, to develop their content, to organize their writing, and to let their voices sing through the rhythm and specificity of the words they choose to carry their ideas. Grammar, of course, plays a central part in all of this, freeing the writer to create masterpieces by using his knowledge of how our language works. The study of grammar and conventions makes us aware of the beauty of our language and the infinite possibilities for expression.

A Treasure Chest of Children's Books for Teaching Grammar and Conventions

We have found the following books useful in our teaching of grammar and conventions.

Auker, Kim R. 2013. *Professor Panda and the Punctuation Station: An Apostrophe Catastrophe.* CreateSpace, a DBA of On-Demand Publishing, LLC.
Designed to help elementary students understand punctuation.

Brennan-Nelson, Denise. 2003. *My Momma Likes to Say.* Chelsea, MI: Sleeping Bear Press.

———. 2004. *My Teacher Likes to Say.* Chelsea, MI: Sleeping Bear Press.

———. 2007. *My Grandma Likes to Say.* Chelsea, MI: Sleeping Bear Press.
Explains idioms with delightful illustrations. Each page states an idiom as the first line of a set of rhymed couplets and then explains the idiom.

Bruno, Elsa Knight. 2009. *Punctuation Celebration.* New York: Henry Holt.
Features fourteen poems, each addressing a mark of punctuation and its uses.

Cleary, Brian P. 1999. *A Mink, a Fink, a Skating Rink: What Is a Noun?* Minneapolis, MN: Millbrook Press.
Examples of nouns on every page; each noun is set off from the rest of the text by colored print. The definition of a noun is easy to intuit from multiple illustrations.

————. 2000. *Hairy, Scary, Ordinary: What Is an Adjective?* Minneapolis, MN: Millbrook Press.
    Chock-full of examples of adjectives and their uses. Illustrated.
————. 2003. *Dearly, Nearly, Insincerely: What Is an Adverb?* Minneapolis, MN: Carolrhoda Books.
    Adverbs abound in this delightful rhyming book. Each adverb is printed in color for ease in helping children find them.
————. 2004. *I and You and Don't Forget Who: What Is a Pronoun?* Minneapolis, MN: Carolrhoda Books.
    This book helps clarify the concept of pronouns for children. Key pronouns appear in color for easy identification.
————. 2005. *How Much Can a Bare Bear Bear? What Are Homonyms and Homophones?* Minneapolis, MN: Millbrook Press.
    Definitions and examples galore in this colorfully illustrated picture book sure to engage young writers and their teachers.
————. 2006. *Stop and Go, Yes and No: What Is an Antonym?* Minneapolis, MN: Millbrook Press.
    Through playful illustrations young readers learn about antonyms and their usefulness.
Dahl, Michael. 2006. *If You Were an Adverb*. Minneapolis, MN: Picture Window Books.
    Brimming with adverbs printed in color this book playfully explains the job of adverbs.
Edwards, Wallace. 2004. *Monkey Business*. Tonowanda, NY: Kids Can Press.
    Familiar sayings are illustrated in imaginative and hilarious ways in this book.
Ghigna, Charles. 1999. *See the Yak Yak*. New York: Random House.
    This Early Step into Reading book provides an explanation of homonyms by giving examples on every page.
Gwynne, Fred. 1970. *The King Who Rained*. New York: Aladdin.
    A humorous work of homophones and homonyms that provides object lessons for expressing the vagaries of the English language.
————. 1976. *A Chocolate Moose for Dinner*. New York: Aladdin Books.
    The illustrations show the literal interpretation of idioms in a humorous interpretation.
Heller, Ruth. 1987. *A Cache of Jewels and Other Collective Nouns*. New York: Grosset & Dunlap.
    A school of fish, a gam of whales, and a kindle of kittens are among the collective nouns in this book. Great for specific word choice.

———. 1989. *Many Luscious Lollipops: A Book About Adjectives*. New York: Scholastic.
This book not only defines adjectives but is overflowing with examples of specific word choice.

———. 1991. *Up, Up and Away: A Book About Adverbs*. New York: Grosset & Dunlap.
Filled with great examples of adverbs, this book also addresses comparative and superlative forms, irregular adverbs, and double negatives.

———. 1995. *Behind the Mask: A Book About Prepositions*. New York: Grosset & Dunlap.
Each preposition is color highlighted. Heller explains the uses of prepositions and provides a list of common prepositions at the end of the book.

———. 1998. *Fantastic! Wow! And Unreal! A Book About Interjections and Conjunctions*. New York: Scholastic.
Addresses issues of punctuation as well as definitions of both interjections and conjunctions in colorfully illustrated rhyming verse.

Hutchins, Pat. 1968. *Rosie's Walk*. New York: Simon & Schuster.
A fox is after Rosie the hen, but Rosie doesn't know it. Hers is a preposition-filled excursion.

Krouse Rosenthal, Amy. 2013. *!*. New York: Scholastic.
The author describes what an exclamation point does with clever illustrations.

Leedy, Loreen, and Pat Street. 2003. *There's a Frog in My Throat: 440 Animal Sayings a Little Bird Told Me*. New York: Scholastic.
Each page of this book is brimming with similes, metaphors, and idioms along with explanations in plain words.

Loewen, Nancy. 2007a. *If You Were a Conjunction*. Minneapolis, MN: Picture Window Books.
Conjunctions are set off in big, colorful print in this book that explains coordinating, correlative, and subordinating conjunctions. A glossary is provided as well.

———. 2007b. *If You Were a Preposition*. Minneapolis, MN: Picture Window Books.
Prepositions are set off in colorful print in this book that addresses preposition use. Teachers might enjoy using the activity page at the end with students.

Martin, Bill. 1970. *The Maestro Plays*. New York: Henry Holt.
A book that highlights adverbs in an entertaining narrative.

Pulver, Robin. 2003. *Punctuation Takes a Vacation*. New York: Holiday House.
Punctuation marks decide to teach students a lesson by going on
vacation. It doesn't take long for them to be missed! A great object
lesson in the importance of punctuation marks.

———. 2006. *Nouns and Verbs Have a Field Day*. New York: Holiday House.
When they are abandoned by the students because of field day, nouns
and verbs decide to have a field day of their own. Chaos ensues until
they realize they need to work together.

Roy, Jennifer Rozines. 2004. *You Can Write Using Good Grammar*. Berkeley
Heights, NJ: Enslow.
An easy-to-follow guide to good grammar. Explanations are illustrated
by good examples.

Ryan, Pam Muñoz. 1997. *A Pinky Is a Baby Mouse*. New York: Scholastic.
Specific word choice for baby animals abound in this book about nouns.

Schneider, R. M. 1995. *Add It, Dip It, Fix It: A Book of Verbs*. New York:
Houghton Mifflin.
Each page pictures action verbs. This is a great introduction to verbs
for younger students.

Schotter, Roni. 2006. *The Boy Who Loved Words*. New York: Random House
Children's Books.
A great collection of luscious words. A glossary is included.

Shaskan, Trisha Speed. 2009. *If You Were A Contraction*. North Mankato,
MN: Picture Window Books.
"If you were a contraction, your best friend would be an apostrophe."
This book is a great resource for students and teachers.

Steinberg, Laya. 2003. *Thesaurus Rex*. Cambridge, MA: Barefoot Books.
A young dinosaur has adventures with verbs.

Terban, Marvin. 1983. *In a Pickle: And Other Funny Idioms*. New York:
Clarion Books.
Through illustrations thirty popular expressions are amusingly explained.

Truss, Lynne. 2006. *Eats, Shoots & Leaves*. New York: G. P. Putnam's Sons.
Why commas are important. Each sentence is punctuated two ways to
illustrate how meaning changes depending on punctuation usage.

———. 2007. *The Girl's Like Spaghetti: Why, You Can't Manage Without
Apostrophes!* New York: G. P. Putnam's Sons.
Use of apostrophe demonstrates how meaning changes depending on
the placement of the apostrophe.

Walton, Rick. 2004. *Suddenly Alligator: An Adverbial Tale*. Layton, UT: Gibbs Smith.
Each sentence ends with an adverb. Entertaining story that will engage
readers. Students can experiment with adverb placement.

Appendix A:

Mentor Texts Conversations (Using Mentor Texts to Notice Grammatical Concepts and Punctuation)

In your classroom library of read-alouds and independent reads, you can choose wonderful mentor texts to use in whole- or small-group conversations (see Chapter 16) about matters of grammar and punctuation. Of course, these books should first be enjoyed for their content. Students may use them at a later point in time to imitate the author's craft. By the time you use a book for grammar conversations, there will already be a familiarity with the book so that students can direct their attention to noticings about syntax and mechanics. Often, it is easy to display a passage, several passages, or a single sentence on a chart or document imager. Dorfman and Cappelli (2009) suggest picture books as good sources for student investigation.

This appendix gives you a close look at a variety of texts for various grade levels. Your own collection is most likely filled with appropriate choices that would stimulate rich conversations. Feel free to use our examples or use them as guidelines to develop your own sets. The students should use the sentences to notice something about the writing, write down their noticings in their writer's notebook, and share with a partner or two before sharing with the larger group. Sometimes, students are able to talk about parts of a sentence without doing any jotting. It is not always necessary to write in the writer's notebook first. Students can use their noticings

265

Grammar Matters: Lessons, Tips, and Conversations Using Mentor Texts, K–6 by Lynne Dorfman and Diane Dougherty. Copyright © 2014. Stenhouse Publishers.

to return to a notebook entry, a current draft, or an already-published piece to revise and edit sentences or paragraphs. Again, the examples show possibilities for noticings. Some concepts and structures may not be discussed or noticed because the students do not have enough background knowledge at that time. We need to be aware of the instructional time involved to discuss a grammar or convention point and the effect it will have on our student writers. Will they be able to transfer the learning to their own writing? Can they imitate the sentence construction or punctuation use independently or with a little help? What are they able to notice and talk about before you point it out to them?

Grammar Matters: Lessons, Tips, and Conversations Using Mentor Texts, K–6 by Lynne Dorfman and Diane Dougherty. Copyright © 2014. Stenhouse Publishers.

Kindergarten and grade one

Heard, Georgia, ed. 2009. "Recipe for Writing an Autumn Poem." In *Falling Down the Page: A Book of List Poems*. New York: Roaring Brook Press.

"Recipe for Writing an Autumn Poem"
by Georgia Heard

One teaspoon wild geese.
    naming words (nouns—teaspoon, geese), adjective (one, wild)
One tablespoon red kite.
    naming words (tablespoon, kite), adjective (one, red)
One cup wind song.
    naming words (cup, song), adjective (one, wind)
One pint trembling leaves.
    naming words (pint, leaves), adjective (one, trembling)
One quart darkening sky.
    naming words (quart, sky), adjectives (one, darkening)
One gallon north wind.
    naming words (gallon, wind), adjective (one, north)

This poem could also be introduced in math class. Kindergartners and first graders could practice using the measurement words that name (*teaspoon, tablespoon, cup, pint, quart, gallon*) by using different sizes of containers. These words can become part of their sight-word vocabulary.

Teach younger children the simple test for describing words:

The _____ NOUN

If a word can fit between the word *the* and the noun, it probably is an adjective (a word that describes a noun). Young writers can also learn that all numbers can be used as adjectives.

You can also use this poem to talk to students about rules for capitalizing words in a title—always the first word, always the last word, and all the important words in between.

If you are using this poem with older students, ask them to rewrite the lines of poetry as complete sentences in different ways. For example: "Use one cup of wind song." OR "Add one cup of wind song." OR "You will need to blend in one cup of wind song."

You can also talk about the use of *wind* as an adjective when it is usually used as a noun or about the pronunciation of this word—use context to determine. For example, "I wind my music box to make it play."

Grammar Matters: Lessons, Tips, and Conversations Using Mentor Texts, K–6 by Lynne Dorfman and Diane Dougherty. Copyright © 2014. Stenhouse Publishers.

Kindergarten and grade one

Juster, Norton. 2005. *The Hello, Goodbye Window*. New York: Hyperion Books for Children.

There are shelves full of glass jars with lots of everything
unusual plural nouns (words that end in -*f* or -*fe*), plural noun just add -*s*

in them, a step stool so I can wash my hands, and all
commas in a series, plural noun (hands) just add -*s*

kinds of pictures from the olden days. Nana says she
plural nouns by adding -*s*, adjective (olden) and position before the noun, prepositional phrase (beginning with "from")

even used to give me a bath in the sink when I was little—
prepositional phrase (in the sink), commentary dash

really!
exclamation point (emphasizing it's true)

Grammar Matters: Lessons, Tips, and Conversations Using Mentor Texts, K–6 by Lynne Dorfman and Diane Dougherty. Copyright © 2014. Stenhouse Publishers.

Grades one and two

Nelson, Robin. 2013. *From Sheep to Sweater*. Minneapolis, MN: Lerner.

In the spring, the sheep's coats are clipped. This is called
prepositional phrase, use of apostrophe for ownership, irregular plural noun (sheep), double consonant to form past tense of "clipped"

shearing. A person shears each sheep's wool off in one big
boldface print (shearing), apostrophe for ownership (sheep's wool), sheep as singular noun here, adjectives (one, big)

piece called a **fleece**. The sheep will grow another coat
boldface print (fleece), sheep as singular, adjectives (each, one, big), nouns (piece, fleece, sheep, coat), sheep as singular noun, future tense verb (will grow)

over the summer to keep it warm in the winter.
prepositional phrases (over the summer, in the winter), use of pronoun *it* to refer to the one sheep, nouns (summer, winter)

Grammar Matters: Lessons, Tips, and Conversations Using Mentor Texts, K–6 by Lynne Dorfman and Diane Dougherty. Copyright © 2014. Stenhouse Publishers.

Grades one and two

Legg, Gerald. 1997. *From Egg to Chicken*. New York: Franklin Watts.

The hen is a good mother. She keeps
> **nouns name (hen, mother), adjectives describe nouns (good), pronoun (she)**

her eggs warm by sitting on them. She
> **pronouns (her) can show possession, sentences start with capitals, end punctuation, prepositional phrase (on them)**

surrounds them with her soft feathers.
> **prepositional phrase, recognizing verbs (surrounds), adjectives describe nouns (soft feathers), use of pronoun ("them" to rename "eggs")**

This is called brooding.
> **recognizing a noun—brooding names what the hen does to keep her eggs warm so they will hatch.**

Grammar Matters: Lessons, Tips, and Conversations Using Mentor Texts, K–6 by Lynne Dorfman and Diane Dougherty. Copyright © 2014. Stenhouse Publishers.

Grades two and three

Murphy, Frank. 2002. *George Washington and the General's Dog*. New York: Random House.

In the fall of 1777, George's troops went to
> **apostrophe to show ownership, capitalize a proper noun, comma after introductory phrases (prepositional phrases)**

Pennsylvania. They were fighting the English
> **proper nouns, use of the helping verb "were" with the *-ing* form of the verb**

troops. Guns fired! RAT-A-TAT-TAT!
> **exclamation marks, N/V sentence, variation in print, use of hyphens**

Cannons roared. BOOM! BANG! Smoke filled the air.
> **past tense (*-ed*) of verbs, exclamation points, variation in print, N/V/N sentence**

Grammar Matters: Lessons, Tips, and Conversations Using Mentor Texts, K–6 by Lynne Dorfman and Diane Dougherty. Copyright © 2014. Stenhouse Publishers.

Grades two and three

Monjo, F. N. 1970. *The Drinking Gourd*. New York: HarperTrophy.

Tommy gave them each an apple.
> **proper noun, pronoun "them," and end punctuation**

"You don't have to be good in church, do you?" Tommy said.
> **direct quotation, contraction, end punctuation, use of question**

The horses stamped and snorted.
> **N/V sentence with compound predicate and past tense of verbs ending in -*ed***

Tommy saw the hay wagon piled high with
> **irregular verb to form past tense (see-saw), adjective (hay)**

hay. He wanted to jump from the hayloft
> **noun (hay), prepositional phrase (from the hayloft) and use of pronoun to rename Tommy, compound word (hayloft)**

down into all that hay in the wagon.
> **adverb (down), prepositional phrases, noun (hay) used before as an adjective**

Grammar Matters: Lessons, Tips, and Conversations Using Mentor Texts, K–6 by Lynne Dorfman and Diane Dougherty. Copyright © 2014. Stenhouse Publishers.

Grades two and three

Hill, Tad. 2012. *Rocket Writes a Story*. New York: Schwartz & Wade Books.

The little yellow bird encouraged him. "Remember,
> **use of adjectives without comma placement, strong verb (encouraged), past tense verb with *-ed* (drop silent *-e*), quotation marks**

stories take time," she'd say.
> **quotation marks for conversation, comma to separate quote from explanatory words, plural noun follows consonant *y* rule, contraction for she would**

She wanted to know more about the owl and asked
> **past tense *-ed*, use of subject pronoun "she" for bird, prepositional phrase, compound predicate**

Rocket questions. "Why do you think the owl wouldn't
> **proper noun (name of a dog), quotation marks, and contraction (wouldn't)**

come down? What color is her beak? What does she do every day?"
> **question mark and question words, use of pronouns—possessive and subject, singular form of verb do (does), adjective (every), nouns (color, beak, day)**

Grammar Matters: Lessons, Tips, and Conversations Using Mentor Texts, K–6 by Lynne Dorfman and Diane Dougherty. Copyright © 2014. Stenhouse Publishers.

Grades four to six

Yolen, Jane. 2010. *Elsie's Bird*. New York: Philomel Books.

Best of all, Elsie took a birdcage
> **introductory phrase followed by a comma, proper noun, irregular past tense of verb (took), direct object (birdcage—a compound word)**

with her new canary, Timmy Tune,
> **prepositional phrase that modifies a direct object, use of commas to set off an appositional phrase, capitalization of a pet's name, use of alliteration, use of specific noun (canary)**

yellow as the sun over Boston Harbor.
> **use of simile, prepositional phrase, proper noun**

They sang to one another, bird and girl,
> **subject pronoun (refers to Elsie and Timmy Tune), commas to set off an appositional phrase (bird and girl—nonspecific nouns)**

along the gathering miles.
> **prepositional phrase, unusual adjective—a verbal—that is often used as a verb**

(See the Your Turn Lesson "Adding Appositives to Paint Pictures and Combine Ideas" following Part 3.)

Grammar Matters: Lessons, Tips, and Conversations Using Mentor Texts, K–6 by Lynne Dorfman and Diane Dougherty. Copyright © 2014. Stenhouse Publishers.

Grades five and up

Schachner, Judy. 2013. *bits and pieces*. New York: Penguin Young Readers Group.

Just as he had learned to be a good cat from his grannyman,
> **Adverbial clause (subordinating conjunction pair, just as) past perfect tense (had learned) infinitive phrase (to be a good cat) prepositional phrase (from his grannyman).**

Tink decided to be a mother-brother to his kitten.
> **Independent clause, infinitive phrase, invented compound noun, prepositional phrase.**

Where did he come from?
> **Interrogative sentence with a split verb (did come).**

Oooh he's so cute.
> **Simple sentence with a contraction (he's) that includes the predicate verb of the sentence (he is). Predicate adjective (cute).**

Huffing and puffing right behind them was a lady
> **Participles (huffing and puffing) describing "lady." Subject of the clause positioned after the verb (was a lady). Prepositional phrase "behind them."**

who looked like she had lost her best friend.
> **Adjective clause (who looked), which modifies "lady" along with an adverbial clause (like she had lost her best friend), which modifies "looked." Note that "like" is a preposition and in formal writing the word *like* in this sentence would be written as "as though."**

Grammar Matters: Lessons, Tips, and Conversations Using Mentor Texts, K–6 by Lynne Dorfman and Diane Dougherty. Copyright © 2014. Stenhouse Publishers.

Appendix B:

Mentor Text and the Common Core Language Standards

The following concepts are suggested by the Common Core State Standards (CCSS) at the noted grade levels. Using mentor texts to have conversations about these concepts provides students with a hook for making this information stick. Encourage students to look for other examples in their reading and to share these examples with the class. Having an anchor chart or bulletin board available for students to add their own examples, gives everyone the opportunity to become an expert.

Grades one, two, three

What makes a sentence? The simple sentence

Palatini, Margie. 2001. *The Web Files*. New York: Hyperion.

6:32 a.m. This is the farm. My partner, Bill, and I were working the barnyard shift. It was peaceful. Quiet. Then we got the call.

    6:35 a.m. The hen's house. We knocked on the door. She answered.

    10:43 a.m. Corner of Barn and Pen. Bill and I talked to the horses.

Grammar Matters: Lessons, Tips, and Conversations Using Mentor Texts, K–6 by Lynne Dorfman and Diane Dougherty. Copyright © 2014. Stenhouse Publishers.

11:47 a.m. The squad room. My partner and I were still trying to quack the case, but we didn't have any idea whom to I.D.

Note that there are multiple fragments (Quiet. The hen's house. Corner of Barn and Pen. The squad room.). Make sure students recognize that these are fragments. In upper grades you may discuss the use of fragments for effect, but in the lower grades, the first consideration is that students recognize the sentence unit.

Grades four, five, six

Sentence unit: Compound sentence and punctuation—coordinating conjunctions

Golenbock, Peter. 1990. *Teammates*. New York: Harcourt.

The Negro Leagues had extraordinary players, and adoring fans came to see them wherever they played. They were heroes, but players in the Negro Leagues didn't make much money and their lives on the road were hard.

Many Americans knew that racial prejudice was wrong, but few dared to challenge openly the way things were.

Back then, many hotels didn't rent rooms to black people, so the Negro League players slept in their cars. Many towns had no restaurants that would serve them, so they often had to eat meals that they could buy and carry with them.

Grades four, five, six

Sentence unit: Complex sentences

Wyeth, Sharon Dennis. 1998. *Something Beautiful*. New York: Doubleday.

Introductory adverbial clauses
When I look through my window, I see a brick wall. When I go back outside, I see some of my friends.

Simon, Seymour. 2000. *Gorillas*. New York: HarperCollins.

When it gets older, it will ride on her back when she travels.

Grammar Matters: Lessons, Tips, and Conversations Using Mentor Texts, K–6 by Lynne Dorfman and Diane Dougherty. Copyright © 2014. Stenhouse Publishers.

As a male gorilla grows older and heavier, the hair on his back slowly turns gray, much like the hair on an older person's head. By the time a male has taken command of a family, his back hair may be totally gray.

When families travel, the silverback often leads, followed by the blackbacks and the females with their young.

When blackbacks become silverbacks, they may leave the group and travel alone or stay and help fight off intruders. When young females grow up, they leave to join other males or other families.

Grade five

Sentence unit (fragment for effect)

MacLachlan, Patricia. 1985. *Sarah, Plain and Tall*. New York: HarperCollins.

I rocked on the porch and Caleb rolled a marble on the wood floor. Back and forth. Back and forth. The marble was blue.

"Hush," said Papa to the dogs.

And it was quiet.

Note that the fragments "Back and forth. Back and forth." are effective because they slow down the action and help the reader to visualize what is happening. The fragment "And it was quiet." acts in the same way.

Grades three, four, five

Quotation marks: Use and punctuation and change of speaker

Wyeth, Sharon Dennis. 1998. *Something Beautiful*. New York: Doubleday.

I go to Miss Delphine's Diner. "Hi there, sugar pie," says Miss Delphine. "What are you up to¿"

"I'm looking for something beautiful," I tell her.

"Sit down for a minute," she says as she goes to the grill. She puts on fish. The fish sizzles. Miss Delphine makes it into a sandwich.

"There's nothing more beautiful tasting than my fried fish sandwiches," she tells me. My teeth sink in.

"Mm! This is good!"

Grammar Matters: Lessons, Tips, and Conversations Using Mentor Texts, K–6 by Lynne Dorfman and Diane Dougherty. Copyright © 2014. Stenhouse Publishers.

Palatini, Margie. 2001. *The Web Files*. New York: Hyperion.

"A lot of squawking going on down in the coop area, Ducktective Web. Looks like fowl play. Report says feathers are flying. Chief says we should check out the chicks."
"Chicks?"
"Check."
"Let's fly."

Grades two, three, four

Use of exclamation point

Murphy, Frank. 2002. *George Washington and the General's Dog*. New York: Random House.

A friend from France gave George an even bigger gift—seven dogs!

Rylant, Cynthia. 1992. *An Angel for Solomon Singer*. New York: Orchard Books.

He could not even paint his walls a different color, and, oh, what a difference a yellow wall or a purple wall would have made!

Grades three, four

Commas in a series

Simon, Seymour. 2003. *Spiders*. New York: HarperCollins.

Spiders live nearly everywhere around the world—in grasslands, forests, mountains, deserts, ponds, schools, and houses, and on ocean-going ships.
Other spiders are yellow, red, or orange.

All insects have three body parts, six legs, and antennae.
They are related to mites, ticks, and scorpions.
Jumping spiders, wolf spiders, and most hunting spiders have large main eyes.
Spiders can run, jump, climb on smooth surfaces, and hang upside down.
They use it to make webs, traps, burrows, and cocoons.

Grammar Matters: Lessons, Tips, and Conversations Using Mentor Texts, K–6 by Lynne Dorfman and Diane Dougherty. Copyright © 2014. Stenhouse Publishers.

They eat small fish, tadpoles, and insects that have fallen into the water.
A water spider eats, mates, and lays its eggs inside the bell.

Grades two, three, four

Commas in dates; commas to separate city and state

Simon, Seymour. 1991. *Earthquakes.* New York: William Morrow.

On the morning of September 19, 1985, a major earthquake struck Mexico City.
The Armenian earthquake of December 7, 1998, measured 6.9 and was followed, four minutes later, by a 5.8 aftershock.
On the afternoon of Good Friday, March 27, 1964, Anchorage, Alaska, was shaken apart by the most violent earthquake ever recorded in the United States.

Grades three, four, five, six

Use of the apostrophe in contractions

Simon, Seymour. 1993. *Weather.* New York: HarperCollins.

It's cloudy today. It's also sunny, rainy, and snowy, hot and cold, calm and windy, dry and damp.
Weather is what's happening at the bottom of the atmosphere, mostly in a layer seven and a half miles thick called the troposphere.
The sun doesn't warm Earth evenly. Land areas can't store much heat and become hot or cold more rapidly. That's why mid-continental regions have warmer summers and colder winters than do coastal areas.
We're going to have it and it's going to change.

Grades three, four, five, six

Use of the apostrophe to show possession

Simon, Seymour. 1993. *Weather.* New York: HarperCollins.

Earth's weather is driven by the intense heat of the sun. The sun's energy travels through space in the form of visible light waves and invisible ultraviolet and infrared rays.

Grammar Matters: Lessons, Tips, and Conversations Using Mentor Texts, K–6 by Lynne Dorfman and Diane Dougherty. Copyright © 2014. Stenhouse Publishers.

At the equator, where the sun's rays are most direct, insolation is several times greater than at either of the poles, where the sun's rays come in at a slant. Most of the Earth's hot spots are located near the equator, and most of the cold spots are in the Arctic or Antarctic.

Simon, Seymour. 1991. *Big Cats*. New York: HarperCollins.

Even the cat's tongue helps out.

A cat's senses are very keen, and it can detect its prey at a distance or at night.

Sensitive hairs in this jaguar's ears can pick up the sound of an animal's movements even before the animal can be seen.

By now, the cub's eyes have opened and their weight has more than doubled.

The tiger's coat blends in well with the dark shadows and light patches of the grasslands or forests in which it lives.

The jaguar's main food is the capybara, the largest rodent in the world, with a weight of 100 pounds.

Simon, Seymour. 2000. *Gorillas*. New York: HarperCollins.

Its fingers have fingernails and fingerprints that look like humans' prints, only larger. The silverback may beat his chest to move family members along, to stop fights that may arise between them, or to attract the females' attention.

Grades five, six

Tense consistency (use of present tense in nonfiction to report on a subject—things that are factual); notice how Seymour Simon keeps everything in present tense (happening now)

(Any of the Simon books work for this.)
Simon, Seymour. 2003. *Spiders*. New York: Scholastic.

Spiders are not the most popular kind of animal. Some people scream or run away from them. They think spiders are ugly and poisonous. Actually, only a very few are poisonous to people. Each year, far more people get sick or die from bee stings or other insect bites than from spiders.

Grammar Matters: Lessons, Tips, and Conversations Using Mentor Texts, K–6 by Lynne Dorfman and Diane Dougherty. Copyright © 2014. Stenhouse Publishers.

Perfect tense
George, Jean Craighead. 1998. *My Side of the Mountain*. New York: Puffin Books.

I had been working since May, learning how to make a fire with flint and steel, finding what plants I could eat, how to trap animals and catch fish—all this so that when the curtain of blizzard struck the Catskills, I could crawl inside my tree and be comfortably warm and have plenty to eat.

During the summer and fall I had thought about the coming of winter.

I left New York in May. I had a penknife, a ball of cord, an ax, and $40, which I had saved from selling magazine subscriptions.

Grammar Matters: Lessons, Tips, and Conversations Using Mentor Texts, K–6 by Lynne Dorfman and Diane Dougherty. Copyright © 2014. Stenhouse Publishers.

Appendix C:

Commonly Confused Homophones for Elementary School Writers

Accept; Except

Accept means "to receive willingly."
I accept the nomination for class president.
Except means "apart from or excluding."
I can resist every dessert except chocolate.
I would be on honor roll except I never study.

Aloud; Allowed

Aloud means simply "out loud."
I read the story aloud to my little sister.
Allowed means "to have permission."
I am not allowed to go to the movies on school nights.

Blew; Blue

Blew is the past tense of the verb *blow*.
He blew his trumpet night and day.
Blue is the color.
We gazed at the crystal blue sky.

283

Grammar Matters: Lessons, Tips, and Conversations Using Mentor Texts, K–6 by Lynne Dorfman and Diane Dougherty. Copyright © 2014. Stenhouse Publishers.

Brake; Break

Brake means "to stop (v.)" or "a device to slow or stop a motion (n.)."
My father braked hard when a cat darted across the road in front of us.
My mother always uses the emergency brake when she parks on a hill.

Break means "to come apart" or "a pause" (as in a gap or a recess from work).
He was sorry to break his mother's favorite vase.
Our family enjoys our winter break in Colorado because we love to ski.

Capital; Capitol

Capital means "an uppercase letter"; or "the city where the seat of the government for a country or state is located"; or "the main, chief [reason]."
Proper nouns begin with a capital letter.
Harrisburg is the capital of Pennsylvania.
Jim had a capital idea for completing the project with photographs.

Capitol is the building at Washington, DC, where Congress meets or in an individual state where the state legislature meets.
When we visited Washington, DC, we toured the Capitol Building.
The state capitol building in Harrisburg, Pennsylvania, is visited by school-children nearly every day.

Dear; Deer

Dear means "much loved or precious." It is also used as a salutation in letters ("Dear Mom,").
Joey's stuffed teddy bear was dear to him.

Deer is a woodland animal.
Bambi tells the story of a young deer's adventures.
The state animal of Pennsylvania is the white-tailed deer.

Its; It's

Its is the possessive form of the pronoun *it*.
The dog injured its paw.

It's can only be a contraction meaning "it is."
It's a beautiful day in the neighborhood.

Knew; new; gnu

Knew is the past tense of the verb *know*.
I was happy that I knew the answer.

New is the opposite of old.
For my birthday my parents bought me a new bike.

Grammar Matters: Lessons, Tips, and Conversations Using Mentor Texts, K–6 by Lynne Dorfman and Diane Dougherty. Copyright © 2014. Stenhouse Publishers.

Gnu is an African antelope that has horns like an ox.
We saw a gnu at the zoo.

Know; No

Know means "to be sure of or to be aware of or have an understanding of."
I know the names of all of the presidents of the United States.

No is the antonym for "yes." It is used to give a negative answer or reply. It can also mean "not any."
My mother said, "No," when I asked her if I could go to the mall after school.
I have no experience with computer skills.

Lead; Led

Lead (when pronounced "led") is a metal that is easily melted.
I used a lead pencil to fill in the bubbles on the answer sheet.

Led is the past tense of the verb *lead*, which means "to show the way."
Mrs. Dougherty led the class to the auditorium.

Pare; Pair; Pear

Pare means "to shave or peel."
My mother pared six apples for the pie.

Pair indicates two of something that go together.
She wore her new pair of shoes to church.

Pear is a fruit.
The ripe pear smelled delicious.

Passed; Past

Passed is the past tense of the verb *pass*, which means "to advance or to be successful or to go by."
I passed the test with flying colors.
The kids passed the lemonade stand on their way to the Ferris Wheel.

Past indicates time gone by or the time before. It can be used as a noun, an adjective, or a preposition meaning "to or on the further side of."
When we study the past, we can learn from the mistakes of others.
In the past year, Steven won many baseball games.
The Boy Scout troop hiked past the old mill on their way to the creek.

Grammar Matters: Lessons, Tips, and Conversations Using Mentor Texts, K–6 by Lynne Dorfman and Diane Dougherty. Copyright © 2014. Stenhouse Publishers.

Peace; Piece

Peace is the antonym for war. It is a synonym for harmony.
The world leaders wanted the warring nations of the Middle East to make peace.

Piece means a part that has been broken, torn, or cut from the original whole.
My dad always asks for a second piece of custard pie.

Read; Red

Read is the past tense of the verb *read* as in "to read a book."
I read three books this month.

Red is the color.
In the fall maple tree leaves turn red.

Right; Write

Right is the opposite of wrong or the opposite of left.
He checked the answer to the long division problem with a calculator to make sure it was right.
In the United States drivers drive on the right side of the road.

Write is the physical act of forming letters or symbols to form words.
He learned to write friendly letters in second grade.

Sea; See

Sea is a large body of water.
My family loves to visit the seashore.

See is to perceive with the eyes or to understand.
In the classroom I can see my friends' faces.
I see your point, but I don't agree with it.

Some; Sum

Some is an indefinite amount (adj.).
I would like some pudding for dessert.

Sum is a total or amount (n.).
The number four is the sum of two plus two.

Stair; Stare

Stair refers to one step or a series of steps for going from one level to another; usually used in the plural form, *stairs*, or as part of the word *staircase*.
Jenny ran down the stairs.

Grammar Matters: Lessons, Tips, and Conversations Using Mentor Texts, K–6 by Lynne Dorfman and Diane Dougherty. Copyright © 2014. Stenhouse Publishers.

Stare means "to look steadily (v.)" or "the act of looking steadily (n.)."
When you stare at people, you often make them feel uncomfortable.

Tail; Tale

Tail is the hind part of anything.
The red fox has a long, fluffy tail.
Tale can be a story or a lie.
The boy who cried "Wolf!" was cautioned to stop telling tales.

Their; They're; There

Their is the possessive form of the personal pronoun *they.*
Their home is located in Downingtown.
They're is a contraction form of the two words *they are.*
They're my favorite team.
There means "in or at a place" or "to go to that place."
Let's not go there.

Threw; Through

Threw is the past tense of the verb *throw.*
The pitcher threw the ball across the plate.
Through is a preposition meaning "between parts" or "over; around."
The dog chased the cat through the kitchen door.

To; Too; Two

To is a preposition indicating direction.
Take the recycling to the curb.
Too is an adverb meaning "excessively" or "also."
This lemonade is too sour to drink.
Diane's younger sister wanted to go to the party too.
Two is the number.
I have two pieces of chocolate left to eat.

Weather; Whether

Weather refers to the state of the atmosphere at any given place in time.
The weather outside is frightful.
Whether is a conjunction that indicates a choice.
I wonder whether Tommy will play the part of a turkey at Thanksgiving.

Grammar Matters: Lessons, Tips, and Conversations Using Mentor Texts, K–6 by Lynne Dorfman and Diane Dougherty. Copyright © 2014. Stenhouse Publishers.

Wear; Where

Wear is a verb meaning "to have on the body" or "to erode."
Some children like to wear school uniforms.
A strong hurricane can wear away the sand dunes.

Where means "in what place, position, or direction." It may be used as a question marker.
We found a place at the park where there was some shade.
Where do you think you are going?

Who's; Whose

Who's is a contraction for the words *who is.*
Who's going to the park today?

Whose is the possessive form of *who*. It is often used to form a question to ask who owns something or has something.
Whose car is parked in the principal's spot?

Your; You're

Your is the possessive form of *you.*
Is this your jacket in the lost and found box?

You're is a contraction of the two words *you are.*
You're my best friend.

Grammar Matters: Lessons, Tips, and Conversations Using Mentor Texts, K–6 by Lynne Dorfman and Diane Dougherty. Copyright © 2014. Stenhouse Publishers.

Appendix D:

Glossary of Terms

Grammar consists of the agreed-upon rules for making meaning clear in speaking and in writing. All languages have grammar. Native speakers of English "know" the grammar of the language, but when they write, they most likely need help in applying what they know about grammar to their writing. The purpose of grammar instruction in the writing workshop is to provide students with a shared language for communicating—the nomenclature of grammar. The key to effective grammar instruction is to integrate that instruction into the writing workshop during the revision and editing stages. Make it relevant; use student samples (with student permission, of course) whenever possible.

The following list of grammatical terms is for quick reference.

Parts of Speech

The Noun

A noun is a word used to name a person, place, thing, or idea.
Proper nouns name particular persons, places, or things and are capitalized: *Lynne, Philadelphia, Hershey Park, Thanksgiving.*

289

Grammar Matters: Lessons, Tips, and Conversations Using Mentor Texts, K–6 by Lynne Dorfman and Diane Dougherty. Copyright © 2014. Stenhouse Publishers.

Common nouns do not name a particular person, place, or thing and are not capitalized: *teacher, city, amusement park, holiday.*
Collective nouns name a group: *team, family, orchestra, congregation (alligators), pod (whales).*

The Pronoun

A pronoun is a word used in place of a noun.
Personal pronouns: *I, me, you, he, him, she, her, it, we, us, they, them.*
Possessive forms of personal pronouns: *my, mine, your, yours, his, hers, its, our, ours, their, theirs.*
Interrogative pronouns: *who, whom, whose, which, what.* (These pronouns are used in asking questions.)
Demonstrative pronouns: *this, that, these, those.*
Reflexive pronouns: Personal pronouns ending in *-self* or *-selves* are reflexive pronouns: *myself, yourself, himself, herself, itself, ourselves, yourselves, themselves.* Note that these pronouns may be used reflexively or intensively. For example, in the sentence *Lynne baked the cookies herself,* "herself" is used reflexively. An example of *herself* used intensively follows: *Lynne herself baked the cookies.*
Other types of pronouns include relative and indefinite pronouns.

The Adjective

An adjective is a word that describes a noun or pronoun. Adjectives tell what kind (*tall* tree), which one (*that* girl), or how many (*two* books).

The Verb

A verb is a word that shows action or that helps make a statement. *Only a verb can show a change of time by a change in its form.*
Linking verbs are verbs that link a word that follows it with the subject. Most common linking verbs are forms of the verb *to be* (*am, is, are, was, were, been*). Some other linking verbs are *seem, appear, look, feel, become.*
Helping verbs are sometimes called auxiliary verbs. They help the main verb to show action or to make a statement (*The teacher* will be *grading papers in her classroom before school starts.*).
Principal parts of verbs—The principal parts of verbs are the present, present participle, past, and past participle. For regular verbs, the present participle is formed by adding *-ing* to the present. It is used with a form of the helping verb *be.* The past and past *participle* of regular verbs are formed by adding *-ed* or *-d* (if the word ends in silent *-e*) to the present, usually with a form of the helping verb have. For example, the verb *talk* has the following forms:

Grammar Matters: Lessons, Tips, and Conversations Using Mentor Texts, K–6 by Lynne Dorfman and Diane Dougherty. Copyright © 2014. Stenhouse Publishers.

| **Verb** | **Present Participle** | **Past** | **Past Participle** |
| talk | (is) talking | talked | (have) talked |

Verb tense—Verbs are the only parts of speech that show a change of time by changing their form. In addition to present, past, and future tense (formed by adding *will* or *shall* to the present form), verb tenses include perfect tenses.

Perfect tense: CCSS for fifth grade stipulates that students demonstrate how to form and use the perfect verb tenses. In discussing verbs, *perfect* means "complete." The past, present, and future perfect tenses describe actions that are already complete at that point in time. Young writers frequently fail to use the perfect tense to show the relationships between two different times. Perfect tenses are formed by combining some form of *to have* with the past participle of the verb.

Present perfect tense: This tense expresses actions occurring in the past that have effects in the present. It is formed by adding *have* or *has* to the past participle of the verb.

Examples:

I *have* always *liked* strawberry shortcake. (I still do)

For years my family *has vacationed* in North Carolina. (we still vacation there)

Past perfect tense: This tense expresses actions completed in the past before some other action. It helps keep straight the time order of events in the past. Past perfect tense is formed by combining *had* with the past participle of the verb.

Examples:

The children *had left* the classroom before the bell rang.

My family *had vacationed* in North Carolina for many years before buying a home there.

Future perfect tense: This tense expresses action that will be completed in the future before some other future action. It is formed by using *will have* or *shall have* along with the past participle of the verb.

Examples:

As of next month, I *will have taken* piano lessons for one year.

By the end of this summer, my family *will have been visiting* North Carolina for ten years.

Active voice—A verb is in the active voice when the subject performs the action: *The pitcher hurled the ball over the plate.*

Passive voice—A verb is in the passive voice when the subject is the result of the action: *The ball was hurled by the pitcher.*

The Adverb

Adverbs are words that modify (or change) a verb, an adjective, or another adverb. Most (but not all) adverbs end in -*ly*. Adverbs tell when (*early, today, later*), where (*here, there, away*), how (*quickly, slowly, fearlessly*), or how much (*frequently, continually, regularly*).

The Preposition

A preposition is a word that shows a relationship between the noun or pronoun that follows it and another word in a sentence. *A preposition never works alone*. It is always part of a phrase that begins with a preposition. The noun or pronoun that follows it is called the *object* of the preposition. Commonly used prepositions include *about, above, across, after, against, along, amid, among, around, at, as, before, behind, below, beneath, beside, between, beyond, by, down, during, except, for, from, in, into, like, of, off, on, over, past, since, through, to, toward, under, until, up, upon, with, within, without.*

Prepositional phrases begin with a preposition and usually end with a noun or pronoun. "We hiked *into the dark, cool woods* but left our supplies behind." Note that *behind* in this sentence is an adverb and not a preposition. In order to be a preposition, *behind* would have to be the beginning of a phrase. Prepositions never work alone.

The Conjunction

A conjunction joins words or groups of words. There are three kinds of conjunctions: coordinating, correlative, and subordinating.

Coordinating conjunctions: *for, and, nor, but, or, yet, so* are the coordinating conjunctions. The mnemonic *fanboys* helps students remember them.

Correlative conjunctions are always used in pairs: *either–or; neither–nor; not only–but also.*

Subordinating conjunctions are used to begin subordinate clauses. Some common subordinating conjunctions are *after, although, as, because, if, since, though, unless, when, while.*

The Interjection

Interjections are words that expresses emotion and are usually followed by an exclamation point: *Hurry! Wait! Help! My goodness!*

Grammar Matters: Lessons, Tips, and Conversations Using Mentor Texts, K–6 by Lynne Dorfman and Diane Dougherty. Copyright © 2014. Stenhouse Publishers.

Parts of a Sentence

The Sentence

A sentence is a group of words that expresses a complete thought. To give a sense of completeness a sentence must make a statement about something. Therefore, it needs two parts: a part that names something and a part that tells something about it.

The Subject of a Sentence

This is the naming part of the sentence. It consists of a noun or pronoun and all its modifiers.

My older sister attends Penn State University.
My favorite cousin plays football for the Eagles.

The Verb (Predicate) of a Sentence

This is the telling part of the sentence. It is built around a verb that either shows action or helps make a statement.

My older sister *attends Penn State University*.
My favorite cousin *plays football for the Eagles*.

Linking verbs involve no action at all. The purpose of a linking verb is to define or describe the subject.

My favorite cousin *is* a football player for the Eagles.
My older sister *was* class president.

The Complement

Complements are words or groups of words that are needed to complete the meaning of the sentence.

My dad taught *high school English for 30 years*.
Everyone enjoyed *the Broadway show*.
The crowd seemed *excited about the game*.

Direct objects receive the action of the verb.

Derek hit *the ball*.
The teacher praised *the class*.

Indirect objects come before the direct object of the verb and usually tell to whom or for whom the action of the verb is done.

Derek gave *me* some batting tips.
The teacher read *us* a story about bears.

Grammar Matters: Lessons, Tips, and Conversations Using Mentor Texts, K–6 by Lynne Dorfman and Diane Dougherty. Copyright © 2014. Stenhouse Publishers.

Subject complements (predicate nouns and predicate adjectives) follow linking verbs only.

> James is *my brother.* (predicate noun)
> Mrs. Jones is the *principal.* (predicate noun)
> Our school is *small.* (predicate adjective)
> The wind felt *cold.* (predicate adjective)

The Phrase

This is a group of related words that do not form a sentence by themselves. Phrases may be modifiers or they may be subjects, verbs, or complements.

Prepositional phrases begin with a preposition and usually end with a noun or pronoun. Prepositional phrases are modifiers.

Appositives are nouns or pronouns (sometimes with modifiers) that explain or help identify another noun that comes before it.

> *Doctor Smith, our choir director, sang in the Vienna Boys Choir.*
> *Our vacation, two weeks at the Outer Banks, was the highlight of the summer!*

Verbal phrases (gerunds, participles, and infinitives) all use verbs to form phrases whose part in the sentence may be that of a noun (gerund), adjective (participle), or either a noun or a modifier (infinitive).

> *Jogging in Central Park is my favorite activity.* ("Jogging" is a gerund.)
> *Huffing and puffing, the man finished the race.* ("Huffing" and "puffing" are participles.)
> *To be successful was his primary goal.* ("To be successful" is the infinitive phrase used as a noun.)
> *Frozen is my favorite Disney movie to watch.* ("To watch" is an infinitive used as a modifier.)

The Clause

A clause is a group of words containing a subject and a predicate. It may be a sentence by itself. It may be part of a sentence when grouped with another clause or other clauses.

Independent clauses—An independent clause makes complete sense by itself. One independent clause is a simple sentence.

> *We vacationed in the Outer Banks of North Carolina.*
> *The cold, brittle air swept over the hillside.*

Dependent (subordinate) clauses—These clauses *depend* on independent clauses to make sense. Dependent clauses cannot stand alone as sentences.

> *When we vacation in the Outer Banks of North Carolina*
> *As the cold, brittle air swept over the hillside*

Grammar Matters: Lessons, Tips, and Conversations Using Mentor Texts, K–6 by Lynne Dorfman and Diane Dougherty. Copyright © 2014. Stenhouse Publishers.

Compound Sentences

These consist of at least two independent clauses joined by a coordinating conjunction (*for, and, nor, but, or, yet, so*).

> *Anne enjoys swimming, but she doesn't like surfing.* (two clauses joined by the conjunction *but*)
>
> *Grandmom may be old, but she is not old-fashioned, nor does she sit in a rocking chair all day!* (three clauses—the first joined by *but* and the next joined by *nor*)

Complex Sentences

These consist of one independent clause and at least one dependent (subordinate) clause.

> *Because our family loves the beach, we rent a house at the shore every summer.*

Compound-Complex Sentences

These consist of two or more independent clauses and at least one dependent (subordinate) clause.

> *We rent a house at the shore every summer, and we also invite our friends to stay with us because they love the beach too.*

Common Usage Errors

Sentence Fragments

These are groups of related words that may contain a subject and a verb but fail to make sense all by themselves.

> *When I go to the beach* (contains a subject, *I*, and a verb, *go*, but doesn't make sense by itself)
>
> *To go to the beach* (contains a verb, *go*, but that verb does not have a subject)
>
> *To the beach* (contains neither a subject nor a predicate)

The most common error in sentence structure among young writers is the failure to recognize a sentence unit. This failure results in students writing a fragment or run-on sentence—see the following entry—that the writer thinks is a complete sentence unit. Teaching students about where one sentence begins and another ends is a serious challenge. If it were easy to recognize fragments and run-ons, students wouldn't make those errors. Because the unintentional use of fragments and run-ons in student writing

Grammar Matters: Lessons, Tips, and Conversations Using Mentor Texts, K–6 by Lynne Dorfman and Diane Dougherty. Copyright © 2014. Stenhouse Publishers.

gives the impression of carelessness and keeps the piece from having "the look of literacy," direct instruction of the sentence unit is a must. Sometimes this instruction needs to be conducted in whole group; sometimes small-group instruction or even one-on-one instruction will suffice. Know your student writers and what they need.

Run-On Sentences

These are the result of the combination of two complete thoughts that are not joined by a coordinating conjunction (*for, and, nor, but, or, yet, so*).

The door to the basement was wide open, I crept down the stairs. (This example contains two independent clauses. The first one ends after *open*. To correct this run-on the writer may add a conjunction before the comma: *The door to the basement was wide open, and I crept down the stairs.* Another way to correct the run-on would be to create two separate sentences: *The door to the basement was wide open. I crept down the stairs.* Teaching about fragments and run-on sentences is a natural venue for talking to students about elements of style: sentence fluency, including variety of sentences by length and structure, word choice, and voice.

Appendix E:

About Editing Skills

Editing is the last stage of the writing process. As we start the school year, we often ask students to engage in an eye conference or a self-conference to look at conventions—spelling, grammar, capitalization, and punctuation—as the last thing they do before publishing. Here students can actually hold each other's drafts in their hands, lightly underline awkward sentences and grammar usage errors, use editing marks to show where letters should or should not be capitalized, and circle spelling errors with a pencil. Sometimes, a dictionary or thesaurus can be helpful; other times reference pages that consist of class notes from a Your Turn Lesson or shorter focus lessons can offer some assistance in editing matters.

As we move through cycles (or units) of study throughout the school year, we should begin to push a certain amount of editing skills further and further back. That means that students should apply these skills automatically and/or correct mistakes independently in all of their work across the curriculum, too!

For example, let's say you are a second-grade teacher and have been working on beginning each new sentence with a capital letter and ending with some mark of punctuation. As you move out of the first cycle, you

297

Grammar Matters: Lessons, Tips, and Conversations Using Mentor Texts, K–6 by Lynne Dorfman and Diane Dougherty. Copyright © 2014. Stenhouse Publishers.

should expect your students to start paying attention to these two skills in the drafting and revision stages. Later, when you move to a third cycle, these skills should be pushed back, to appear in their writer's notebook entries. Finally, you should expect to see an attempt to begin every sentence with a capital letter and end with some mark of end punctuation in everything your second-grade students do. You may keep a list of grammar and mechanics skills as you introduce and practice them during each unit of study.

Keep track of these skills as you proceed to a new unit of study and revisit them during conferences and additional mini-lessons or brief focus lessons. Occasionally during a teacher-student conference, ask the student to continue to monitor an earlier skill as a writing goal. Of course, not all goals should focus on editing. Another goal would be to focus on imitating the writer's craft in a mentor text, focusing on a trait such as word choice, voice, or organization.

Checklists for Spelling

Checklists can specifically look at spelling, punctuation, and grammar issues. It is important to limit the list for students to make it more doable. In elementary school grades, it is a good idea first to reread for spelling mistakes only. The next read can be a punctuation check with a particular emphasis on one or two areas or skills, such as commas in a series or end punctuation. Students can work through an editing conference with a peer by actually exchanging papers and noting errors on sticky notes. After offering suggestions to the writer, he then has to try out the suggestion to see if it makes sense. He may want to consult with a grammar reference book or another peer, or wait for a teacher-student conference. Here is an example of a third-grade classroom's spelling checklist:

The Spelling Checklist
1. No excuse to misspell these words—spell these words correctly all the time! These are provided by the teacher and can come from the Dolch Sight Word List (such as *about, myself, today, only, try, laugh, full, warm, clean,* and *hurt*).
2. Homophone pairs (and triplets) that are often misused, even by adults: *too/to/two, your/you're, their/they're/there, hear-here, plain-plane, meat/meet, it's/its, wear/where, piece/peace.*
3. Irregular past tense verbs: *bring-brought, keep-kept, come-came, go-went, swim-swam, take-took, break-broke, see-saw, swing-swung.*

Grammar Matters: Lessons, Tips, and Conversations Using Mentor Texts, K–6 by Lynne Dorfman and Diane Dougherty. Copyright © 2014. Stenhouse Publishers.

4. Nouns that remain the same in their plural form such as *deer, moose,* and *sheep.*

5. Environmental print—any words in the room on posters or chart and titles of books that students are reviewing.

6. Words that students individually need that are discussed in conferences. For example, if a student writes a lot of soccer stories, then for that student *soccer* becomes a word he needs to know how to spell.

The Self-Edit

The Self-Edit

Name _____ **Date** _____

1. Frame each sentence with your fingers.
   - Check for a capital letter at the beginning.

2. Frame each sentence with your fingers.
   - Check for a period, question mark, or exclamation point at the end.

3. Read each sentence to see if it sounds right.
   - Does it seem too long? You might need two shorter sentences.
   - Are there any words that are missing?
   - Are there any words that don't belong?

4. Read each sentence again and tap each word lightly with the eraser end of your pencil as you read it aloud. Tap for a space between words.

5. Read each sentence again and tap each word lightly with the eraser end of your pencil as you read it aloud. Tap for a space between sentences.

6. Check your words for spelling.
   - Circle any words that don't look right to you. Check with a spelling buddy.

Grammar Matters: Lessons, Tips, and Conversations Using Mentor Texts, K–6 by Lynne Dorfman and Diane Dougherty. Copyright © 2014. Stenhouse Publishers.

Appendix F:

Understanding Differences in Other Languages to Help Our ELLs

In *Grammar Alive! A Guide for Teachers*, Brock Haussamen looks at some of the common languages we encounter in our classrooms to help us differentiate instruction for our English language learners (ELLs). The following list from Haussamen's book may help you understand the origin of certain constructions in the written work your ELLs produce for you. By understanding a little about other language structures, you may be able to provide these students with the tools they need to gain mastery of the English language. We cannot overstate the importance of learning about ELL students' interests, hobbies, culture, and country of origin and language as a way to welcome them and raise their comfort level in our classroom and in our school. Here are some aspects of other languages Haussamen suggests we consider:

- Nouns might take the gender.
- Some languages do not use articles or may use articles differently.
- Plurals may be formed by adding words or by adding syllables to the sentence or by giving context clues in the sentence.
- Word order may not follow the typical noun-verb-object sentence pattern common to English (*The boy sharpened his pencil.*).
- The pronoun may not have to agree in gender or number with its antecedent.

300

Grammar Matters: Lessons, Tips, and Conversations Using Mentor Texts, K–6 by Lynne Dorfman and Diane Dougherty. Copyright © 2014. Stenhouse Publishers.

- Other languages may have fewer prepositions, making it confusing for the novice to know which preposition to use in English. Also the preposition may not precede its object.
- There are differences in inflection and pacing.
- There are differences in written conventions, such as punctuation and capitalization.
- Nonverbal communications—such as gesture, eye contact, silences, and what people do to indicate that they understand—differ from culture to culture. (2003, 55)

Idioms are another aspect of language that do not translate from one language to another. For example, the meaning of our idiom, "It's a horse of a different color" would not be understood by a native from a Spanish-speaking country if you said, "Es un caballo de otro color." A student who speaks Spanish as his first language would say, "Tengo hambre" (I have hunger) for "I am hungry." In English we say, "Money doesn't grow on trees." In France they would say, "L'argent ne tombe pas du ciel." (Money doesn't fall from the sky.) If we choose to not teach our English language learners our idioms, they will miss an important cultural element of the language they are trying to speak fluently. Include the explanation of idioms as an everyday occurrence as they appear in literature, songs, and current events, especially to students in intermediate elementary grades and higher who are ready to take their English fluency to the next level.

Grammar Matters: Lessons, Tips, and Conversations Using Mentor Texts, K–6 by Lynne Dorfman and Diane Dougherty. Copyright © 2014. Stenhouse Publishers.

Appendix G:

Comma Rules for Students in Grades 4–6

Fold in half lengthwise, then fold in half and fold again to create a book on comma rules. Special thanks to Teresa Moslak for this comma book.

Grammar Matters: Lessons, Tips, and Conversations Using Mentor Texts, K–6 by Lynne Dorfman and Diane Dougherty. Copyright © 2014. Stenhouse Publishers.

Commas
1

Punctuation that signals a short break.

Name _____

Use a comma after the greeting and closing of a friendly letter.

Dear Sally, (greeting)
Your friend, (closing)

Use commas to separate the two complete parts of a compound sentence.

I love to swim, but I'm afraid to dive.

Use commas to separate introductory words like *yes, no, well,* and *oh*.

Yes, you may go trick or treating on Halloween.

Use commas to separate items in a series.

We have apples, butter cookies, or pudding for snacks.

Use commas after an adverb that tells how at the beginning of the sentence.

Wearily, we trudged home with our sacks full of candy.

Use commas to set off an appositive, a phrase that gives extra information.

Halloween, my favorite holiday, is next week!

Use a comma to set off the name of a person who is being spoken to.

Don't worry, Alfredo, you can study and pass the next test.

Appendix H:

Writing Abbreviations Correctly

An abbreviation is a shortened form of a word or expression followed by a period. Abbreviations are never used in formal writing.

The entire word must be spelled unless it is part of a title as in *Mr., Mrs., Dr., Rev., Sen., Hon.,* or *Ms. (mister, missus, doctor, reverend, senator, honorable).* Often *Ms.* is used before a woman's name when it is not known if she is married or single. *Miss* is not an abbreviation.

Jr. and *Sr.* stand for *junior* and *senior,* and you can often find these abbreviations following someone's name as in Jon Koch, Sr.

If you are writing to several doctors, you would use *Drs.* as the abbreviation or *Messrs.* as the plural form of *Mr.*

Abbreviations are often used for someone's first and (sometimes) middle name, followed by a space and a period (E. B. White, C. S. Lewis, S. E. Hinton).

St. is the abbreviated form for *saint* (as in jolly old St. Nicholas!).

Use no periods with abbreviations that appear in full capitals, whether two letters or more, as in US and USA or in names of organizations such as NCTE (National Council of Teachers of English), IRS (Internal Revenue Service), WWF (World Wildlife Fund). When using an acronym, write the entire name the first time it appears in the text. After that, you can use the acronym.

Grammar Matters: Lessons, Tips, and Conversations Using Mentor Texts, K–6 by Lynne Dorfman and Diane Dougherty. Copyright © 2014. Stenhouse Publishers.

Common abbreviations in student writing are TV, VCR, PC, and DVD. Abbreviations used in text messaging such as LMK (Let me know), BFN (Bye for now), or DWBH (Don't worry, be happy) are never used in formal compositions. These acronyms have their place—the text message is really the only genre where their use is acceptable.

If any abbreviation falls at the end of a sentence, use only one period.

Grammar Matters: Lessons, Tips, and Conversations Using Mentor Texts, K–6 by Lynne Dorfman and Diane Dougherty. Copyright © 2014. Stenhouse Publishers.

Appendix I:

Sentence Combining in Grades 4–6 (and Beyond!)

Find passages from interesting books, magazines, and newspapers to practice sentence combining. Read some information from the text to establish interest first. Possibly show photos or illustrations. Take apart a passage from the text by separating all of the ideas that were listed or combined in compound subjects, compound predicates, or compound and complex sentences—but do not change the order. Ask students to rewrite the sentences by combining ideas that logically go together. This work should follow a Your Turn Lesson on creating compound or complex sentences. (Also see Chapter 2 for more information.)

For the Students

The following are ideas that David McCullough wrote into a paragraph in his book *The Johnstown Flood* (1968). Take all of these ideas and form them into sentences to write a paragraph. You will then compare your paragraph to the one that is in the book. (Hint: If you are having trouble, highlight repeated words in the same highlighter color and try to figure out a way to phrase the ideas using the repeated words only once.)

306

Grammar Matters: Lessons, Tips, and Conversations Using Mentor Texts, K–6 by Lynne Dorfman and Diane Dougherty. Copyright © 2014. Stenhouse Publishers.

- A jury had come to investigate the cause of death of the bodies that had been recovered.
- There were 121 bodies.
- It was a coroner's jury that came to investigate.
- The jury was from Westmoreland County.
- The bodies were recovered at Nineveh.
- Nineveh was in Westmoreland County.
- Nineveh was just across the county line.
- The jury poked about the ruins of the dam.
- The jury talked to the people.
- The jury made notes.
- The jury went home.
- The formal investigation was to be held on the 5th.
- The 5th was a Wednesday.
- The investigation included testifying witnesses.
- When the witnesses testified, they were under oath.

McCullough, David. 1968. *The Johnstown Flood*. New York: Simon & Schuster.

The coroner's jury from Westmoreland County had come to investigate the cause of death of the 121 bodies that had been recovered at Nineveh, which was just across the line in Westmoreland County. They poked about the ruins of the dam, talked to the people, made notes, and went home. The formal investigation, with witnesses testifying under oath, was to be held on Wednesday, the 5th.

Note: Special thanks to Teresa Moslak for this lesson on sentence combining.

Grammar Matters: Lessons, Tips, and Conversations Using Mentor Texts, K–6 by Lynne Dorfman and Diane Dougherty. Copyright © 2014. Stenhouse Publishers.

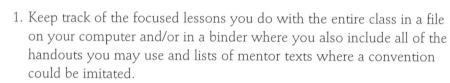

Appendix J:

Top Ten Tips
for a Teacher of Writers

1. Keep track of the focused lessons you do with the entire class in a file on your computer and/or in a binder where you also include all of the handouts you may use and lists of mentor texts where a convention could be imitated.
2. Use the hard copy handouts to view using a document imager, as a display on the bulletin board, or to give to students as an easy reference.
3. Don't put your notebook away. Place it in a key location where students can use it as easy access for reference or as a memory jogger.
4. Post the Your Turn Lesson or mini-lesson you will teach a week in advance. Put it on your class website or blog, or even create a fifteen-second Instagram video to pique interest in the lesson early on. Encourage students to try out a strategy or two before you teach the lesson, and then to share what they have tried out independently or with a partner.
5. During the lesson, writer's notebooks should be open to a clean page where students can try out new learnings in a safe place with no grade attached.

Grammar Matters: Lessons, Tips, and Conversations Using Mentor Texts, K–6 by Lynne Dorfman and Diane Dougherty. Copyright © 2014. Stenhouse Publishers.

6. Use an inquiry-based approach where students can "play" with words and discover how a grammar or convention rule works (and, for older students, how the rule was broken purposefully) and the effect on the reader.

7. Make sure that the students have ownership during the lesson—not only in the shared, guided, independent, and reflection parts, but also sometimes in the planning process as well.

8. Make sure students are sharing what they know about grammar and conventions and how that knowledge is shaping their writing.

9. Encourage students to continue to investigate aspects of grammar and conventions on their own by studying favorite mentor texts.

10. Create an expert list (authority list) by posting names of the students who effectively use certain conventions—such as quotation marks or commas—on a bulletin board or another key location. These students can help others when you are busy.

Grammar Matters: Lessons, Tips, and Conversations Using Mentor Texts, K–6 by Lynne Dorfman and Diane Dougherty. Copyright © 2014. Stenhouse Publishers.

References

Allen, Janet. 1999. *Words, Words, Words: Teaching Vocabulary in Grades 4–12*. Portland, ME: Stenhouse.

———. 2005. *Best Little Wingman*. Honesdale, PA: Boyds Mill Press.

Anderson, Jeff. 2005. *Mechanically Inclined: Building Grammar, Usage, and Style into Writer's Workshop*. Portland, ME: Stenhouse.

———. 2007. *Everyday Editing*. Portland, ME: Stenhouse.

———. 2011. *10 Things Every Writer Needs to Know*. Portland, ME: Stenhouse.

Angelillo, Janet. 2002. *A Fresh Approach to Teaching Punctuation: Helping Young Writers Use Conventions with Precision and Purpose*. New York: Scholastic.

Atwell, Nancie. 2002. *Lessons That Change Writers*. Portsmouth, NH: Heinemann.

Babbitt, Natalie. 1985. *Tuck Everlasting*. New York: Farrar, Straus and Giroux.

Beecroft, Simon. 2009. *Star Wars: Luke Skywalker's Amazing Story*. New York: DK Publishing.

Beers, Kylene, and Robert E. Probst. 2013. *Notice and Note: Strategies for Close Reading*. Portsmouth, NH: Heinemann.

Boelts, Maribeth. 2007. *Those Shoes*. Somervile, MA: Candlewick Press.

Braddock, Richard, Richard Lloyd-Jones, and Lowell Shoer. 1963. *Research in Written Composition*. Urbana, IL: NCTE.

Brinckloe, Julie. 1986. *Fireflies*. New York: Aladdin Books.

Bryant, Jen. 2005. *Georgia's Bones*. Grand Rapids, MI: Wm. B. Eerdmans.

Bulla, Clyde Robert. 1975. *Shoeshine Girl*. New York: HarperTrophy.

Bunting, Eve. 1989. *The Wednesday Surprise*. New York: HMH Books for Young Readers.

Calkins, Lucy. 2005. *One on One: The Art of Conferring with Young Writers*. Portsmouth, NH: Heinemann.

Calkins, Lucy, Mary Ehrenworth, and Christopher Lehman. 2012. *Pathways to the Common Core*. Portsmouth, NH: Heinemann.

Carlstrom, Nancy White. 1995. *The Snow Speaks*. New York: Little, Brown.

Cleary, Brian. 2004. *I and You and Don't Forget Who: What Is a Pronoun?* Minneapolis, MN: Carolrhoda Books.

Cole, Joanna. 1990. *The Magic Schoolbus Lost in the Solar System*. New York: Scholastic.

Common Core State Standards Initiative. 2014. *English Language Arts Standards*. www.corestandards.org/ELA-Literacy/.

Coville, Bruce. 2003. *The Monsters of Morley Mann: A Madcap Adventure*. New York: HMH Books for Young Readers.

Creech, Sharon. 2001. *Love That Dog*. New York: HarperCollins.

Crews, Donald. 1996. *Shortcut*. New York: Greenwillow Books.

———. 1998. *Night at the Fair*. New York: HarperCollins.

Crimi, Carolyn. 1995. *Outside, Inside*. New York: Simon & Schuster.

Dahl, Michael. 2006. *If You Were an Adjective*. Minneapolis, MN: Picture Window Books.

Dahl, Roald. 1961. *James and the Giant Peach*. New York: Alfred Knopf.

———. 1966. *Matilda*. New York: Farrar, Straus and Giroux.

———. 1982. *The BFG*. New York: Farrar, Straus and Giroux.

Davies, Nicola. 2001. *One Tiny Turtle*. Cambridge, MA: Candlewick Press.

———. 2007. *White Owl, Barn Owl*. Cambridge, MA: Candlewick Press.

Day, Alexandra. 1986. *Good Dog, Carl*. New York: Simon and Schuster.

Dorfman, Lynne, and Rose Cappelli. 2007. *Mentor Texts: Teaching Writing Through Children's Literature, K–6*. Portland, ME: Stenhouse.

———. 2009. *Nonfiction Mentor Texts: Teaching Informational Writing Through Children's Literature, K–8*. Portland, ME: Stenhouse.

———. 2012. *Poetry Mentor Texts*. Portland, ME: Stenhouse.

Ehlert, Lois. 2004. *Hands: Growing Up to Be an Artist*. New York: Dell.

Ehrenworth, Mary, and Vicki Vinton. 2005. *The Power of Grammar: Unconventional Approaches to the Conventions of Language*. Portsmouth, NH: Heinemann.

Falconer, Ian. 2000. *Olivia*. New York: Atheneum Books for Young Readers.

———. 2001. *Olivia Saves the Circus*. New York: Atheneum Books for Young Readers.

———. 2012. *Olivia and the Fairy Princess*. New York: Atheneum Books for Young Readers.

Fisher, Douglas. 2013. "Text Complexity and Close Reading." KSRA Annual Conference General Session. Penn Stater Conference Center, State College, PA.

Francois, Chantal, and Elisa Zonana. 2009. *Catching Up on Conventions: Grammar Lessons for Middle School Writers*. Portsmouth, NH: Heinemann.

Frazee, Marla. 2003. *Roller Coaster*. New York: HMH Books.

Friedman, Ellen G., ed. 1984. *Joan Didion: Essays and Conversations*. Princeton, NJ: Ontario Review Press.

Gallagher, Kelly. 2003. *Reading Reasons: Motivational Mini Lessons for Middle and High School*. Portland, ME: Stenhouse.

———. 2011. *Write Like This: Teaching Real-World Writing Through Modeling and Mentor Texts*. Portland, ME: Stenhouse.

George, Jean Craighead. 1998. *My Side of the Mountain*. New York: Puffin Books.

Glaubitz, Grace Ellen. 1967. "Walking." In *Our Language Today 3*, eds. David Conlin, H. T. Fillmer, Ann Lefcourt, and Nell C. Thompson. New York: American Book Company.

Golenbock, Peter. 1990. *Teammates*. New York: Harcourt.

Graham, Steve, and Dolores Perin. 2006. "Writing Next: Effective Strategies to Improve Writing of Adolescents in Middle and High School: A Report to Carnegie Corporation of New York." Report published on October 9. Washington, DC: Alliance for Excellence in Education.

Graves, Donald H. 1994. *A Fresh Look at Writing*. Portsmouth, NH: Heinemann.

———. 2001. *The Energy to Teach*. Portsmouth, NH: Heinemann.

Hannigan, Katherine. 2004. *Ida B. and Her Plans to Maximize Fun, Avoid Disaster, and Save the World*. New York: HarperCollins.

Haussamen, Brock. 2003. *Grammar Alive! A Guide for Teachers*. Urbana, IL: National Council of Teachers of English.

Heard, Georgia, ed. 2009. "Recipe for Writing an Autumn Poem." In *Falling Down the Page*. New York: Roaring Brook Press.

Henkes, Kevin. 1991. *Chrysanthemum*. New York: Greenwillow Books.

High, Linda Oatman. 1999. *Barn Savers*. Honesdale, PA: Boyds Mills Press.

———. 2003. *The Girl on the High Diving Horse*. New York: Philomel.

Hill, Tad. 2012. *Rocket Writes a Story*. New York: Schwartz & Wade Books.

Hillman, Ben. 2007. *How Big Is It? A Book About Bigness*. New York: Scholastic Reference.

Hillocks, George, Jr., and Michael Smith. 1991. "Grammar and Usage." In *Handbook of Research on Teaching the English Language Arts*, ed. Diane Lapp and Douglas Fisher. New York: Macmillan.

Hopkinson, Deborah. 2006. *Skyboys: How They Built the Empire State Building*. New York: Schwartz and Wade.

Horowitz, Ruth. 2004. *Crab Moon*. Somerville, MA: Candlewick Press.

Hutchins, Pat. 1987. *Rosie's Walk*. New York: Alladin Books.

Janeczko, Paul B. 2001. *Dirty Laundry Pile: Poems in Different Voices*. New York: HarperCollins.

Juster, Norton. 2005. *The Hello, Goodbye Window*. New York: Hyperion Books for Children.

Kann, Victoria. 2001. *Silverlicious*. New York: HarperCollins.

Kinney, Jeff. 2009. *Dog Days*. New York: Amulet Books.

Lane, Barry. 1993. *After the End: Teaching and Learning Creative Revision*. Portsmouth, NH: Heinemann.

———. 1999. *Reviser's Toolbox*. Shoreham, VT: Discover Writing Press.

———. 2001. *Why We Must Run with Scissors: Voice Lessons in Persuasive Writing 3–12*. Shoreham, VT: Discover Writing Press.

———. 2008. *But How Do You Teach Writing? A Simple Guide for All Teachers*. New York: Scholastic.

Legg, Gerald. 1997. *From Egg to Chicken*. New York: Franklin Watts.

L'Engle, Madeleine. 1962. *A Wrinkle in Time*. New York: Dell.

Lewis, C. S. 1950. *The Lion, the Witch, and the Wardrobe*. New York: HarperCollins.

Little, Jean. 1986. *Hey World, Here I Am!* New York: HarperCollins.

Loewen, Nancy. 2007. *If You Were a Conjunction*. Minneapolis, MN: Picture Window Books.

Lyons, Shelly. 2009. *If You Were an Apostrophe*. North Mankato, MN: Capstone Press.

MacLachlan, Patricia. 1985. *Sarah, Plain and Tall*. New York: HarperCollins.

———. 2003. *Painting the Wind*. New York: HarperCollins.

Martin, Jacqueline Briggs. 1998. *Snowflake Bentley*. New York: Houghton Mifflin.

Mayer, Mercer, and Marianna Mayer. 1971. *A boy, a dog, a frog, and a friend*. New York: Dial Books for Young Readers.

McCullough, David. 1968. *The Johnstown Flood*. New York: Simon and Schuster.

McFarland, Lyn Rossiter. 2006. *Widget*. New York: Square Fish.

McGarry, Richard. 2012. *Teaching English as a Second Language: Giving New Learners an Everyday Grammar*. Jefferson, NC: McFarland.

McNaughton, Colin. 2007. *Suddenly! (A Preston Pig Story)*. Nantucket, MA: Anderson.

Messner, Kate. 2011. *Over and Under the Snow*. San Francisco: Chronicle Books.

Monjo, F. N. 1970. *The Drinking Gourd*. New York: HarperTrophy.

Murphy, Frank. 2002. *George Washington and the General's Dog*. New York: Random House.

———. 2003. *Thomas Jefferson's Feast*. New York: Random House.

Murphy, Patti Beling. 2001. *Elinor and Violet: The Story of Two Naughty Chickens*. New York: Little, Brown.

Naylor, Phyllis Reynolds. 1991. *Shiloh*. New York: Simon and Schuster.

Nelson, Robin. 2013. *From Sheep to Sweater*. Minneapolis, MN: Lerner.

Noden, Harry R. 2011. *Image Grammar: Teaching Grammar as Part of the Writing Process*. Portsmouth, NH: Heinemann.

O'Connor, Jane. 2005. *Fancy Nancy*. New York: HarperCollins.

———. 2010. *Fancy Nancy: Poet Extraordinaire!* New York: HarperCollins.

———. 2012. *Fancy Nancy: Tea for Two*. New York: HarperCollins.

———. 2013. *Fancy Nancy: Budding Ballerina*. New York: HarperCollins.

Orloff, Karen Kaufman. 2004. *I Wanna Iguana*. New York: Putnam.

Palatini, Margie. 2001. *The Web Files*. New York: Hyperion.

Park, Barbara. 1995. *Mick Harte Was Here*. New York: Scholastic.

Patawaran, A. A. 2012. *Write Here Write Now: Standing at Attention Before My Imaginary Style Dictator*. www.nationalbookstore.com.

Paulson, Gary. 1989. *The Winter Room*. New York: Scholastic.

———. 1996. *Hatchet*. New York: Simon and Schuster.

Polacco, Patricia. 1990. *Thunder Cake*. New York: Philomel Books.

Ray, Katie Wood. 1999. *Wondrous Words*. Urbana, IL: National Council of Teachers of English.

Reagan, Jean. 2012. *How to Babysit a Grandpa*. New York: Knopf Books for Young Readers.

Riordan, Rick. 2005. *The Lightning Thief*. New York: Hyperion.

Romano, Tom. 2000. *Blending Genre, Altering Style*. Portsmouth, NH: Heinemann.

Rylant, Cynthia. 1985. *Every Living Thing*. New York: Simon and Schuster.

———. 1992. *An Angel for Solomon Singer*. New York: Orchard Books.

———. 1993. *When I Was Young in the Mountains*. London: Puffin Books.

———. 1993. *The Relatives Came*. New York: Alladin Paperbacks.

———. 2000. *In November*. New York: Harcourt.

Sams, Carl R., and Jean Stoick. 2000. *Stranger in the Woods*. Self-published.

Schachner, Judy. 2013. *bits and pieces*. New York: Penguin Young Readers Group.

Schuster, Edgar. 2003. *Breaking the Rules: Liberating Writers Through Innovative Grammar Instruction*. Portsmouth, NH: Heinemann.

Seuss, Dr. 1957. *The Cat in the Hat*. New York: Random House.

Simon, Seymour. 1991. *Big Cats*. New York: HarperCollins.

———. 1991. *Earthquakes*. New York: William Morrow.

———. 1993. *Weather*. New York: HarperCollins.

———. 2001. *Crocodiles and Alligators*. New York: HarperCollins.

———. 2006. *Sharks*. New York: HarperCollins.

———. 2006. *Volcanoes*. New York: HarperCollins.

———. 2007. *Spiders*. New York: HarperCollins.

———. 2008. *Gorillas*. New York: HarperCollins.

Smith, Michael W., and Jeffrey D. Wilhelm. 2007. *Getting It Right: Fresh Approaches to Teaching Grammar, Usage, and Correctness*. New York: Scholastic Teaching Resources.

Smith, Robert Kimmel. 1982. *Jelly Belly*. New York: Yearling.

Spandel, Vicki. 2013. *Creating Writers: 6 Traits, Process, Workshop, and Literature*. Upper Saddle River, NJ: Pearson.

Spinelli, Eileen. 2004. *Do You Have a Hat?* New York: Simon and Schuster.

———. 2007. *Someday*. New York: Dial.

Strunk, William, Jr., and E. B. White. 2000. *The Elements of Style*. 4th ed. New York: Penguin Books.

Topping, Donna H., and Sandra J. Hoffman. 2006. *Getting Grammar: 150 Ways to Teach an Old Subject*. Portsmouth, NH: Heinemann.

Van Allsburg, Chris. 1984. *The Mysteries of Harris Burdick*. New York: Houghton Mifflin.

———. 1985. *The Polar Express*. New York: Houghton Mifflin.

———. 1992. *The Widow's Broom*. New York: Houghton Mifflin.

Walton, Rick. *Suddenly Alligator: An Adverbial Tale*. Layton, UT: Gibbs Smith.

Weaver, Constance. 1996. *Teaching Grammar in Context*. Portsmouth, NH: Boynton/Cook.

Weaver, Constance, and Jonathan Bush. 2008. *Grammar to Enrich and Enhance Writing*. Portsmouth, NH: Heinemann.

Whatley, Bruce. 1993. *Looking for Crabs*. New York: HarperCollins Childrens Books.

White, E. B. 1945. *Stuart Little*. New York: HarperCollins.

———. 1952. *Charlotte's Web*. New York: HarperCollins.

Wiesner, David. 1999. *Tuesday*. New York: Houghton Mifflin.

Wilde, Sandra. 2012. *Funner Grammar: Fresh Ways to Teach Usage, Language, and Writing Conventions*. Portsmouth, NH: Heinemann.

Wing, Natasha. 1999. *The Night Before Halloween.* New York: Grossett and Dunlap.

Wyeth, Sharon Dennis. 1998. *Something Beautiful*. New York: Random House.

Yolen, Jane. 1988. *Owl Moon*. New York: Philomel Books.

———. 2010. *Elsie's Birds*. New York: Philomel Books.

Zolotow, Charlotte. 1985. *William's Doll*. New York: HarperCollins.

———. 1993. *The Moon Was the Best.* New York: Greenwillow Books.

Index

Page numbers followed by an *f* indicate figures.

Probst, Robert E., 248
procedural writing, 140–161
  photography and, 154
  topics, 160
  videorecording of, 154
Professor Panda and the Punctuation Station (Auker),
  261
progress monitoring, 54
pronoun-antecedent agreement, 100
pronoun-noun pairs, 168–169
pronouns, 31, 57, 117, 168–169
  defined, 290
  demonstrative, 290
  interrogative, 290
  personal, 290
  possessive, 164, 290
  reflexive, 290
  usage, 5, 25, 54, 168
pronunciation, 38
proper nouns, 34, 39, 60–61, 109–112, 124
  defined, 289
*Publication Manual of the American Psychological
  Association*, 184
Pulver, Robin, 264
punctuation, 25, 27–30, 42, 48–50, 54, 60–61, 63,
  66–67, 69, 78–79, 84–86, 89, 100, 104, 106–108,
  111–114, 122, 143–144, 147–151, 158, 187, 222.
  See also individual terms
  checklists, 298
Punctuation Celebration (Bruno), 164, 261
Punctuation Takes a Vacation (Pulver), 264

Q
question marks, 50
question sentences. *See* interrogative sentences
quotation marks, 34, 49, 60–61, 63, 78–79, 83, 85,
  252–255, 278

R
Raschka, Chris, 51
Rathmann, Peggy, 52
Ray, Katie Wood, 4, 73
readers, 22–23
reading. *See also* mentor texts
  close, 248–253
  critical, 73
  independent, 33, 80, 88, 90, 95
  levels, 23
  programs, 54
  workshop, 60

reading aloud, 26, 29, 41, 50, 53–54, 84, 92, 111, 120,
  122, 124, 138, 158, 214, 250
  choral reading, 105, 249
  correctness, for, 227–228, 240
Reagan, Jean, 154, 158, 216
"Recipe for Writing an Autumn Poem" (Heard), 267
Red Book, The (Lehman), 51
reflection, 9, 161
reflexive pronouns, 290
regular verbs, 36, 45
Relatives Came, The (Rylant), 214
repetition, 63
research, 3, 203–204
Reviser's Toolbox (Lane), 64
revision, 1–2, 26, 41–42, 45, 56, 58, 68–69, 73, 75,
  79–80, 85, 138, 140, 143, 154
rhythm, 39, 80
Riordan, Rick, 207
Rocket Writes a Story (Hill), 273
Rogers, Gregory, 51
Rohmann, Eric, 52
role-play, 85, 171
Roller Coaster (Frazee), 23, 62, 64
Rosenthal, Amy Krouse, 263
Rosie's Walk (Hutchins), 171, 263
Rowling, J. K., 29f, 78, 80, 87, 208
Roy, Jennifer Rozines, 264
run-on sentences, 4, 136, 138, 295–296
run-together sentences, 136–137
Ryan, Pam Muñoz, 264
Rylant, Cynthia, 31f, 39, 116–117, 127–128, 214, 237,
  279

S
Sarah, Plain and Tall (MacLachlan), 31f, 34f, 166, 278
scaffolds, 12–13, 102, 111, 203–204
Schachner, Judy, 275
Schneider, R. M., 264
Schotter, Roni, 264
Schuster, Edgar, 4–5
second grade, 54–62, 76, 92, 102, 109, 116–119,
  190–194, 248–253
  mentor texts, 269–273, 276–277, 279–280
Sector 7 (Wiesner), 52
See the Yak Yak (Ghigna), 262
self-conferences, 10, 73, 297
self-edit checklists, 297, 299
sentences, 58, 83, 92, 225, 278
  combining, 306–307
  complements, 131
  complete, 133, 137, 148, 151

Franklin Pierce University

00207638

DATE DUE

PRINTED IN U.S.A.